DESPITE DESTRUCTION, MISERY AND PRIVATIONS...

The Polish Army in Prussia During the War Against Sweden 1626–1629

Michał Paradowski

'This is the Century of the Soldier', Fulvio Testi, Poet, 1641

Helion & Company

Helion & Company Limited
Unit 8 Amherst Business Centre
Budbrooke Road
Warwick
CV34 5WE
England
Tel. 01926 499 619
Email: info@helion.co.uk
Website: www.helion.co.uk
Twitter: @helionbooks
blog.helion.co.uk/

Published by Helion & Company 2020
Designed and typeset by Mach 3 Solutions Ltd (www.mach3solutions.co.uk)
Cover designed by Paul Hewitt, Battlefield Design (www.battlefield-design.co.uk)

Text © Michał Paradowski 2020
Images © as individually credited
Colour artwork by Sergey Shamenkov © Helion & Company 2020
Maps drawn by Alan Turton © Helion & Company 2020

ISBN 978-1-913336-45-5

British Library Cataloguing-in-Publication Data.
A catalogue record for this book is available from the British Library.

For details of other military history titles published by Helion & Company Limited
contact the above address or visit our website: http://www.helion.co.uk.

We always welcome receiving book proposals from prospective authors.

Contents

Acknowledgements

Through the years many friends and fellow history enthusiasts provided help, encouragement and support in my research. I would like to use this opportunity to express my gratitude for their support, apology if I missed anyone from this list (let me know, I will send a 'thank you letter' via post). Special thanks to Daniel Staberg for always interesting discussions and many priceless sources and to Przemysław Gawron for his generous support and feedback. My salutations to friends, colleagues and fellow researchers from Poland: Artur Świetlik, Michał Molenda, Rafał Szwelicki, Zbigniew Hundert, Paweł Duda, Radosław Sikora, Witold Biernacki, Emil Kalinowski, Łukasz Pabich, Mariusz Balcerek, Karol Łopatecki, Arkadiusz Czwołek, Tomasz Bohun, Jerzy Czajewski, Michał Chlipała, Tomasz Ratyński, Maciej Flis, Jakub Pokojski, Krzysztof Kmąk, Zbigniew Chmiel, Krzysztof Cheliński and Robert Jakubas. I appreciate all your help, comments, criticism and inspiration through all those years. I'm also very grateful to E.J. Blaauw for his translation from Dutch and to Mats Elzinga for explanation of some seventeenth-century Dutch terms.

My wholehearted thanks to all the lovely folks at Helion and Company, for giving me a chance to be part of 'Century of the Soldier'. I would especially like to thank Charles Singleton for his constant encouragement and huge support during the dark days.

Finally massive thanks to the two most important people in my life: wife Patrycja and son Ezra. Without your love, help, understanding and patience ('Dad, when can I finally play on computer?') I would never be able to finish this project.

Chronology of the Polish–Swedish Conflict, 1621–1635

1621

21 August – Swedish army led by Gustav Adolf begins the siege of Ryga (Riga) in Livonia
25 September – capitulation of Riga
October – Swedes capture Mitawa (Mitau), capital of Courland
28 November – Lithuanian victory at Kropimojza (Kropenhof)

1622

January–July – Lithuanian siege of Mitawa (Mitau), Swedish garrison surrenders on 5 July
July–August – Unsuccessful Swedish relief of Mitawa, resulting in inconclusive battle with Lithuanians
10 August – Signing of Lithuanian–Swedish ceasefire

1623

Ceasefire extended into truce, signed until March 1625

1625

27 June – Swedes start new campaign in Livonia
August–October – Swedish army captures Kokenhauz (Koknese), Dorpat, Birże (in Lithuania), Bowsk (Bauske) and Listenhoff

1626

13 January – Decisive Swedish victory at Walmozja (Wallhof)

6 July – Gustav Adolf and his army land at Piława (Pillau) in Prussia

July – Practically unopposed, the Swedes capture the majority of the important towns in Prussia, including Braniewo (Braunsberg) on 10 July, Frombork (Frauenburg) and Tolkmicko (Tolkemit) on 11 July, Elbląg (Elbing) on 15 July, Malbork (Marienburg) on 18 July, Tczew (Dirschau), Orneta (Worditt) and Dobre Miasto (Guttstadt) on 27 July, Puck (Putzig) on 29 July

14 September – Fortress Głowa Gdańska (Danziger-Haupt) captured by Swedish forces

22 September–1 October – inconclusive battle at Gniew (Mewe), where forces led by King Sigismund III clash a few times with those led by Gustav Adolf

21 October – Hetman Stanisław Koniecpolski arrives in Prussia and takes over command of the Polish army

Late November – Beginning of the Polish siege of Puck, the first unsuccessful assault on the town in early December

1627

19 January – Lithuanians sign six-month truce with the Swedes, leading to the cessation of military operations in Livonia

2 April – Poles capture Puck

18 April – Swedish troops marching from Mecklenburg surrender at Czarne (Hammerstein), with the majority of the soldiers joining the Polish army

22/23 May – Gustav Adolf wounded during the first action at Kiezmark (Käsemark)

June – Lithuanian–Swedish war in Livonia resumes, the campaigns until the end of the war in 1629 focus mostly on 'small war', with no direct impact on the situation in Prussia

12 July – Poles recapture Gniew

End of July – Second action at Kiezmark, this time it ends with Swedish victory and heavy Polish losses

17–18 July – Battle of Tczew. After a successful first day of battle the Swedes are forced to retreat from the battlefield on the next day, after Gustav Adolf is heavily wounded

28 November – Victory of the Polish fleet at Oliwa (Oliva)

1628

January–July – Temporary truce between the Poles and Swedes in Prussia

6 July – Polish ships ambushed at their mooring near Wisłoujście (Weichselmünde) fortress by Swedish troops and artillery. Fire exchange leads to heavy Polish losses

August–September – Swedish attempt to attack Pomorze Gdańskie (Danzig Pomerania), ended with heavy losses for Gustav Adolf's army, with their only success being the capture of Brodnica (Strasburg in Westpreussen)

1629

12 February – Swedish army under Herman Wrangel succeeds in the relief of Brodnica, which was blocked by Polish troops. The Poles, led by Stanisław Potocki in Koniecpolski's absence, are defeated at the battle at Górzno

16–17 February – Unsuccessful Swedish attempt to capture Toruń (Thorn)

18 March – Signing of three-month truce in Prussia

June – Allied Imperial forces led by Hans Georg von Arnim enter Prussia to support the Poles

27 June – Polish–Imperial victory at the battle of Trzciana (Honigfelde)

6 September – Signing of six-year truce in Stary Targ (Altmark)

1635

12 September – Signing of the treaty of Sztumska Wieś (Stuhmsdorf), introducing the 26.5-year truce between the Polish–Lithuanian Commonwealth and Sweden

Introduction

On 9 August 1587, Swedish Royal Prince Sigismund Vasa was elected as ruler of the Polish–Lithuanian Commonwealth and became known as Sigismund III. His father was the Swedish King John III, while his mother was Catherine Jagiellon, youngest daughter of Polish King Sigismund I the Old. The young (21-year-old) Swedish prince, raised as Roman Catholic, was crowned in Cracow in December of the same year. No one could foresee that his reign would start a series of Polish–Swedish conflicts that would echo throughout the seventeenth century. King John III died in 1592, so Sigismund, as his heir, was due to inherit Swedish Crown. The main problem was that unlike the majority of his Swedish subjects, he was Roman Catholic, but before his coronation in Sweden he had promised that Lutheranism would remain the official religion of the Scandinavian Kingdom. He was finally crowned King of Sweden at the beginning of 1594 but decided to return to Poland where he appointed his uncle, Charles Duke of Södermanland, as leader of the Swedish privy council. As history shows, it was one of the worst decisions of the young king. Charles soon started to turn public opinion against the Catholic king, and in 1595 the *Rigsdag* elected him as regent. After a few years Sigismund decided to use armed force to keep Charles in place. In 1598 the King arrived in Sweden, leading troops paid from his own treasury and some provided by a few supporting Polish magnates, but the poorly led campaign led to his defeat at the battle of Linköping (Stångebro). Many Swedish and Finnish supporters of Sigismund were killed or forced into exile to Poland. In 1599 Sigismund was dethroned by the *Rigsdag*, while in 1603 his uncle became the new king of Sweden, known as Charles IX.

Sigismund did not stop thinking about a return to Sweden, and his next step was to encourage his Polish subjects to support his claims. In 1600 he

Mounted portrait of King Sigismund III. Peter Paul Rubens, circa 1624. (Author's archive)

announced incorporation of the Swedish part of Livonia – the Duchy of Estonia – into Poland. Charles decided to strike first, though and his troops entered Polish Livonia. It started first of the Polish–Swedish conflicts, known as the 1600–1611 war. For the majority of Polish and Lithuanian nobles this war was just private affair of their king, so they were not eager to support it. For years the conflict was focused in Livonia, where Polish–Lithuanian forces were winning each and every pitched battle, including the famous encounter at Kircholm in 1605, when they completely destroyed Charles IX's army besieging Riga. Unfortunately they were unable to dislodge the Swedes from many castles and towns. The death of Charles IX in 1611 brought only a temporary pause, and in 1617 the new Swedish monarch, Gustav II Adolf, attacked Livonia again. The first breakthrough for the Swedes came in 1621. While the main Polish and Lithuanian forces were engaged in the south, defending Chocim (Khotyn) against a massive Turkish invasion, Gustav II Adolf landed with his forces

near the important port of Riga and after a short siege managed to capture it. A further campaign took place in Courland, where the Swedes took control of the capital city of Mitawa (Mitau). A Lithuanian counterattack, after a long siege, recovered Mitawa in July 1622 and after some further fighting both sides signed a truce that was kept until 1625. In this year Gustav II Adolf led a new attack against Polish Livonia, opposed by small Lithuanian forces.

King Gustav II Adolf. Copy of the portrait by Michiel Jansz van Mierevelt, circa 1633 (Rijksmuseum)

In January 1626 the Swedish king was victorious at Walmozja (Wallhof), defeating the main Lithuanian army. In spring 1626 he then decided to attack Prussia, for the first time striking directly into Poland's main territory. In July 1626 his troops landed at Piława (Pillau) and within a month managed to take control of the main towns and castles in Royal Prussia. With the Polish nobility seeing such actions as a direct threat to their economy, especially with the Swedes blocking main Baltic port of Gdańsk (Danzig), Sigismund III could finally receive the support he needed. No one could suspect that this new phase of the Polish–Swedish conflict would be a bitter and bloody struggle, with war waged in Prussia until 1629. For the first time Gustav II Adolf was to face the Polish army, led by one of the best commanders in the history of the Commonwealth – Hetman Stanisław Koniecpolski.

From the military point of view this conflict was a very important stepping stone for both the Poles and the Swedes. Of course in this book we will focus on the Polish experience and army. For the first time in a long time Polish army was to fight prolonged campaigns on its own main territory (unlike Livonia), fairly close to an important centre of the country. The terrain and character of the war dictated a style of fighting that was not a strong Polish suit, as it required plenty of infantry for both garrisons and siege operations.

It also, in a very painful way, showed the ineffective Polish fiscal system, as even with the Swedish army and fleet threatening the crucial port of Gdańsk – the Polish 'window on the Baltic' – the nobles were not so eager to raise taxes for a large army.

In this book we will first of all look into the unique Polish military establishment, with all the different types and ways of raising troops. Then we will present main Polish commanders from 1626–1629, led by Hetman Stanisław Koniecpolski; also discussing both the planned and real strength of the army in Prussia. We will look into details of each formation of the army (yes, there will be plenty of 'winged hussars' there), presenting their organisation, equipment and tactics. The next part of the book will focus on the conditions of the service, describing financial problems, provisions and other issues of the Polish army during the war. Additionally readers will be able to find there some information about the uniforms and flags of the troops. In the final part we will look into some examples of the army's performance, including sieges and 'small war', so important during the conflict in Prussia.

A few additional notes regarding terminology used in the book. All Livonian and Prussian towns and villages are called by their Polish name, followed by seventeenth-century German names (in brackets) which should make it easier to research for anyone using Swedish and German sources from the period. Polish, German and Latin terms (except personal and geographical names) are written in italics. Certain Eastern European and German words that are already established in English-language nomenclature are not marked in italics, for example hetman, haiduks, reiters. For many Polish military and measurement words that do not have an English equivalent, the original form will be used, and on its first appearance it will be accompanied by a footnote explaining its meaning. The currency mentioned in the text is the Polish *złoty* (abbreviated to zl), which was divided into 30 *groszy* (abbreviated to gr). In that period 1 *grosz* equals 0.27 grams of silver, so 1 *złoty* was approximately 8.1 grammes of silver. If a different currency is mentioned, its equivalent in the Polish currency will be given as well. All dates in the book will be written according to the Gregorian calendar, used at that time in the Polish–Lithuanian Commonwealth. The Swedes were still at that point using the Julian calendar, so events in their primary sources tend to be dated 10 days earlier than in Polish ones.

Chapter 1

The Commonwealth's Military System During the 1626–1629 War

The Union of Lublin, signed on 1 July 1569, created the Polish–Lithuanian Commonwealth, with the Kingdom of Poland and Grand Duchy of Lithuania joined by a real union and ruled by an elected monarch. One of the issues of the union was resolving the military matters of the new state. It was decided that both the Crown (Poland)[1] and Lithuania would have separate military forces, with their own command[2] and a slightly different military establishment (only Poland was to have a standing army, see below). In this chapter we will focus solely on the Polish army, referencing Lithuanian troops only in certain parts that relate to the situation in Prussia in the 1626–1629 period. The Lithuanian army, while no less interesting and worth its own book, will have to wait for another occasion to receive more in-depth treatment.

When researching seventeenth-century Polish warfare, one has to recognise first of all the very complicated structure of its military establishment. There were many elements of Polish armed forces: commanded, recruited and paid by the King, central and local authorities, towns and cities, even by wealthier individuals. Some of them had regular or semi-regular character, other could be raised only in specific situations.

I. The Quarter Army

In the fifteenth and sixteenth centuries the south-eastern Polish border was protected by a so-called 'Continuous Defence' (*obrona potoczna*): regular units of cavalry, supported by some infantry, that were paid mostly from the Royal Treasury. Their main task was to defend against Tatar raids but

---

1   Both names will be used to describe Polish troops.
2   Each army would have its two hetman: the Grand Hetman in command, and Field Hetman as second in command.

frequently in its history the force had to fight against Turks, Wallachians and Moldavians. Its size varied, depending on period, available funds and dangers to the country. In 1505 it had only 500 cavalry and 400 infantry, while five years later it had 3,000 cavalry and 300 infantry. It was a great practical military school for both officers and soldiers, who served there on a seasonal basis. Unfortunately its strength relied too much on an irregular flow of money from the Royal Treasury and taxes set up in the south-eastern districts of Poland.

A new, permanent force was required to protect the border though. It was named the 'quarter army' (*wojsko kwarciane*) after the method of financing the troops, a special tax on income from Crown estates. It was established in 1563, when a tax was set at the rate of one quarter of all income. In 1567 it was changed to a rate of one fifth but the name of the army remained the same. The election of Stephan Bathory in 1576 led to changes in this military formation, as the new monarch was very interested in this 'standing army'.

The majority of the new force was composed of hussars and cossack cavalry, with some small infantry garrisons deployed at the crucial fortresses of Kamieniec Podolski and Lubowla. Here are examples of the size of the 'quarter army' at the beginning of the seventeenth century:

Year(s)	Hussars	Cossacks[3]	Infantry	Other formations
1604	500	400	200	–
1606	900	300	400	–
1607	1,596	1,300	200	–
1609–1611	900	300	250	–
1618	1,750	1,200	200	150 reiters
1623	600	1,350	350	–
Summer 1626	1,500	3,100	1,300	1,000 dragoons, 100 reiters
Autumn 1626	–	600	300	–
1627	–	1,800	300	–
1629	600	2,300	600	–

The increase in the size of the army was always dictated by the growing danger of Tatar attacks, especially following the escalation of Cossack raids against the Tatars and Turks. The huge decrease from summer to autumn 1626 was the effect of the redeployment of the majority of available troops from Ukraine to Prussia, to fight against the Swedes. Field Hetman Stanisław Koniecpolski took with him all 12 banners[4] of hussars (1,500 horses), 23 banners of cossacks (2,600 horses), three units of dragoons (1,000 men) and six banners of Polish infantry (1,000 men). Left to defend Ukraine, under the command of Stefan Chmielecki, were just four 'old' cossack banners (500 horses), reinforced by one newly recruited banner (100 horses).

The 'quarter army' was, like its predecessor, a great proving ground for many Polish soldiers, who gathered there invaluable experience in fighting

---

3   Polish cossack cavalry, not Zaporozhian Cossacks, as they were a separate formation. More details about this formation in Chapter 3.

4   (Pol.) *Chorągiew*, equivalent of a company.

'small war' against elusive Tatar warriors. It continue to defend the Polish border until 1652, when it was merged with supplementary troops into a new standing army, the so-called *wojsko komputowe*.[5]

II. Supplementary Troops

The 'Quarter army', while serving as a standing military force, was far too small to fight on its own during longer campaigns or against strong enemy armies (for example, Turks). Therefore in the case of open conflict so-called supplement troops (*wojsko suplementowe*) were raised. The *Sejm* during its proceedings decided the size, composition and cost of the newly raised army. Raised troops were then gathered under the command of the Grand and/ or Field Hetman, rarely under command of the King himself (for example the 1609–1611 siege of Smolensk). They could be joined by the 'quarter

Hussars from the beginning of the seventeenth century, from the so-called 'Stockholm Roll', portraying the Royal entry into Cracow in 1605. Unfortunately we do not know the name of the artist who painted it. (Author's archive)

army' but often, when the latter was required to defend the border, while the main campaign was taking place elsewhere (Livonia, Muscovy), it was supplementary troops that comprised the bulk of the army, supported by additional forces such as Zaporozhian Cossacks, volunteer private troops and a levy of the nobility. Such a *komput*, as the army was normally called, changed its size and organisation during each campaign. Some units were disbanded due to losses or ending their agreed time of service; others were newly raised, often based on the previously serving soldiers but under a new commander or even reformed into a different formation.[6]

Sometimes some units could also be moved between the Polish and Lithuanian armies, starting the campaign serving in one, to finish it in the other. For example two units of foreign infantry, under the command of Arthur Aston Jr and James Butler, were initially recruited in 1621 to be part of the Crown army against the Turks. As they arrived too late to take part in the Khotyn campaign, they were instead sent to Courland and, as part of the Lithuanian *komput*, fought in 1622 against the Swedes. In 1626 a large contingent of Lithuanian troops was sent from Livonia to Prussia, to aid King Sigismund against Gustav Adolf. This force contained three banners of hussars, one regiment and one banner of reiters, three banners of Polish/Lithuanian infantry, with

---

5   From the Polish word *komput*, used to describe an army serving at the given time.

6   For example cossack cavalry converted into a hussar banner (a so-called *pohusarzenie*).

total strength of 1,950 horses and men. Those units took part in the initial phase of the war, including the battle of Gniew, but then the majority of them were sent back to Livonia or disbanded. In fact only one banner of hussars and a regiment of reiters reminded in the Polish *komput* and fought under Koniecpolski's command until the end of the war.

Supplementary troops were normally disbanded at the end of a campaign/war. Some of them could be kept in service for a longer period, for example joining the 'quarter army' or stationed as a garrison. Unfortunately the common motif during the whole seventeenth century was that due to lack of pay soldiers mutinied, creating so-called *konfederacja*, moving away from the theatre of war into Poland/Lithuania and mercilessly plundering the local populations, waiting for delayed money. We will look in more detail into this problem in Chapter 4.

III. *Wybraniecka* Infantry

The Polish army was severely lacking infantry, relying heavily on cavalry. When Stephan Bathory took over the Polish throne in 1576, he tried to reform the military system of his new kingdom and introduce conscription of peasant infantry from all lands: owned by the Crown, nobility and clergy. The Polish nobles strongly opposed such a far-reaching idea so the King was allowed to create a new formation based on peasants from Crown-owned lands only. The new troops were called *wybraniecka* infantry, from the Polish word *wybraniec*, which means 'chosen'. From each 20 lans (*łany*)[7] one man 'who would volunteer himself, [being] amongst others braver and more eager to serve in the time of war',[8] and was to be freed from any tax obligation on his lan in exchange for military service. Peasants from the other 19 lans were to take the burden of his tax and work duties. Once every three months a designated *rotmistrz*[9] or lieutenant for the land was to muster and train all troops, who should be equipped 'with good handgun, sabre, axe, in the uniform that his *rotmistrz* or lieutenant had chosen for him, similar to those that other infantryman [in his unit] will have, [also] needing to have powder and lead'.[10]

The initial deployment of the *wybraniecka* was fairly successful, with the units bravely fighting during the sieges of Velikiye Luki in 1580 and Pskov in 1581–1582. Quickly though the new formation encountered many issues. The main problem was to gather enough soldiers from each region to create a banner (equivalent of the company) from them. Recruits were poorly trained and, despite the initial decree issued by Bathory, they were not paid for their participation in the campaign. They were normally quickly relegated to

---

7   The Polish unit of field measurement, depending on region varied between 18 and 28 hectares.
8   'Uniwersał JKMści o wybraniu piechoty w dobrach królewskich' in *Sprawy wojenne króla Stefana Batorego. Dyjaryusze, relacyje, listy i akta z lat 1576–1568* (Kraków: Akad Umiejętności, 1887), p.117.
9   Equivalent of a captain. The rank of *rotmistrz* was used in the cavalry (including reiters) and all types of Polish infantry. Foreign infantry and dragoons used Western terminology, so their companies' commanders were called captains.
10 'Uniwersał JKMści o wybraniu piechoty…', p.118.

Polish infantry from the beginning of the seventeenth century, 'Stockholm Roll'. (Author's archive)

garrison duties, where units suffered a high percentage of desertions and non-combat deaths due to sickness and starvation. In December 1625 a gathering of nobles from Ruthenian Voivodship described the *wybraniecka* as 'hungry, tired and what is more they are not trained to fight'. They suggested replacing them with regular infantry or to ensure that methods of training were changed and improved.[11] We will look into more details into their service in Prussia in the 1626–1629 period in Chapter 3.

IV. Zaporozhian Cossacks

King Stephan Bathory attempted to create semi-regular militia from Zaporozhian Cossacks, which could be then used to support Polish troops in defending the border against the Tatars. He wanted to use the Transylvanian experience with free haiduks and apply it to Cossacks. The idea was to control those unruly warriors, prevent them from igniting the situation with Turks and Tatars; finally to be able to use them in his planned wars against Muscovy. The initial register (*rejestr*) of Cossacks from 1578 was very small, with only

---

11 *Akta grodzkie i ziemskie z czasów Rzeczypospolitej Polskiej*, volume XX (Lwów: Towarzystwo Naukowe, 1909), p.222.

500 men. They were to receive small annual fee and cloth for uniforms. The King also designated a lieutenant (*porucznik*)[12] and special muster clerk, to control the register.[13]

The size of the register could be only changed by the decision of the *Sejm*. In 1590 it was increased to 1,000 men but of course it was still very small, leading to dissatisfaction from the Cossacks' side. It was one of the main reasons for the Cossack uprisings, which (until 1648) were always defeated by a combination of the Polish standing army, private troops and registered Cossacks. Depending on circumstances, the number of registered Cossacks could be increased, usually varying between 5,000 and 6,000 men.[14] In 1630 the register achieved its maximum size of 8,000 men but it was then decreased to 6,000 in 1638 and it kept that size until Khmelnytsky's uprising in 1648.

While Cossacks did not take part in the 1626–1629 war in Prussia, there were at least two projects that involved their deployment against the Swedes. In 1628 an anonymous author, probably Grand Crown Chancellor Jakub Zadzik, in his *Discurs na sejmie in Iulio de subsodo na wojnę pruską* suggested to the *Sejm* that 4,000 Cossacks should be sent to Prussia. They were to sail on their chaika (*czajka*) boats via the rivers Bug and Vistula, to be used against the Swedish fleet.[15] Another, rather similar, *Discurs*, written by Prince Jerzy Zbaraski, was issued at the time of the 1629 *Sejm*. The Prince wanted to employ 3,000 Cossacks, who, via the same route suggested in 1628, would arrive in Prussia and start to harass Swedish communication lines on the coast.[16] While widely discussed by nobles during the *Sejm*, those projects were never fulfilled, instead the Cossacks supported the 'quarter army' in defending the Polish border against Tatar incursions in 1629.

V. Levy of Nobility

In case of grave danger to the country, the King could raise a levy of the nobility. Since 1493 he could only do that with agreement from the *Sejm*. The levy was, at least in theory, composed of all able-bodied nobles in the land, arriving with their retinues (if they could afford one). Additionally towns were obligated to supply a levy of infantry, which, depending on the size and importance of the town, could bring between a few and a few hundred men.

In time of peace, nobles from each voivodships were obliged to attend musters (usually annual ones), where their number and equipment could be checked. Official documents mentioned that nobles should arrive *armatus*

12 Later called hetman.

13 'Uniwersał królewski o wojsku zaporoskim z 1578 r', Zdzisław Spieralski, Jan Wimmer (ed.), *Wypisy źródłowe do historii polskiej sztuki wojennej. Zeszyt piąty. Polska sztuka wojenna w latach 1563–1647* (Warszawa, 1961), pp.54–56.

14 *Acta historia res gestas Kozacorum Ukrainiensum illustrantia* (Lwów: Nauk. Tovarystvo im. Shevchenko, 1908), volume I, pp.281, 290.

15 Henryk Wisner, Dwa polskie plany wojny szwedzkiej z 1629 r. (Projekty Jerzego Zbaraskiego i Krzysztofa Radziwiłła)', *Zapiski Historyczne*, volume XLII, part 2 (Warszawa, 1977), p.16.

16 *Ibidem*, p.17.

Tin figurines of a Polish officer (hetman) and horseman. Decorations from Hetman Stanisław Żółkiewski's sarcophagus, circa 1621. (Muzeum Narodowe, Kraków)

et hastatus (armed and mounted), with a fully equipped retinue.[17] While in theory the majority of the levy was due to appear either 'hussar style' or 'cossack style', in practice some of them arrived at the muster without horses or even weapons. Sometimes the *Sejm* in its acts regarding the levy did mention service on foot, 'with sabre and *rusznica* (handgun)'. Additionally towns in Poland were, since the late fifteenth century, obliged to send some infantry as a part of the support to the levy of the nobility. Of course the size of such contingents varied, depending on the importance and wealth of the city. For example Nowy Sącz in 1621 despatched four musket-armed haiduks, two mounted cossacks, one small-calibre cannon and three supply wagons (each with four horses).[18] The military value of such 'troops' varied depending on the period and region. Usually nobles from the south-east of Poland were the best fighting part of the levy, due to their experience in fighting against

---

17   Its size depended always on individual wealth of the noble. Some of them took few retainers but many poorer ones arrived on their own.

18   Jan Sygański, *Historya Nowego Sącza od wstąpienia Dynastyi Wazów do pierwszego rozbioru Polski*, volume I (Lwów, 1901), p.22.

Tatar raiders. The levy from each land/district was in time of war organised into territorial banners (companies) and regiments, led by prominent nobles and magnates. Unfortunately they were more often a hindrance than a real support to the normal army: unruly, ill-disciplined and poorly trained, with hundreds of tabor wagons accompanying their units.

The levy took part in the initial part of the war in 1626, with nobles of the northern provinces defending Prussia against the Swedes. At the muster that took place near Grudziądz on 21 August 1626, Chełmno Voivodship supported by troops sent by Chełmno Bishopric fielded 767 horses (including 242 hussars and 525 cossacks) and 530 infantry.[19] Those forces at the beginning of September joined the army led by King Sigismund. Nobles from the Prince-Bishopric of Warmia took part in the defence of Prussia, at the end of August besieging the Swedish-held town of Orneta, but after a few days were forced to retreat by the garrison of Elbląg.[20] It is possible though that at least some of those soldiers were in fact district troops, raised and paid by Voivodships (see next section). Other areas of Poland also sent some levies to join the King in 1626, it seems that nobles from Poznań, Kalisz, Brześć Kujawski and Inowrocław Voivodeships were present in Prussia during the summer–autumn of that year.[21] The majority of levies gathered during the war never left their land, though, protecting it against attacks by Tatars and Protestant (for example ex-Danish) troops. Hetman Koniecpolski mentioned that levies from some of the regions – Płock and Chełmno Voivodship – arrived to support his army in October 1628 but it was too little and too late, and despite their eagerness they were not really any help in the struggle against the Swedes during this campaign.[22] It is almost certain that the sudden eagerness of the nobles to support the main army was mostly dictated by the aggressive strategy of Gustav Adolf and the fact that he managed to capture the vital town of Brodnica.

VI. District troops

In times of dire need, for example when the standing army was destroyed during the war or where their district was threatened by marauders and/ or approaching enemy, the local *Sejmiki* could raise so-called district troops (*wojska powiatowe*). They were enlisted soldiers, paid and controlled directly by the *Sejmik*. Such troops were equipped and organised in the same way as the standing army, usually composed of banners of cossacks and infantry,

---

19   Jan Seredyka, *Sejm w Toruniu z 1626 roku* (Wrocław-Warszawa-Kraków: Zakład Narodowy im. Ossolińskich, 1966, 1966), p.23

20   Archiwum Państwowe w Gdańsku, 300/53, no 48, *Diariusz Wojny Pruskiej z roku 1626*, pp.346, 349.

21   Jan Seredyka, *Sejm w Toruniu*, p.23.

22   'Relacja IMP. Wojewody Sendomirskiego, Hetmana Polnego Koronnego, o wojnie przeszłego roku w Warszawie, dnia 4 Februari 1629 uczyniona', Otto Laskowski (ed.) *Przyczynki do działań hetmana polnego koronnego Stanisława Koniecpolskiego w Prusach Wschodnich i na Pomorzu przeciwko Gustawowi Adolfowi*, *Przegląd Historyczno-Wojskowy*, volume IX, part 3 (Warszawa, 1937), p.422.

with hussars and reiters also raised depending on the region. Their pay was usually much higher than that of regular troops, which helped to entice veteran soldiers. Time of service was often short, with just one quarter (three months), sometimes two. District troops were from time to time sent to support the regular army, when they would be under command of the hetman. On other occasions they would be stationed in their district, with their main task being protection of it.

During 1626–1629, especially in the early stage of the war, King Sigismund encouraged voivodships to raise district troops that could then be used to strengthen his army in Prussia. Chełmno, Pomeranian and Brześć Kujawski Voivodships did oblige, paying for some additional troops that served next to the levy of nobility. In December 1626 Poznań Voivodship decided to raise two banners of cossack cavalry (100 horses each) under *rotmistrz* Adam Olbracht Przyjemski and Łukasz Górski but they were most likely kept to defend the province.[23] Also some Masovian districts agreed to do so, raising hussar banners that did see service in 1626.[24] The Prince-Bishopric of Warmia kept some troops on their pay through the majority of the war, used solely for defence purposes and being in fact an independent force, not under Koniecpolski's command. They were probably mostly infantry units, used for garrison duties. Some other regions raised their own district troops to protect themselves from marauding forces pillaging the Polish border. The main source of the problem was ex-Danish troops of the late Ernest von Mansfeld, who in late 1626–mid 1627 were fighting with Imperial forces in Silesia and Moravia, often marching through parts of Wielkopolska. Both district troops and the levy of nobility were used, without much success, to fight them off. It is possible that some district troops did serve alongside the regular army in Prussia after 1626, unfortunately we lack detailed information about such activities.

VII. Town Troops

Royal towns normally employed a very small city guard, guarding the gates and patrolling the streets. Town guilds and local ethnic minorities (Jews, Armenians, etc.) were tasked with defending the city walls in case of siege and had to pay for their own weapons, equipment and ammunition. Only the wealthiest of towns could afford to employ mercenaries, not to mention keeping them in service for a longer period of time.

Gdańsk, one of the main targets of the Swedish invasion, dug deeply into city coffers to protect itself from Gustav Adolf's attack. Already in 1624 the city council had hired 2,000 German mercenaries, with a further 3,000 employed by summer 1626. Additionally to those 5,000 soldiers, more than

---

23 BK 341, pp.224v–226, *Universauł seymiku szredzkiego pro die XXIX mensis Decemb. w Srzedzie złożonego.*

24 Jan Seredyka, *Sejm w Toruniu...*, p.24.

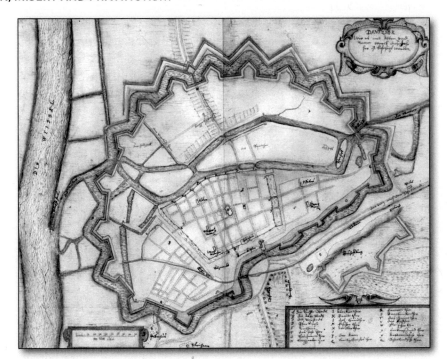

City plan of Gdańsk (Danzig) circa 1630, with fortifications built during the 1626–1629 war, drawn by Heinrich Thome. (Krigsarkivet, Stockholm)

6,000 city militia,[25] divided into five foot regiments of 12 companies each, supplemented the defence. The majority of those troops were infantry but sources mention also some Western-style cavalry.[26] Gdańsk also spent a large amount of money on building fortifications, in 1626 approximately 500,000 florins and a year later up to 800,000 florins.[27] This army was not under Koniecpolski's command though, we should rather think about them as allied troops. The city council employed Dutch veteran officer Liesemann, who was nominated as a colonel in charge of the Gdańsk soldiers. The main areas of recruiting troops were Hamburg, Bremen, Wismar and Rostock, with mercenaries transported via ships to Gdańsk. The final attempt to recruit in Silesia and Brandenburg, made in 1626, brought only 105 men, as demand for new soldiers greatly exceeded the available supply.[28]

Of course Gdańsk was not the only town in Prussia that fought against the Swedes. Malbork had 100 enlisted infantry, designated as the garrison of the castle; also 40 so-called *ceklarze*, town servants, who were serving as day and night watch. Both groups were poorly trained, equipped with old weapons and had very minimal impact on the short-lived defence of the town in July 1626.[29] Toruń as early as 1626 hired 100 infantry and 50 cavalry, that were sent alongside Sigismund's army to Prussia. In 1628 Colonel Friedrich von

---

25   Jerzy Teodorczyk, 'Wyprawa szwedzka z Meklemburgii do Prus Królewskich 1627 r.', *Studia i Materiały do Historii Wojskowości*, volume VI, part 2 (Warszawa 1960), p.118.

26   Probably both mercenaries and wealthier citizens.

27   Jerzy Teodorczyk, 'Wyprawa', op. cit., p.106.

28   *Ibidem*, p.118.

29   Jerzy Teodorczyk, 'Walki o Malbork w roku 1626, z uwzględnieniem opisu stanu fortecy, piechoty polskiej i szwedzkiej oraz politycznego tła wydarzeń', in *Studia do Dziejów Dawnego Uzbrojenia i Ubioru Wojskowego*, volume 7 (Kraków, 1978), pp.39–67.

Rossen (Ross) was employed to command Toruń's troops and to oversee building of the fortifications. The town kept some mercenaries on its payroll throughout the whole war and those soldiers proved crucial in the repelling of a Swedish attack in February 1629.[30] Their strength varied between 80 and 350 men, supported by militia raised from the city's population.

The Royal City of Toruń (Thorn) with fortifications built during the 1626–1629 war. Jacob Hoffman, 1631. (Biblioteka Narodowa, Warszawa)

Both sides of a medal commemorating the successful defence of Toruń (Thorn) against the Swedes in 1629. (Muzeum Narodowe, Kraków)

---

30   Jacob Heinrich Zernecke, *Das bey denen schwedischen Kriegen bekriegte Thorn oder zuverläszige Erzehlung desjenigen was sich bey dieser Stadt im Jahr 1629, 1655, 1658 und 1703 in anfällen Bloqvir- Bombardir- und Belagerungen denckwürdiges zugetragen: dabey ein nöthiger Anhang zur thornischen Chronicke* (Thorn, 1712), pp.1–18.

VIII. Royal Guard (Household Guard)

In the first half of the seventeenth century the Royal Guard, known also as the Household Guard (*gwardia przyboczna*) was a division of private troops of the monarch, paid from his own treasury. Stephen Bathory, reigning 1576–1586, largely increased the size of the Royal Guard. Numerous cavalry and infantry units were enlisted in his native Transylvania and served with great distinction in the wars against Gdańsk (1576–1577) and Muscovy (1577–1582). When Sigismund III was elected in 1587, he took over some of Bathory's Hungarian troops and also raised some new units, mostly of the Western type. The new king kept his Household Guard busy, with soldiers fighting against Turks and Tatars in 1595–1596, landing with Sigismund in Sweden in 1598, from 1609 engaged in Polish intervention in Muscovy and in 1620–1621 again against Turks and Tatars.

Foreign infantry in Polish service during the Smolensk War, 1632–1634. Wilhelm Hondius, 1636. (Author's archive)

In the 1620s the King kept in his service a few hundred (usually between 400 and 600 men) Hungarian infantry, a banner (company) of reiters-drabants (approximately 100 horses), and a banner of Tatar-cossacks used to deliver royal mail (between 70 and 100 horses).[31] There were also some additional troops such as halberdiers and musicians, which were garrisoned in Warsaw, but they were not treated as combatants. A unit we could also add to the Royal Guard, but not to the Household troops, was a unique banner of hussars, the so-called 'Court banner'. It was composed of the royal courtiers, who did not receive pay for their service, but instead had to pay for their own equipment and retinues. It was more a ceremonial than a battle unit although it could accompany the King during the war.

---

31 Mirosław Nagielski, 'Gwardia przyboczna Władysława IV (1632–1648)', *Studia i Materiały do Historii Wojskowości*, volume XXVII (Warszawa, 1984), pp.115–117.

In certain situations, such as in 1598 during Swedish expedition or in 1625–1626, the King could raise additional troops paid from his treasury. We would not go so far as to call them Royal Guard though, it is better to think of them as private troops raised by the King. As we will see in 1626, as soon as it was possible such units were moved to become part of the standing army, and paid from regular taxes, not from the royal purse.

In spring to summer 1626 Sigismund was forced to loan money from his own wife, Queen Constance of Austria, to be able to raise foreign troops to defend Prussia. At least 12 'free companies' were created, with their strength varying between 100 and 500 men with a total strength of approximately 2,700 men. Some of them may in fact have been in royal service since 1624, connected to his plans against Sweden. Also some cavalry units, mostly *lisowczycy* light horse, were employed that way. As we mentioned before, we would not count those units as a part of the Household Guard – by the end of 1626 some of them were disbanded, while the majority became part of the standing Polish army in Prussia, paid from taxes ordered on *Sejm*. Of course that does not mean that the King arrived in the theatre of war without his Royal Guard. In fact he took almost all available troops, with the Court hussar banner (probably 200 horses), Otto Denhoff's reiters banner (200 horses) and four Hungarian infantry banners (total of 600 men). They took part in the battle of Gniew, where Denhoff was killed on 22 September, when leading the charge of his reiters. Some guard units were assigned to Royal Prince Władysław, when he stayed in Prussia in 1627 and 1629. Since at least 1621 he had several dozen Scots as his personal bodyguard,[32] there is also information about 'Hungarians from His Royal Prince infantry' in 1629, which could indicate that at least one of the banners from his father's troops was serving under Władysław's name.[33] When Sigismund III returned to the theatre of war in 1629 he also was accompanied by some of his guards. Interesting fact: the 'Court banner' of hussars was so undermanned (due to courtiers being late to arrive in Prussia), that on 17 July 1629 the newly arrived banner of hussars under Dobrogost Grzybowski[34] was disbanded and all the soldiers used to strengthen the 'Court banner' itself.[35]

IX. Private Troops

Wealthy magnates tended to keep private armies on their pay. Their role varied from purely ceremonial activities (such as assisting their employer during his journeys), through more or less violent internal affairs (such as skirmishes between neighbours) to full scale military operations, when they supported the regular army during the campaigns or defended the employer's

---

32 Mirosław Nagielski, 'Gwardia przyboczna Władysława IV', pp.116–117.
33 'Kontynuacja Diariusza o dalszych postępach wojennych ze Szwedami a die 1 Julii (1629)', Otto Laskowski (ed.), *Przyczynki do działań hetmana polnego koronnego Stanisława Koniecpolskiego w Prusach Wschodnich i na Pomorzu przeciw Gustawowi Adolfowi, Przegląd Historyczno-Wojskowy*, volume IX, part 3, (Warszawa, 1936), p.440.
34 Either his private unit or (more likely) district troops.
35 'Kontynuacja Diariusza', p.437.

Officer of the Polish infantry from the beginning of the seventeenth century. 'Stockholm Roll'. (Author's archive)

land against raiders such as Tatars or Cossacks. Of course the size of such private forces depended on the wealth and importance of each noble, also on their willingness to spend coin on equipping, training and keeping in service their own soldiers. There were a few main sources of recruiting troops into private armies:

- So-called 'clients', nobles living on magnates' land, being his neighbours, relatives and/or depending on his political and economic patronage. They would normally create a unit of hussars, cossack cavalry, also serving as officers in private troops. If serving as companions in the cavalry, they would provide their own retinue, from their relatives, friends, servants, etc.
- Professional soldiers, often foreigners, employed mostly as officers and NCOs of the Western-type troops (infantry, dragoons, reiters), also as gunners with the magnate's artillery park. Sometimes whole units were employed that way (for example from Transylvania) but it was not a very common occurrence.
- Subjects, usually peasants from lands that belonged to the magnate. Some of them could serve in permanent/semi-permanent units (like haiduks), others could simply be armed ad hoc, as some sort of land militia, to defend land against Tatars or Cossacks.
- Military settlers, often former soldiers or foreigners (such as Tatars or Wallachians) that in exchange for a land allowance from the magnate were required to provide him with military service.

Let us look into some examples of the size and composition of private troops. The magnate in question will be Tomasz Zamoyski (1594–1638), voivode of Kijów, starost of Kraków and one of the wealthiest Polish nobles in 1620s. In September 1618, to support Hetman Stanisław Żółkiewski's army against the Tatars, he brought 1,200 well-equipped men 'paid from his own coffer'.[36] In 1624 he joined the army led by King Sigismund III himself, bringing 1,000 men and six cannons.[37] There is an even more detailed roster of his private troops,[38] which in summer 1626 marched to Prussia to fight against the Swedes (again, under command of the King):

---

36   Tomasz Żurkowski, *Żywot Tomasza Zamoyskiego* (Lwów, 1860), p.35.
37   *Ibidem*, p.95.
38   *Ibidem*, p.107.

- cossack banner of Stanisław Czernecki, 150 horses
- cossack banner of Adam Kisiel, 150 horses
- cossack banner of Andrzej Drwalowski, 150 horses
- cossack banner of Aleksander Pluciński, 150 horses
- Polish infantry banner of Bohdarowski, 120 men
- Foreign infantry company under Scottish captain Gryma (Graham?), 100 men

It is important to note though, that the biggest military show of power was often connected with non-warfare endeavours. After Sigismund's death in 1632, when Polish magnates and nobles were gathering in Warsaw to elect the new king, Zamoyski arrived in October with a small army, raised to 'make sure that factions of heretics and schismatics[39] will not triumph [in the election]':

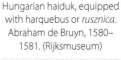

Hungarian haiduk, equipped with harquebus or *rusznica*. Abraham de Bruyn, 1580–1581. (Rijksmuseum)

- Hussar banner of Paweł Słotowski, 150 horses (enlisted unit)
- Hussar banner of Jan Dzik, 150 horses (gathered from Zamoyski's subjects in Ukraine and Volhynia)
- *Petyhorcy* banner, 200 horses (gathered from Zamoyski's subjects in Ukraine and Volhynia)
- cossack banners, 100 horses
- Polish infantry, 200 enlisted men
- Foreign infantry, 800 men raised from Zamoyski's subjects and trained by foreign officers and NCOs
- Dragoons, 100 men
- 30-man strong retinue comprising 'friends and neighbours'[40]

To put that in some perspective, the 'quarter army' had at the same time 1,540 winged hussars, 2,250 cossack cavalry, 1,350 dragoons and 600 Polish infantry.

Private troops appeared in larger numbers in Prussia in 1626 and in 1629. On both occasions it was connected with the presence of Sigismund III in the theatre of war: his courtiers and high ranking officials arrived alongside the monarch and brought their troops with them. In 1626, due to the absence of the 'quarter' army, private troops were a large part of the field army. We can identify at least 14 banners of hussars, 34 banners of cossack cavalry, eight banners of Polish-Hungarian infantry and one company of German infantry that belonged to private armies. While the strength of most of those units is unknown, even with a minimal assumption of 100 horses/men per banner (which was fairly standard at that time

---

39   He meant non-Roman Catholic Christians, in that case mostly Protestant.
40   *Ibidem*, p.144

across the Commonwealth), we have here at least 4,800 cavalry and 900 infantry – all recruited and paid from the private coffers of Polish magnates.

In summer 1629 we can find following units that arrived to support the army:

Owner	Formation	Strength	Date of the arrival in army camp
Kasper Działyński	Hussars	6 (retinue)	1 July 1629
Sierakowski	? (possibly hussars)	6 (retinue)	1 July 1629
Aleksander Ludwik Radziwiłł	Haiduks	Unknown (banner)	3 July 1629
Stefan Pac	Hussars	30 (retinue)	9 July 1629
Dobrogost Grzybowski[41]	Hussars	Unknown (banner)	12 July 1629
Tomasz Zamoyski	Haiduks	Unknown (banner)	28 July 1629
Paweł Stefan Sapieha	Haiduks	Unknown (banner)	30 July 1629
Woyna	Hussars	6 (retinue)	30 July 1629

There is also some limited information about magnates supporting Koniecpolski in autumn 1628. In the official report to the *Sejm* he praised Stanisław Łubieński, Bishop of Płock, for sending a large retinue of private troops, which was then used to fight off Swedish raids from recently captured Brodnica. Others that sent their troops (probably cavalry) to Prussia were Erazm Domaszewski, Crown Equerry; Kacper Denhoff, *starosta* of Dorpat and Henryk Buryan Count Schampach (Szampach).[42] It is more than probable that those magnates that held official posts in Prussia and the near neighbourhood, such as Samuel Żaliński (voivode of Malbork) and Melchior Wejher (voivode of Chełmno) also kept some private troops in their own holdings and used them to protect them against Swedes, unfortunately it is very hard to find details about such actions. They tend to also have some troops under their name in the regular army and it is often very difficult to distinguish if the primary source mentioned private or *komput* soldiers.

X. 'Fee tail' Troops

A very specific type of private troops, normally counted as a separate military 'branch', were so-called 'fee tail' troops (*wojska ordynackie*). Four wealthy magnate families (three in Poland and one in Lithuania) were granted by the Polish king the privilege of fee tail (*ordynacja*), which allowed them to keep all their estates without any dispersion, making sure that all those lands were always passed to the next male heir. In exchange for that, they had to keep a standing military force, which was used as a garrison in the main fortress of the estates. The magnates also had to, in time of war, raise additional troops to be sent to the main army, where they would be under the command of a

---

41　It is possible though, that this unit was composed of district troops and not private ones.
42　'Relacja IMP. Wojewody Sendomirskiego', p.426.

hetman, like any other regular troops. A list of fee tails and their military obligation:[43]

Name of fee tail	Name of the family	Year of creation	Number of troops in the peacetime	Main fortress	Additional troops to be raised during the war	Notes
Radziwiłł[44]	Radziwiłł	1586	6,000[45]	Słuck	None	Lithuanian
Zamoyska	Zamoyski	1589	200 infantry	Zamość	None	Polish
Pińczowska	Myszkowski	1601	100 infantry, 50 cavalry	Pińczów	None	Polish
Ostrogska/Dubieńska	Ostrogski	1618	600 infantry	Dubno	300 infantry, 300 cavalry	Polish

As no fee tails were located in Prussia, none of their troops took part in the 1626–1629 war, despite their owners (such as Tomasz Zamoyski or Władysław Myszkowski) taking part in some campaigns. At the end of 1626 there was a plan to send one banner of hussars from Ostrogski's family fee tail to Prussia. The unit was to be composed of 160 or 170 horses, with 60 zl pay per month and a planned six months of service.[46] It is highly unlikely that it arrived in Prussia though, instead – amongst other local troops and 'quarter army' soldiers – defending the Polish borders against Tatars.

XI. Vassals and Fiefs

The Commonwealth had one vassal state – the Duchy of Courland and Semigalia – and one fief – the Duchy of Prussia, known also as Ducal Prussia.[47] Both of them had a small military obligation towards the Polish king.

Based on the Treaty of Vilnius from 1561 Courland became the personal fief of the Grand Duke of Lithuania (later the king of Poland). One of the paragraphs of the treaty mentioned the military obligation of the newly created country. Except for normal defensive duty, Courland was to raise a token force of 100 horse that could be sent to the Polish king even if he fought away from Livonia. Those soldiers could be taken either from the Horse Service (*Rossdienst*) which was the Courland levy of nobility, or from enlisted troops. The Polish king could also request a stronger contingent, but in that case he would have to pay for the additional troops himself. In reality, when the Courland auxiliary force was requested to take part in Bathory's war against Muscovy in 1579, local nobles decided to pay for 200 mercenaries, while Duke Gotthard Kettler financed an additional 100.[48] Courland troops took part in the 1600–1611 war in Livonia, where they supported Hetman Chodkiewicz's army during the famous battle of Kircholm in 1605. During

---

43   Aleksander Mełeń, *Ordynacje w dawnej Polsce* (Lwów: Pamiętnik Historyczno-Prawny, 1929), pp.5–14, 54.
44   It was in fact divided into three smaller fee tails, for each main branch of the family. They were named after the 'capital' of the land: Kłeck, Nieświerz and Ołyka.
45   Divided between all three fee tails of the family.
46   Archiwum Narodowe w Krakowie, Archiwum Sanguszków, Volumin 563, file 3.
47   Since 1618 in personal union with the Margraviate of Brandenburg.
48   Mariusz Balcerek, *Księstwo Kurlandii i Semigalii w wojnie Rzeczypospolitej ze Szwecją w latach 1600–1629* (Poznań: Wydawnictwo Poznańskie, 2012), p.61.

Musketeer from Friedrich Jungermann's 'Paraten Schlachtordung', dated between 1617–1625. It gives some idea how Polish (foreign), Gdańsk, Brandenburg and Imperial soldiers would look during the war. (Biblioteka Cyfrowa Uniwersytetu Wrocławskiego)

the period 1621–1629 they were not so successful, facing overwhelming Swedish forces and having no impact on the military struggle in Livonia.

The Duchy of Prussia was, according to the 1525 Treaty of Cracow, to raise an army to defend its own territory 'with all its subjects and all its power'. Additionally the Duke was to raise an auxiliary force of 100 horse, that could be used either to defend Prussia or to accompany the Polish king when facing 'heathens or other'. On the latter occasion, those troops would be paid by the Polish treasury, however.[49] As was the case with Courland, the King could request a stronger contingent from Prussia, which again would be taken on the Polish payroll.

Defence of Ducal Prussia itself relied on so-called Land Defence (*Landesdefension*) divided into levy of nobility serving as cavalry (*Dienstpflichtige*) and infantry militia, recruited from peasants and some towns (*Wybranzen/Amtsmuketiere*).[50] They were supported by a few companies of enlisted troops defending Kłajpeda (Memel) and Piława (Pillau). Poorly equipped and trained, they were no match for the Swedish army in 1626 however, quickly losing vital locations. Defenders of Pillau – two companies of infantry (Günther von Bronsart's and Achatius von Wallenrodt's) – were composed of only 350 infantry, so it was no surprise that they did not even attempt to fight against the main Swedish army.[51] As King Sigismund III requested more support from Elector George Wilhelm, the Prussian *landtag* decided to increase taxes, raise some troops locally and even allow for some mercenary troops from Brandenburg to arrive in the Duchy, to provide better defence against the Swedes. The latter were soldiers initially raised as protection against Protestant and Catholic troops during the early stages of 'Danish' phase of the Thirty Years' War.

By the beginning of 1627 the Elector's forces in Prussia were composed of the following units:

A. Contingent from Brandenburg[52]
- *Leibregiment zu Fuss* (Foot Lifeguard regiment) of seven companies under Lieutenant Colonel Konrad von Burgsdorff. Each company was 200 men strong. The first company (*Leibgarde zu fuss*) had a white standard, rest of the companies received carmine-red flags

49 Polish translation of the Treaty of Cracow (last entry from 3/06/2019) <https://historia.org.pl/2009/10/27/traktat-krakowski-8-kwietnia-1525-r/>
50 Sławomir Augusiewicz, *Przebudowa wojska pruskiego w latach 1655–1660* (Oświęcim: Wydawnictwo Napoleon V, 2014), pp.26–40.
51 *Ibidem*, pp.78, 98.
52 Curt Jany, *Geschichte der königlich preussischen Armee bis zum Jahre 1807*. Volume I, von den Anfängen bis 1740 (Berlin: K. Siegismund, 1928), pp.52–53.

- Colonel Hillebrandt von Kracht's infantry regiment of 12 companies (also 200 men strong each), each with blue standards
- Horse regiment (harquebusiers) under Hans Wolf von der Henden, with *Leibgarde zu Ross* (Horse Lifeguard) company of 116 men and four horse companies, each with 96 men.
- These troops were also supported by a small field artillery company of four cannons and four mortars

B. Locally Enlisted Troops[53]
- Infantry companies of Hans Erhard von Pröck (150 men, garrison of Kłajpeda), Günther von Bronsart (200 men), Achatius von Wallenrodt (150 men), Nicklas von Tettelbach (size unknown)[54]
- Horse (harquebusier) company of Georg von Kospoth (100 men), that was raised as a Prussian auxiliary force for the Polish Crown
- Additionally one new infantry company, 200 men under Fabian von Lehndorff, was raised in spring 1627.

C. *Wybranzen* and *Dienstpflichtige* troops[55]
- Approximately 11 infantry companies, their strength varied between 100 and 300 musketeers
- Approximately 22 horse companies, with average strength of 100 men

Georg Wilhelm, Elector of Brandenburg. Simon van Passe, after original by Crispijn van de Passe (I), 1615. (Rijksmuseum)

In July 1627, to fulfil his military obligation to Sigismund III, George Wilhelm decided to sent an auxiliary contingent to join Koniecpolski's army. Six infantry companies were chosen for that mission: three enlisted in Prussia (under Lehndorff, Wallenrodt and Pröck), one from the Life Regiment (Elias von der Burgh) and two from von Kracht's regiment (Joachim von Wintz and von Gröben). Additionally von Kospoth's horse was to be sent with them as well. The soldiers were not very eager to join the Poles and fight against their 'Protestant brothers', so the Elector decided to send them with strong escort, to prevent possible desertions. Four horse companies and three infantry companies from the Life Regiment were to act in this capacity. The whole force was accompanied by three cannons and the troops were under command of Lieutenant Colonel Albrecht von Kalckstein and Lieutenant Colonel Konrad von Burgsdorff. The Elector also sent

---

53 Sławomir Augusiewicz, *Przebudowa wojska*, pp.78–82.
54 The unit was to be created in July 1626.
55 Sławomir Augusiewicz, *Przebudowa wojska*, pp.63–73.

with them his War Commissioner Wilhelm von Hatzfeldt, most likely to act as his envoy to Koniecpolski.

The whole escapade ended up in embarrassing disaster. The Brandenburg soldiers were on 25 July surprised by Swedish reiters under command of Franz Bernhard von Thurn. The Elector's troops were forced to retreat in panic, losing the artillery, tabor wagon and captured Kalckstein. On 26 July Brandenburg troops were in the area of Morąg (Mohrungen), facing a fast-approaching Swedish main force, led by Gustav Adolf himself. The soldiers' morale was low, most of the infantry wanted to negotiate and only the horsemen from 'convoy' units supported idea of armed resistance. When the Brandenburg infantry, under command of von Burgsdorff, deployed in ranks, they were surrounded by Swedish reiters. An often quoted passage from Israel Hoppe's chronicle explains best what happened next:[56]

> Count von Thurn shouted "[Are you] Friends or Foes?" to which [the Elector's] infantry answered "Friends". He continued "Shoulder your muskets then" and when they had done that, he approached them and said "Are you King's [of Sweden] men?" for which they answered "Yes, yes". [The Brandenburg] Horse did the same and before even one shot all of them surrendered to the Swedish king's mercy.

After short negotiations seven companies of infantry (including all from the auxiliary force) and more than half the horsemen decided to switch sides and join the Swedish army, where the infantry became the new 'Green' regiment. The remaining troops, all cannons and all officers were sent back by Gustav Adolf to Georg Wilhelm with a friendly warning 'to be more careful of their units and their cannons in the future'.[57]

The Poles received detailed information about this whole affair, the Polish relation mentioned that the Brandenburg troops surrendered 'without giving a shot' and that the Swedes captured 12 companies of infantry, three of cavalry and four cannons. When the Elector's officers were sent back to him by Gustav Adolf, Georg William ordered them thrown in prison. Trying to excuse himself from the accusation of supporting Swedish side, he wrote to Sigismund III and to Hetman Koniecpolski, asking for Polish commissioners to be sent to him, in order to assist in investigation. The officers were to be scapegoats of course, with the Elector planning to 'judge and sentence them to death for treason'.[58] For the rest of the war Brandenburg/Prussian troops kept a very 'low profile', remained as garrison troops and avoided wherever possible any confrontation with the warring side. They could not do much to prevent Swedes and Poles from fighting in Upper Prussia (Oberland), especially as the officers and soldiers were not even sure who exactly they should treat as an enemy. Only at the end of the war, in summer 1629, was Konrad von Burgsdorff sent with a company of 150 harquebusiers to the Polish camp, to fulfil the obligation towards the Polish king.

---

56   Israel Hoppe, *Geschichte des ersten schwedisch-polnischen Krieges in Preussen: nebst Anhang* (Leipzig: Duncker & Humblot, 1887), p.188.

57   *Ibidem*, pp.188–189.

58   Biblioteka Czartoryskich, TN, part 118, document 176, p.761, *Nowiny z Prus*.

XII. Allies

The main Polish allies during war against Sweden were the Austrian Habsburgs, although the initial relationship was far from friendly. Archduke of Austria, Maximilian III, was in fact Sigismund's rival to the Polish throne during the election of 1587. Maximilian and his Polish supporters disputed the outcome of the election and decided to resolve matter on the battlefield. The Archduke was not able to capture Cracow though and soon after, on 24 January 1588, he was defeated by Crown Grand Hetman Jan Zamoyski at the battle of Byczyna (Pitschen). Sigismund worked very hard on building an alliance with Austria, however, despite the opposition of many Polish nobles. In 1592 Anne of Austria became his first wife, sadly dying in 1598 during the birth of her fifth child.[59] The Polish king continued his policy of supporting the Habsburgs and, despite the outrage of his opposition, in 1605 he married Anne's younger sister, Constance. When the Bohemian Revolt started in 1618, Sigismund allowed Imperial officers to recruit troops in Poland, sending the infamous *lisowczycy* (Lisowski's cossacks) light cavalry to support Ferdinand II. It is no surprise then, that when fighting against Swedes, he was eager to secure help from the Emperor. Negotiations started in summer 1626 and finally on 12 July 1627 agreement was signed by Polish envoy Krzysztof Lode and Imperial Colonel Adolf, Duke of Holstein-Gottorp.[60]

The Duke's regiment that was sent to Prussia was a fairly new unit, raised in 1626 and composed of 15 companies, with 'paper strength' of 3,000 men. It appears that there were also attached cavalry troops (maybe some sort of life company) which accompanied the infantry. During its march to Poland in July 1627 it was ambushed and badly mauled by Danish troops led by Joachim Mitzlaff near Byczyna (the same place where the 1588 battle occurred).[61] The colonel himself lost all his possessions and fled to Głuchów, where he looked for help from Polish Chancellor Wacław Leszczyński.[62] It seems that Duke Adolf managed to gather the scattered troops and continue with his march to Prussia, as both Polish and Swedish sources confirmed that the regiment arrived at Koniecpolski's camp, where it was welcomed by the Hetman himself. Unfortunately the Imperial troops appear to have been ill-disciplined, and on only the second day after their arrival at the Polish camp the soldiers started to fight with their Polish allies. It led to a serious brawl, where Holstein's troops attacked the military jail to recapture one of their own, previously arrested by a Polish auditor (military judge). Shots being fired, many more Imperials, including the colonel himself, were then

---

59 Only one of them survived to adulthood: Władysław, that later reigned in the Commonwealth between 1632 and 1648 as Władysław IV.

60 Jan Seredyka, 'Wezwanie posiłków cesarskich do Polski w 1629 roku', *Zeszyty Naukowe Wyższej Szkoły Pedagogicznej im. Powstańców Śląskich w Opolu, Seria A, Historia XIV* (Opole, 1977), p.94.

61 Alphonse Wrede, *Geschichte der K. Und K. Wehrmacht. Die Regimenter, Corps, Branchen und Anstalten von 1618 bis Ende des 19. Jahrhunderts, Band II* (Vienna: L.W. Seidel, 1898), p.22.

62 Adam Szelągowski, *O ujście Wisły. Wielka wojna pruska* (Dąbrówno: Oficyna Retman, 2012), p.119.

Albrecht von Wallenstein.
Pieter de Jode (I), after
original by Anthony van Dyck.
(Rijksmuseum)

arrested on the order of Hetman Koniecpolski.[63] The Imperials were not happy with what they saw as unfair treatment, and at the same time Poles immediately disliked their unruly allies. It appears that the regiment took no part in any actions against the Swedes, and as early as October 1627 it was marching back to rejoin the Imperial troops in Pomerania. Wallenstein was outraged that the Poles released Holstein's unit so quickly, as all of the sudden he had to find winter quarter for yet another regiment of his army. In a letter to Krzysztof Lode he even mentioned that he would never send further reinforcements to Poland.[64]

The Imperial Generalissimus had to quickly change his mind though, as Sigismund III soon started to negotiate the hiring of a 10,000-man corps from the Imperial army. The Polish king was looking for some breakthrough in the protracted war against Sweden, at the same time fighting very strong and very vocal opposition amongst his subjects. Polish magnates and nobles were criticising the large number of foreign mercenaries and the enormous cost connected with raising and sustaining those troops. Nonetheless the King had his own plans and, considering that he sent his own fleet to support Wallenstein's Baltic plans, the Imperial commander was now much more willing to lend support.

The initial plan, drawn in 1628, mentioned six infantry regiments, one cuirassiers and two harquebusier regiments, accompanied by 40 cannons.[65] After long negotiations, focused on both the size and cost of the planned corps, Wallenstein agreed to send the following troops to Prussia:[66]

---

63   'Diariusz albo Summa spraw i dzieł wojska kwarcianego w Prusiech na usłudze Jego Królewskiej Miłości przeciwko Gustawowi Książęciu Sudermańskiemu będącego', Stanisław Przyłęcki (ed.), *Pamiętniki o Koniecpolskich* (Lwów, 1842), p.36; Jan Seredyka, 'Wezwanie…', p.87.

64   Jan Seredyka, 'Wezwanie…', p.88.

65   AGAD, Teki Naruszewicza, part 120, document 114.

66   Wallenstein to Maximilian I, 20th April 1629 roku, *Documenta Bohemica Bellum Tricennale Illustrantia* (Prague Academia, 1974), volume IV, p.295.

Name of Colonel/Regiment[67]	Type of Regiment	Number of Companies
Johann Georg von Arnim	Infantry	12
Rudolph von Tieffenbach	Infantry	10
Franz Albrecht von Sachsen-Lauenburg (Alt-Sachsen)	Infantry	9
Hannibal von Dohna	Infantry	9
Franz Albrecht von Sachsen-Lauenburg (Alt-Sachsen)	Cuirassiers	10
Heinrich Schlick	Harquebusiers	5
Franz Albrecht von Sachsen-Lauenburg (Neu-Sachsen)	Cuirassiers / Harquebusiers	3
Johann Georg von Arnim	Harquebusiers	5
Ernst Georg Sparr	Harquebusiers	5

Israel Hoppe in his chronicle[68] mentioned that initially the corps was composed of infantry regiments Alt-Sachsen, Tieffenbach, Dohna and Arnim and of cavalry regiments Alt-Sachsen, Schlick (five companies), Sparr (five companies) and Arnim (five companies). Finally Swedish Field Marshal Herman Wrangel, in a letter to chancellor Axel Oxenstierna dated 28 May 1629,[69] described the composition of the Imperial corps as infantry regiments Arnim, Tieffenbach, Alt-Sachsen and Donna (Dohna), with cavalry regiments Arnim (five companies), Alt-Sachsen (10 companies), Neu-Sachsen (five companies), Sparr (five companies) and Franz Carl von Sachsen-Lauenburg (four companies).

Sources vary regarding size of the corps as well. Stanisław Żurkowski, who was not present in Prussia but had very good sources there, mentioned 12,000 men and adds that, due to starvation and sickness, only 4,000 Imperials left Prussia at the end of the campaign.[70] Bishop Piasecki in his chronicle[71] wrote of 5,000 infantry and 2,000 cavalry. Wallenstein described the 'paper strength' of his troops as 15,000.[72] King Sigismund III, writing to Chancellor Jan Zadzik in October 1629, gives a maximum figure of 11,500.[73] Papal Secretary of State Francesco Barberini, based on information from Vienna, estimated in May 1629 the Imperial corps as 12,000 infantry and 2,000 cavalry.[74] Swedish sources, the letters of Brengt Bagge and Herman Wrangel to Axel Oxenstierna in May 1629,[75] provide the number of 9,000

---

67 The surname or title of the colonel was normally used as the name of the regiment, sometimes with *Alt* (Old) or *Neu* (New) added to it.

68 Israel Hoppe, *Geschichte des ersten*, p.396.

69 *Rikskansleren Axel Oxenstiernas skrifter och brefvexling* (RAOSB), volume II, part 9 (Stockholm: Norstedt, 1898), p.162.

70 Stanisław Żurkowski, *Żywot Tomasza Zamoyskiego*, pp.129–130.

71 *Kronika Pawła Piaseckiego biskupa przemyślskiego* (Kraków, 1870), p.339.

72 *Documenta Bohemica Bellum Tricennale Illustrantia* (Prague, 1974), volume IV, pp.325–326.

73 Biblioteka ks. Czartoryskich, 357, p.556, Zygmunt III do J. Zadzika, 10 października 1629 z Warszawy

74 Paweł Duda, 'Działalność oddziałów Hansa Georga von Arnima w Rzeczypospolitej z punktu widzenia nuncjusza papieskiego Antonia Santacrocego', *Od Kijowa do Rzymu. Z dziejów stosunków Rzeczypospolitej ze Stolicą Apostolską i Ukrainą* (Białystok: In-t Badań nad Dziedzictwem Kulturowym Europy, 2012), p.518.

75 Generalstaben, *Sveriges Krig 1611–1632. Band 2, Polska kriget* (Stockholm, 1936), str. 456.

Hans Georg von Arnim.
Unknown painter. (Author's
archive)

soldiers, supported by 26 cannons. A Polish source from the end of May 1629 mentioned that the Imperials were 'solid, good looking both horse and infantry, [with] 24 good cannons'.[76]

Hetman Koniecpolski in his letter to King Sigismund III, dated 28 June 1629, wrote of Imperial troops in the battle of Honigfelde, that '[the] foreign troops show great valour and eagerness [to fight]'.[77] Royal Commissar Jan Zawadzki, writing on the same day to Chancellor Jakub Zadzik, also praised the Imperial allies:

I can see that the Imperial troops were badly needed, without them we would struggle; but it is worth mentioning, that they would not join the fight, if our cossacks could not keep the enemy occupied; and when [the cossacks] were attacked by Gustav's [cavalry] cornets, the Imperials bravely charged and broke [the Swedes] so much, forcing them to retreat.[78]

An official relation describing the battle, sent by Hetman Koniecpolski,[79] mentioned Imperial 'reiters' supporting both Polish hussars and cossacks and taking more than 200 prisoners. Further information about Imperial troops in July 1629 can be found in a diary written by an anonymous courtier of Royal Prince Władysław.[80] It mentions an episode from the battle of Honigfelde, where 'some of the Imperials were killed by our own [Polish] eager troops, as it was hard to distinguish between our Germans [Imperials] and Swedes, who is an ally and who is an enemy. So a few Imperial soldiers were killed [that way], so then when Imperials were seen approaching Poles they were shouting: Jesus, Mary, Kaiser'.[81] There is also an interesting description of marching Imperial troops during allied operations in Malbork area:

First there was Colonel Kiedrych(s), then cornet of reiters – their flag was red, with Virgin Mary on one side and Fortune on the other – then two large cannons, with them thirty wagons with match, powder and other military equipment, then [soldiers'] private wagons with women and sick, after them [marched] a bunch of

---

76 Riksarkivet Stockholm, Extranea IX Polen, 135, Z listu P. Wojewody Chełmińskiego debata 23 May 1629 o Woyjsku Cesarskim z Arneimem w Prusiech.
77 Od Pana Hetmana do Króla Jego Mości, z pod Nowejwsi na pobojowisku, dnia 28 czerwca 1629, *Pamiętniki o Koniecpolskich*, p.155.
78 Od P. Jana Zawadzkiego do Xiędza Kanclerza Koronnego, z obozu pod Nowąwsią, dnia 28 czerwca 1629, *Pamiętniki o Koniecpolskich*, pp.157–158.
79 'Relacja bitwy trzciańskiej posłana od P. Hetmana', Otto Laskowski (ed.) *Przyczynki do działań hetmana polnego koronnego Stanisława Koniecpolskiego w Prusach Wschodnich i na Pomorzu przeciwko Gustawowi Adolfowi*, *Przegląd Historyczno-Wojskowy*, volume IX, part 3 (Warszawa, 1937), pp.430–431.
80 'Kontynuacja Diariusza', pp.431–444.
81 *Ibidem*, p.432.

a few hundred women, riding horses; after them more than 300 infantrymen, and at the end one more cornet of reiters.[82]

Cuirassiers charging at a musketeer. Johann Jacobi von Wallhausen, Ritterkunst, 1616. (Author's archive)

The Imperial forces were decimated due to lack of food, diseases spreading through their units and a very high level of desertion. In August the Papal nuncio in Poland, Antonio Santacroce, wrote that Arnim only had 5,000 men left, while a month later he mentioned in a letter sent to the Vatican that Sigismund III himself advised him that there are no more than 3,000 Imperials left.[83] In October 1629, once the troops from Prussia rejoined the main army, Wallenstein reported to Emperor Ferdinand II that, 'due to hunger and grief', no more than 5,000 were left in ranks.[84] Albrycht Stanisław Radziwiłł was very critical of Arnim, claiming that the Imperial commander 'was not very eager to fight and was not a very good guest, as he almost on purpose did not provide any useful [help], destroying Prussia almost as much an enemy'.[85] Additionally there was command crisis, as Arnim did not want to cooperate with Koniecpolski and refused point blank to take any orders from him. Poles were also unhappy that the Imperial general refused to take an oath 'to Polish King, his children and Kingdom'.[86] Wallenstein decided to replace him with the other officer but his first candidate – Duke Franz Heinrich von Sachsen-Lauenburg – was not accepted by Polish side. Finally both allies agreed that Imperial corps will be under command of experienced Philip Mansfeld. Soon after though, the signing of the Polish–Swedish truce led to the Imperial army, although severely depleted due to non-combat losses, leaving Prussia. An additional problem was an issue with pay for Imperial help, which we will describe in more detail in Chapter 4.

---

82 *Ibidem*, p.433.
83 Paweł Duda, 'Działalność oddziałów Hansa Georga von Arnima', p.519.
84 Wallenstein to Ferdinand II, 10 October 1629, *Documenta Bohemica*, volume IV, p.326.
85 Albrycht Stanisław Radziwiłł, *Rys panowania Zygmunta III* (Opole: Wyd. Uniwersytetu Opolskiego, 2011), p.125.
86 Paweł Duda, *Krzyż i karabela* (Katowice: Wydawnictwo Uniwersytetu Śląskiego, 2019), p.135.

Chapter 2

The Commanders and their Army

The Commanders

Royal Prince Władysław (later King Władysław IV) at the battle of Chocim (Khotyn) in 1621. Peter Paul Rubens, circa 1624. (Author's archive)

During the first few months of the war, including the battle of Gniew, the Polish field army was led by King Sigismund III (1566–1632). The Polish monarch had some previous military experience, including the fateful expedition to Sweden and successful siege of Smolensk (1609–1611). Normally the army would be under the command of the Crown Grand Hetman and Crown Field Hetman. The first office, after the death of Stanisław Żółkiewski in 1620, was still vacant, while Field Hetman Stanisław Koniecpolski was busy defending the Polish border from Tatars. The King decided then to lead troops into Prussia himself. It appears to have been the right decision, as only royal authority could stop the magnates and nobles from bickering and trying to sabotage military efforts for their own political gains. The person most upset by this decision was the King's son, Royal Prince Władysław (1595–1648),[1] who despite nomination for Royal Lieutenant felt pushed away. He also had some previous military experience, leading an expedition against Moscow in 1617–1618 and taking part in the Chocim (Khotyn) campaign against the Turks in 1621. Władysław expected to play a more important role in Prussia, but as Royal Lieutenant he was only in charge of the march of the troops, safe crossing of rivers and sending reconnaissance forces. In his letter to Lithuanian Field Hetman Krzysztof II Radziwiłł prince mentioned that '[I]

---

1   Between 1632 and 1648 King of Poland, Grand Lithuanian Duke, (nominal) King of Sweden, etc. etc.

need to complain that I am so unhappy, that His Royal Highness does not want to use me for any [military] service and so I am here on this expedition as some sort of novice or, as the foreigners call it, *reformato* General.[2] It is more than certain though, that the King wanted to protect his heir from danger, even for the price of his unhappiness.

The army that Sigismund III led in Prussia in summer–autumn 1626 was divided into four regiments. The King decided to appoint as their colonels a few trusted magnates:[3]

- Tomasz Zamoyski, voivode of Kiev (1594–1638)
- Eustachy Jan Tyszkiewicz, voivode of Brześć (1571–1631)
- Łukasz Opaliński, Crown Court Marshal (1581–1654)
- Jan Dzieduszycki, castellan of Lubaczów (1575–1641); at the beginning of October replaced by Konstanty Plichta, *starosta* of Sochaczew (1580–1631)

It was more a political than a military decision, based on the support they were giving the King and the size of their private troops that they brought to Prussia. The regiments varied in size, for example Zamoyski's regiment, marching as a vanguard of whole army, was composed of his private units (described in Chapter 1), four or five cossack banners raised by the Działyński family, two hussar banners (both private), one more cossack banner (also private), one small regiment/squadron and one company of reiters (from the Lithuanian army). Additionally during the battle of Gniew Zamoyski's regiment was supported by a few units of foreign infantry (Aston's, Fittinghoff's and Keith's) and at least one of Polish infantry. Those regiments were of course only an ad hoc establishment and in November were no longer active, as many of their banners and companies were disbanded or left Prussia.

Stanisław Koniecpolski (1591–1646), who in November 1626 took over the command of the Polish forces in Prussia, was one of the most famous Commonwealth commanders in the seventeenth century. He started his military career as a 19-year-old, accompanying his brother Przebóg on campaign in Muscovy. He took part in Lithuanian Grand Hetman Jan Karol Chodkiewicz's attempts to break into the Polish garrison in Moscow, both in October 1611 and September 1612. Then in 1613 he started his service in the 'quarter army' under Crown Field Hetman Jan Żółkiewski. He helped to defend the Polish border against Tatar incursion and in spring 1615 defeated marauding groups of ex-Polish soldiers, after

Stanisław Koniecpolski as Grand Field Hetman, circa 1640. Unknown painter. (Author's archive)

2   *Listy Władysława IV do Krzysztofa Radziwiłła, hetmana polnego W. X. Litewskiego pisane 1612–1632* (Kraków: W. Jaworski, 1867), p.72.
3   *Diariusz Wojny Pruskiej*, pp.354, 373; Stanisław Żurkowski, *Żywot*, pp.107–108.

their service in the Muscovy war. He quickly became Żółkiewski's protégée, learning both military and diplomatic craft at his side. In February 1615 he even became the Hetman's son-in-law, sadly Koniecpolski quickly became a widower as his wife Katarzyna died in 1616 during childbirth. The *Sejm* of 1618 brought with it an amazing promotion for the young officer. When Żółkiewski became Grand Hetman, he made sure that Koniecpolski was promoted to Field Hetman. It was a great advancement for a fairly inexperienced noble, and no surprise that many of those that opposed Żółkiewski were against Koniecpolski's nomination. However Żółkiewski, having good relations with King Sigismund III, manage to convince the King and get his way during the *Sejm*.

For the next two years Koniecpolski served under his mentor, defending the borders against Tatars and taking part in negotiations with unruly Cossacks. In autumn 1620 he was part of an ill-fated expedition to Moldavia, where the Polish army was defeated, Żółkiewski died and Koniecpolski was captured. For the next two and a half years he was kept at Yedikule Fortress in Constantinople, but in spring 1623, after paying a large ransom of 30,000 zl, he returned to Poland. Almost immediately he took charge of defending the Polish border, reorganising the 'quarter army' and preparing it to fight against the Tatars. At the beginning of 1624 he foiled early Tatar incursions, then in June the same year, at the battle of Martynów, he decisively defeated Kantymir Mirza, one of the greatest Polish victories over the Tatars. The Hetman quickly mastered very efficient ways of fighting against Tatars, using surprising attacks, good reconnaissance (including well established intelligence network) and even (at Martynów) defensive tabor as central point of the battle line.

In autumn 1625 he led a strong Polish army against the Zaporozhian Cossack mutiny of Marek Zhmaylo (Żmajło). While in heavy fought battles at Kryłów and Lake Kurukove Koniecpolski was not able to defeat Cossacks, he forced them to negotiations, which resulted in the signing of the Treaty of Kurukowe. In winter 1626 the Hetman was too late to stop initial Tatar raids and was only able to defeat the rearguard of Khan Mehmed Giray II's army. Nonetheless he presented this campaign as his great success, with the news of a 'heavy Tatar defeat' being spread throughout the whole of Europe. It seems that the Hetman knew how to use propaganda as one of his military tools as well. In summer 1626 he again gathered a strong army in Ukraine and such a show of force was enough to prevent new Tatar attacks. Koniecpolski then had to relocate with the majority of soldiers to Prussia, but he left of one his best officers – Stefan Chmielecki – who successfully stopped further Tatar attacks between 1626 and 1629.

After the Prussian war, in 1630 Koniecpolski fought against the mutiny of Zaporozhian Cossacks led by Tataras Fedorovych, and on 5 April 1632 he finally received nomination for Crown Grand Hetman. The newly appointed hetman successfully defended the southern border against the Tatars and Turks, when they were trying to attack in 1633 and 1634. Alongside the new king, Władysław IV, he then led the Polish army in a military demonstration against the Swedes in Prussia in 1635. He then focused on reforms of the Polish army, supporting Władysław IV in changing the army's structure, and

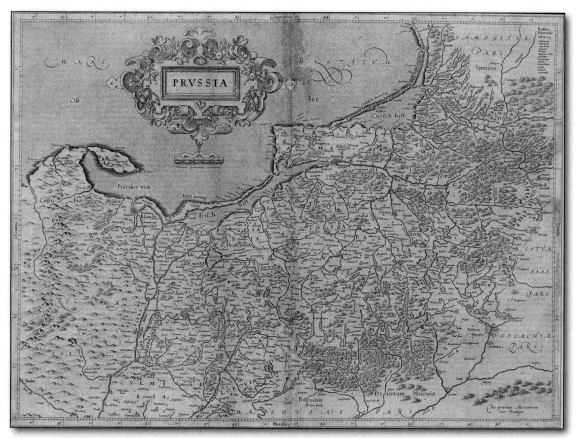

Map of Prussia from 1628, based on the sixteenth-century map by Gerard Mercator. (Biblioteka Narodowa, Warszawa)

improving the artillery and main fortresses. His 'quarter army' often had to clash with Cossacks, although due to illness Koniecpolski did not take part in campaigns against them in 1637 (Pavlyuk uprising) and 1638 (Ostryanyn and Hunia uprising). He often fought against Tatars though, dealing them a heavy defeat at Ochmatów on 30 January 1644. Koniecpolski supported King Władysław's plans to wage war against the Tatars and Turks, even suggesting an alliance with Muscovy, seeing them as the 'enemy of my enemy'. However, due to a rather odd accident the Hetman was unable to fulfil his plans. On 16 January 1646 he married the 30-year-younger Zofia Opalińska, and soon after, on 11 March, died suddenly in his main estate in Brody. He survived Turks, Tatars, Swedes, Muscovites and Cossacks but was defeated by … an overdose of aphrodisiac during one of the nights with his new wife.

During the 1626–1629 war Koniecpolski could count on a very experienced officer corps, especially in regard to the cavalry. It was up to him to appoint commanders of his regiments (*pułki*) so he made sure to choose those officers whom he knew and had served with before. Cavalry serving in Koniecpolski's army was, from November 1626 onwards, divided into six regiments, it appears it was an organisation already active in the 'quarter army' of 1625. His chosen colonels were also in charge, as nominal *rotmistrz*, of their own hussar banners, which clearly indicates the significant role of this particular formation.

Łukasz Żółkiewski (?–1636), who was in charge of the Hetman's regiment, served previously during the 1620 campaign against the Turks and Tatars, when

High-ranking officers in Polish and Western clothes, here in the entourage of King Władysław IV during the Smolensk War, 1632–1634. Painter unknown. (Muzeum Narodowe, Kraków)

he was taken prisoner and kept in same prison as Koniecpolski. After being released he rejoined the 'quarter army', probably fighting against the Tatars at Martynów in 1624 and leading his hussars against Cossacks in 1625 and Tatars in early 1626. Marcin Kazanowski (1563–1656) was one of the oldest and most experienced of all Koniecpolski's officers. Born in 1563, in 1608 he was royal *rotmistrz*. He fought in Muscovy during the Times of Troubles, taking part in the famous battle of Kłuszyn (Klushino) in 1610. He then accompanied Prince Władysław in his unsuccessful final attempt to capture Moscow in 1617–1618. Captured after the Cecora campaign in 1620, from 1625 he was again *rotmistrz* under Koniecpolski's command. Stanisław Rewera Potocki (1589–1667) started his military career from defeat: he took part in a disastrous campaign in Moldavia in 1612, where mostly privately financed Polish troops, led by his uncle Stefan Potocki, were annihilated by Tatars in the battle of Sasowy Róg. In 1617–1618 he took part in a campaign against the Muscovites. Since 1624, under the command of Koniecpolski: at Martynów against the Tatars, then in 1625 against the Cossacks and in 1626 against the Tatars again. Mikołaj Potocki (1593–1651) started his military career as 16-year-old, between 1609 and 1611 fighting in Sigismund III's army besieging Smolensk. From 1617–1620 he served in the 'quarter' army' as *rotmistrz* of a hussar banner. In 1620 he was captured by the Turks after the Cecora campaign, and released after paying a ransom at the end of 1621. From 1624 he was again under Koniecpolski's command, fighting against the Tatars and Cossacks. Stefan Koniecpolski (?–1629) a distant relative of the Hetman, served during the Chocim (Khotyn) campaign of 1621 against the Turks. Mikołaj Kossakowski (?–1639) also served in 1621 against the Turks. Additionally many officers, especially of the cossack cavalry, had years of experience fighting as part of the 'quarter army' against the Tatars, some of them also serving in 1621 in the Chocim (Khotyn) campaign against the Turks.

Most of the *rotmistrz* had taken part in at least one campaign or, especially in the cossack cavalry, they were veterans of skirmish-style war against the Tatars. Such experiences would prove to very useful during the war in Prussia, where officers such as Mikołaj Moczarski, Paweł Czarniecki, Samuel Łaszcz or Jerzy Budziszewski would be leading cavalry raids against the Swedes and harassing their forces.

As for commanders of foreign troops, Mikołaj Abramowicz (?–1651), who during 1626–1629 was in charge of the reiter (Western-style cavalry) regiment, had some good experience from the period 1621–1625, when he fought against the Swedes in Livonia. In 1621–1622 he was *rotmistrz* of a hussar banner. In 1625 he raised a cossack cavalry banner, and was also initially in charge of the Lithuanian artillery. When Hetman Krzysztof II Radziwiłł left his division in January 1626, to attend the *Sejm*, Abramowicz was nominated to lead the Hetman's troops in his absence. He then took command of disbanded Karol Sey's reiter regiment and led them to Prussia, when he then served until the end of the war. 'German' infantry colonels had some limited experience in leading regiment-level units. Gerhard (1598–1648) and Ernest Magnus Denhoff (1581–1642) were in charge of infantry regiments during the Chocim (Khotyn) campaign. Swedish loyalist Gustav Sparre (1582–1629) spent some time in Imperial service, then in 1616 was recruiting private troops for Sigismund III. In 1622 he commanded a 'German' unit but his troops never reached Livonia, being stationed in Prussia instead. James Butler[4] was by far the most experienced colonel, with campaigns in Muscovy (1617–1618), Livonia (1622) and Podolia against the Cossacks (1625).

High ranking official from 'Stockholm Roll'. It is good representation of how officers of Koniecpolski's army could look like. (Author's archive).

The hetman had at his disposal a small staff, with small amount of money designated specially to pay them. For example at the beginning of 1627 campaign there were three such special offices in the army in Prussia:

- Military Guard (*strażnik wojskowy*), whose task was to deal with reconnaissance, protecting the army during both march and camping. It was a role well established during the border wars against the Tatars. Throughout the war, this officer received an allowance for a six-horse retinue, with quarterly pay of 50 zl per horse. In 1628 and 1629 the office was held by Andrzej Jeżewski.[5]
- Military Camp-master (*oboźny wojskowy*), taking care of choosing and setting up the army camp, the orderly movement of the military tabor and setting up defences of the camp. His pay allowance was for a retinue

---

4   Both his year of birth and death are unknown.
5   Biblioteka ks. Czartoryskich w Krakowie, 1772, *Regestrum rationis thesauri Regni in Conventu anni MDCXXIX expeditae*, p.537.

of five horses, also with 50 zl per horse per quarter. In 1628 and 1629 the office was held by Grzegorz Brzozowski.[6]

- Military Captain (*kapitan wojskowy*), which was a rather enigmatic office. We are not really sure of the scope of his duties, it is possible that he was in charge of the hetman's guard. The officer that held this title during the period 1626–1629 was Samuel Nadolski (1590–1655), *rotmistrz* of one of the Polish infantry banners. It appears that he was de facto commander of the whole Polish infantry contingent, often leading a few banners as an ad hoc 'regiment' during sieges or battles. We cannot confirm though if it was connected with his Military Captain's office or just with the fact of being the most senior officer present in the army. His pay in 1627 was the same as the Camp-master's. In November 1628 he received a payment of 800 zl, which represents the back pay of just over three quarters of the service.[7] Interestingly enough, in the official document from 1629 he is called *capitaneus peditatus ungarici*, captain of Hungarian infantry.[8] It is another indicator that the difference between Polish and Hungarian infantry was at that time disappearing in the Polish army, and both names were used to describe the same formation.

There was also the Auditor (military judge), dealing with any disciplinary issues. It appears that this office was held by Wojciech Przeciszewski,[9] although it has not been possible to confirm if he was in that role throughout the war. Neither could we find information regarding his wages. Another special rank was Master of the Ordnance (*starszy nad armatą*), in charge of the artillery train of the army. In 1629 this office was held by Bazyli Judycki,[10] however it has not been possible to establish when he was nominated for this post.

Additional to the military staff there were also special civilian commissioners, appointed by the *Sejm* to control financial aspects related to the army and to help with purchasing and providing provision for the troops. We will look into more details of their role in Chapter 4.

Recruitment and Organisation

The King issued a letter of recruitment (*list przypowiedni*) which stated the name of the chosen *rotmistrz* or captain/colonel, the size of the unit, term of the initial service (usually three or six months) and rate of pay. Often such

6   *Ibidem*, p.537.
7   Biblioteka Kórnicka, BK 341, *Diariusze z lat 1625–1630 oraz korespondencja dyplomatyczna*, p.341v, *Percepta w Toruniu z poborow na seymie warszawskim w roku teraznieyszym uchwalonych*.
8   Biblioteka ks. Czartoryskich w Krakowie, 1772, *Regestrum rationis thesauri Regni in Conventu anni MDCXXIX expeditae*, p.537.
9   CDIAUL, f. 9, 1, 381, pp.1489–1491, oblata 7 września 1630 przez Jana Otwinowskiego, dekret komisji w sporze pomiędzy nim a Wilskim, sądzili Kazanowski, Rey oraz Wojciech Przeciszewski iudex exercitus Pruthenici, Lwów 3 września 1630.
10   In his previous articles, published both in Polish and in English, the author incorrectly identified Judycki as Mikołaj, who in fact was not present in Prussia during the war. Thanks to Przemysław Gawron for pointing out and correcting this error.

letters also contain information about weapons and armour that soldiers should be equipped with. Finally it gave a place and time when the unit should start its service. The hetman often provided the king with a list of suggested candidates for *rotmistrz*, often from those he fought alongside before. Foreign officers often presented themselves at court, offering their service and even the size of the unit they could raise. Finally other candidates could be recommended by local magnates or even foreign monarchs, who provided them with a letter of recommendation. A *rotmistrz* could always reject a letter of recruitment, as long as he provided sufficient excuse: health problems, lack of funds (especially when due to raise hussars or reiters) or recruitment issues.

Once the officer accepted his commission, the process of recruitment started. We can distinguish three main ways of doing it, depending on the formation: whether cavalry, Polish/Hungarian infantry or foreign infantry/ dragoons. All 'national' cavalry (hussars, cossacks, *arkabuzeria* and those units of reiters that were raised locally) would be created in the same way. A *rotmistrz* had to register a letter of recruitment in the local court[11] of the district he was planning to raise the unit in. The letter was then added to the district's record, in a process called *oblatowanie*. It gave the officer the right to look for volunteers, and also described the timeframe within which he should be creating the unit. The next step was to find a candidate for lieutenant (*porucznik*), who would be second in command of the unit and would later deal with the majority of recruitment. He was normally chosen from amongst family, friends or former soldiers. The next step was to recruit the core of the units, so-called companions (*towarzysze*). They were the nobles that would be the basis of the fighting force, again friends, family, neighbours, etc. were the first choice here, especially as many Polish/Lithuanian nobles had some former military experience. Each of those companions would provide his own retinue (*poczet*), composed of retainers called *pocztowi*. It may be slightly simplified, but we can describe companions as NCOs and retainers as privates. One of the companions was designated as the standard-bearer (*chorąży*), who would carry the unit's standard. As such he was not treated as an officer, however. In the absence of *rotmistrz* and lieutenant, one of the companions was normally designated as deputy (*namiestnik*) in charge of the troops. Retinues in each banner were part of a so-called *rolla*, a list of all retinues ordered by the importance of the companions: so it starts with the *rotmistrz*'s and lieutenant's retinues but the next place could be taken by a wealthier or a somehow more important companion, not necessarily by the standard-bearer. It was all part of the delicate social structure of the unit, where in theory officers could only ask their soldiers to follow the orders because, as all officers and companions were nobles, they were (at least in theory) equal. A man's position in the banner's *rolla* could help in future promotions (for example to replace a lieutenant or standard-bearer), a man higher in the hierarchy had a better chance of becoming the deputy or the unit's envoy sent to deliver pay.

---

11 So-called *sąd grodzki*.

Mounted officer of the Polish infantry from the beginning of the seventeenth century. 'Stockholm Roll'. (Author's archive)

The number and size of the retinues varied from unit to unit, it was not – at least in that part of the seventeenth century – much regulated. The *rotmistrz*'s was usually the largest, with surviving muster rolls the majority of them are 12 horses strong. We need to realise that the majority of them were in fact 'blind portions' (dead pays), used as additional pay for the *rotmistrz* or lieutenant (if he was in charge of the unit during the campaign). Other large retinues were usually six or seven horses strong, one of them normally provided by the lieutenant. There were usually a few five-horse retinues as well but the majority of the units were composed of those three or four horses strong, with units two and even one horse strong (so just a companion without any retainers) especially present in cossack banners. Here is an example of a 100 horse banner of cossack cavalry from the Lithuanian army in 1625, under command of Eliasz Zabłocki:[12]

Size of the retinue	Number of retinues	Additional notes
12	1	*Rotmistrz*'s retinue
5	1	Lieutenant's retinue
4	8	Including standard-bearer's retinue
3	9	
2	11	
1	2	

In total this unit had 32 companions, including *rotmistrz* and lieutenant, as both took part in the campaign. Additionally, each retinue had number of camp servants (*czeladź*), employed by a companion to deal with all mundane tasks of camp life – from taking care of equipment and weapons to foraging for both men and horses. They were not part of the unit's muster roll and did not receive pay as soldiers, but could be used as an additional armed force, especially when defending the camp, during sieges and armed supply runs. Such a 'tail' followed each unit on tabor wagons and spare horses, again all that was to be paid by the companion. We will look into other examples of units and retinues sizes in the next chapter, describing all army formations.

---

12   Henryk Wisner, 'Wojsko litewskie I połowy XVII wieku', part III, *Studia i Materiały do Historii Wojskowości*, volume 21 (Warszawa, 1979), p.104.

A *rotmistrz* of Polish infantry also had to register his letter of recruitment in the local court, but in the seventeenth century he was no longer raising units by recruiting retinues. Instead his lieutenant and NCOs were trying to find volunteers in both bigger and smaller towns, recruiting 'by the drum', in a very similar way to foreign troops. The difference was that Polish infantry was always raised locally, with approximately 70 percent of soldiers being minor artisans from towns and the other 30 percent[13] a mix of peasants from lands owned by the King, the priesthood and even nobles.[14] A *rotmistrz* was always trying to enlist experienced soldiers for his lieutenant and NCOs, the main problem was the fairly small pool of such available veterans, which gradually led to Polish infantry becoming a marginal part of the army. Hungarians, often employed in the 1570s and 1580s, were much rarer in the seventeenth century. The chosen *rotmistrz* normally took his letter of recruitment to the territory he came from (for example Transylvania) and recruited soldiers there. By 1626 Hungarians were in fact present only in the Royal Guard and some magnates' armies.

Foreign infantry in Polish service during the Smolensk War, 1632–1634. Painter unknown. (Muzeum Narodowe, Kraków)

Officers of foreign troops, usually ranked as colonels or captains, received a letter of recruitment that mentioned planned strength of the unit but often also stated where the troops should be recruited. As we will see in the chapter describing formations of the infantry and dragoons, it was normally done on basis of a 'national' pattern, with English, Scots and Irish officers recruiting in the British Isles and German-speaking ones (like nobles from Prussia and Livonia) in German-speaking countries (Saxony, Pomerania, Northern Germany) and territories (Prussia, Livonia, Silesia). Soldiers were recruited 'by the drum', normally after receiving permission from the local administration, although for some recruitment operations official permission from the king/prince of the land was required. Such a permit would normally come with certain limitations, such as forbidding the recruitment of this country's soldiers or people of certain professions (for example, miners).

In the cavalry, soldiers would be expected to provide their own horses, weapons, clothing (for both the companion and his retainers) and practically all equipment, including supply wagons, engineering tools, etc. There were a few exceptions though: hussars' lances (*kopie*) were to be provided from the funds allocated from the National Treasury, also a unit's standard was provided in the same way (although it had to be returned when the banner/company was disbanded). In certain situations, for example when raising an expensive unit (hussars, reiters) or when recruitment had to be done in very

---

13   Jan Wimmer, *Historia piechoty polskiej do 1864 roku* (Warszawa: Wyd. MON, 1978), pp.142–143.

14   The latter had to flee from their land to enlist, as it was illegal for the officers to look for recruits in the villages owned by magnates and nobles.

short period of time, additional advance pay could be provided to a *rotmistrz*, to help with equipping the soldiers. Very often a *rotmistrz* himself dug deep into his own pocket and helped companions in purchasing required items.

In regard to infantry, soldiers were also expected to join the ranks with their own weapons, although they could be supplied with weapons provided by a recruitment officer or the main army, although the cost of it was to be deducted from his pay. In theory the National Treasury should provide the newly raised unit with uniforms or with cloth to make them, also troops already serving should at least once a year receive replacements for worn out clothes. As with the cavalry, infantry companies received standards paid for by the National Treasury and those flags were to be returned to the hetman or king once the unit was disbanded.

We already mentioned that the cavalry was divided into six regiments. Each of them had between three and four hussar banners, supported by up to seven cossack banners, with only one regiment – under Mikołaj Kossakowski – composed from just three hussar banners. While hussars served in the same regiment throughout the war, cossack banners would often be swapped between or even detached for longer periods of time as some ad hoc regiment. For example *rotmistrz* Jan Bąk-Lanckoroński from late autumn of 1626 was in charge of such a small unit, composed of three cossack banners, initially serving as part of a force besieging Puck and then left there as a garrison. Reiters could be temporarily attached to one of the 'main' cavalry regiments or fight as part of their own regiments and provisional squadrons. Infantry (both foreign and Polish) and dragoons could also be for some period of time attached to a cavalry regiment, especially when such a mixed-force 'division' was sent away from the main army, as during the siege of Puck or Polish raids on Warmia. We will look into more detailed organisation of infantry and dragoons in Chapter 3.

The Size of the Army in Prussia

Based on surviving documents we can attempt to reconstruct the organisation and, at least theoretically, the strength of the regular Polish forces in Prussia during the war. There are a few problems with such an attempt though. It will not include district and private troops, that showed up in the theatre of war for a very limited period of time. Also, if a regular unit served only for one or two quarters[15] it could sometimes be omitted from the army *komput* presented to the *Sejm*. Interestingly enough, we can include all information about planned forces and see how many of such ideas were in fact put into practice.

November 1626 brought the first shake-up of the Polish army in Prussia. Ad hoc troops gathered by Sigismund III to defend against the Swedes were now supported by the main force of the 'quarter army' led by Crown Field Hetman Stanisław Koniecpolski, who took over general command in Prussia.

---

15   Each quarter (3-month period) was used as basic measure of the service for cavalry, treated as a main part of the army. In regard to the infantry, their service was normally based on the monthly period.

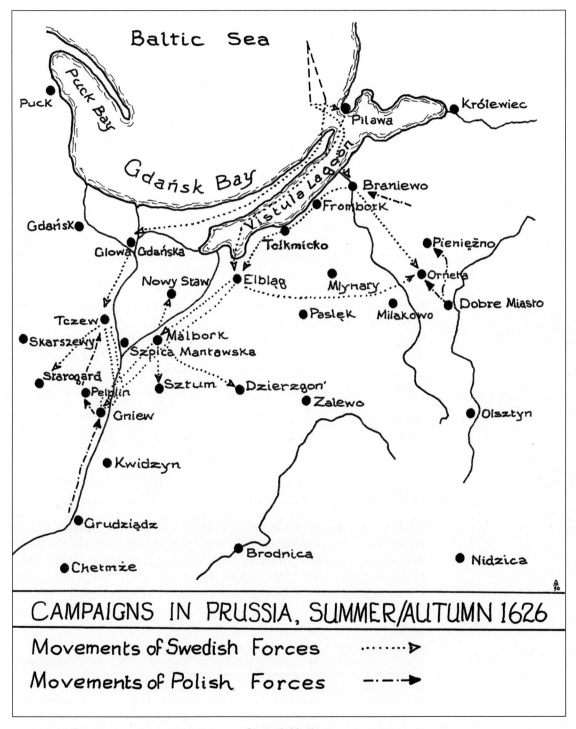

CAMPAIGNS IN PRUSSIA, SUMMER/AUTUMN 1626

Movements of Swedish Forces ·······▷

Movements of Polish Forces –·–·▶

Source: Polska Kriget.

The majority of the units fighting in the initial phase of the war, especially those private and district ones, were now disbanded. The extraordinary *Sejm* that gathered in the same month in Toruń had to decide the size and shape of the new army. During the proceedings, Prince Krzysztof Zbaraski presented his project of the organisation of the armed forces. Next to the troops left to defend the border against Tatars (4,000 horse, probably just cossack cavalry) and another part of the border 'from Silesia and Hungary' (another 3,000 horse, which also appears to be cossack cavalry) his proposal included a larger army to fight in Prussia against the Swedes. His suggestion was to field 3,000 hussars and reiters,[16] 2,000 cossacks, 13,000 foreign infantry and 2,000 Polish infantry, supported by 20 heavier cannons and 25 lighter cannons and mortars.[17] It was clearly an army tailored to a new way of warfare, one that should be won thanks to the large size of the infantry, and suggested with many sieges of Prussian towns in mind. Of course such a project had to be met with opposition from many traditionally minded nobles, for whom cavalry was still the most important part of the army, and the idea of recruiting so many foreigners was impossible to agree with. However both Sigismund and Hetman Koniecpolski understood that without a large infantry force, fighting against the Swedes in Prussia would be very difficult, so tried to shift the *Sejm*'s project towards introduction of a large percentage of all types of infantry and dragoons. The *komput* of the army in Prussia agreed at the end of November 1626 was as follows:[18]

Formation	Strength of old units (already in service)	Strength of new units (agreed at the Sejm)	Total strength (old + new units)
Hussars	1,976	100	2,076
Reiters	825	950	1,775
Cossack cavalry	3,650	–	3,650
Polish infantry	1,200	1,400	2,600
Dragoons	1,152	–	1,152
Foreign infantry	2,509	9,100	11,609
Wybraniecka infantry	–[19]	1,385	1,385
Total	11,312	11,550	22,862

At the beginning of December 1626 Colonel Mikołaj Abramowicz in his letter to Lithuanian Hetman Krzysztof II Radziwiłł described the Royal Army in the camp as 1,775 hussars, 800 reiters, 3,200 cossack cavalry, 3,461 German infantry[20] and 1,200 haiduks, with a total of 5,775 cavalry and 4,661 infantry, giving the overall strength as 10,436 horses and portions.[21] We can

---

16 He included both formations, as they were to have the same level of pay.
17 'Komput wojska z 1626 r.', Zdzisław Spieralski, Jan Wimmer (ed.), *Wypisy źródłowe do historii polskiej sztuki wojennej*, volume V (Warszawa, 1961), pp.141–143.
18 Riksarkivet Stockholm, Extranea IX Polen, 82, *Comput Woyjska K.J.M. Koronnego*.
19 While some *wybraniecka* from Prussia or neighbouring voivodships were most likely in service since summer 1626, they are not included in this *komput*.
20 Considering that he did not mention dragoons as a separate formation, they were most likely counted as part of the infantry here.
21 National Library of Russia in St. Petersburg, fond 971, op. 2, manuscript 96, p.22, Mikołaj Abramowicz to K. Radziwiłł, Toruń, 9 December 1626.

THE COMMANDERS AND THEIR ARMY

see that this number was much lower than what was decided during the *Sejm*. It is fairly easy to explain why the Polish army never reached the planned number. First of all we need to remember the already mentioned system of 'blind portions', that normally reduced the real size of cavalry units by 10–15 percent and probably at least a similar percentage in infantry. Secondly the high level of attrition, due to battle losses, sickness and desertion, was taking a massive toll on the army. Nonetheless, officers always insisted on receiving pay for the 'paper strength' of their units and more often than not the Treasury officials and war commissioners tended to agree to that. We will discuss more examples of such a practice in the following chapters. Many planned units, especially in regard to foreign infantry, were never created, as due to the Thirty Years' War there was a shortage of available candidates in the customary recruitment areas. So throughout 1627 the 'paper strength' of the Polish army in Prussia varied between 11,000 and 17,000 horses and portions, with the real numbers much lower. We have an interesting note from Dutchman Abraham Booth, who on 29 July 1627 witnessed a muster of Polish troops.[22] The army presented in front of Dutch envoys was reinforced by newly arrived infantry units raised by Colonel Denhoff, also by the Imperial regiment of Duke Adolf:

> [The Polish army] Being with new arrived German foot-troops, not stronger than 16 companies of hussars, 24 companies of cossacks, 6 companies of German riders, 4 companies of dragoons, 29 companies of haiduks and 32 companies of German infantry, making together hundred and eleven companies, who have a great number of whores and boys and a lot of baggage with them. Close to midday the entire army was in order, very far spread out.

As it would be very interesting to see how accurate these numbers of companies are, we will look into them in more detail in Appendix III.

Different formations of the Polish army, including hussars and foreign infantry, in 1627, as drawn by Abraham Booth. (Author's archive)

---

22   Abraham Booth, *Journael van de Legatie in Jaren 1627 en 1628* (Amsterdam, 1632), pp.40. The author would like to thank E.J. Blaauw for his enormous help in translation from Dutch.

Another *komput* that survived seems to be created for the purpose of the ordinary *Sejm* from October–November 1627. According to this document, Koniecpolski's forces in Prussia consisted of:[23]

Formation	Strength
Hussars	2,380
Reiters	1,445
Cossack cavalry	3,550
Polish infantry	1,550
Dragoons	1,432
Foreign infantry	5,101
Wybraniecka infantry	_[24]
Total	15,458

Unfortunately only part of the main text (units of hussars, foreign infantry and dragoons) and the final summary of this document have survived, so we are unable to trace the full history of the units in service. We can reconstruct some of them from musters from 1628 but it is possible that it still leaves us with some gaps and there may be units that appeared in Prussia for a short time and then were quickly disbanded. It is interesting that during this *Sejm* a group of senators presented another project concerning the organisation of the Polish army in Prussia. It was based on the suggestion of Hetman Koniecpolski, who was asking for the creation of a 30,000-man force. The majority of them, 20,000, were to be a mix of foreign and Polish infantry and dragoons, so the troops most useful in fighting against many Swedish-held locations. The remaining 10,000 was to be composed of 4,000 hussars, 4,000 cossack cavalry and 2,000 reiters.[25] This suggestion was not even put to a vote, however, and Koniecpolski had to continue his campaigns with forces already available in place.

During an extraordinary *Sejm* in June–July 1628 a new project regarding the planned size of the army, called *Discurs na sejmie Iulio de subsidii na wojne pruską*, was presented during the proceedings.[26] It is possible that the author was Jakub Zadzik, Grand Crown Chancellor, supported by Hetman Koniecpolski himself. This plan estimated that military action should only take place between April and November, the cavalry serving for three quarters and the infantry and dragoons eight months. *Discurs...* presented the idea of the army as such:

23 Riksarkivet Stockholm, Skoklostersamlingen, E 8600, *Comput Woyska K.J.M. Zaciągu do prus, w służbie będąceo i wiele sie mu winno.*

24 Not included in the *komput*.

25 Jan Seredyka, *Sejm zawiedzionych nadziei* (Opole: Wyższa Szkoła Pedagogiczna im. Powstańców Śląskich w Opolu, 1981), p.102.

26 Henryk Wisner, 'Dwa polskie plany', pp.200–201.

Formation	Strength
Hussars	2,000
Reiters	2,000
Cossack cavalry	2,000
Polish infantry	4,000
Hungarian infantry	1,000
Dragoons	–
Foreign infantry	5,000
Zaporozhian Cossacks	4,000
Total	20,000

We can see here the idea of further reduction of the overall size of cavalry, a general shift towards Polish infantry and the introduction of Zaporozhian Cossacks into Prussia. It was a very detailed plan that included detailed information about the estimated cost of such an army and even what types of taxes and amounts of tax would have to be collected to fund it. Again, it remained just a theory and was never discussed as a possible option to be introduced in Prussia.

The campaign of 1628, despite the lack of a major battle and a focus on 'small war', was very costly for both the Polish and Swedish armies. This time we can compare how the army looked 'on paper' with relations describing its real strength. Starting with the theory, here are the numbers from September 1628:[27]

Formation	Strength
Hussars	2,240 (2,320)
Reiters	1,302 (1,295)
Cossack cavalry	3,600 (3,600)
Polish infantry	1,850 (n/a[28])
Foreign infantry and dragoons	7,882 (7,453)
Wybraniecka infantry	Not included in the *komput*
Total	16,374 (14,668[29])

During the time of the ordinary *Sejm* of January–February 1629, another unofficial project of new organisation of the army in Prussia emerged in Warsaw. Its author was Prince Jerzy Zbaraski, who was a brother of the author of the already mentioned project from November 1626, Prince Krzysztof Zbaraski. This new idea, known as 'A method of help for war in Prussia'[30] or

---

27 The first figure is based on a detailed list of army units, as described in Biblioteka ks. Czartoryskich w Krakowie, 1772, *Regestrum rationis thesauri Regni in Conventu anni MDCXXIX expeditae.* The second figure (in brackets) is based on a summary of delivered and overdue payments from Biblioteka ks. Czartoryskich, 2246, pp 115–118, *Summariusz, co brało wojsko pruskie ad rationem z skarbu Rzptej po sejmie blisko przeszłym i co mu Rzpta winna od 1 decembris 1626 a 1 septembris 1628.*
28 *Summariusz…* only mentioned pay already issued and still owed to the Polish infantry, without giving the number of troops.
29 Without Polish infantry.
30 Henryk Wisner, 'Dwa polskie plany', pp.200–201, 201–203.

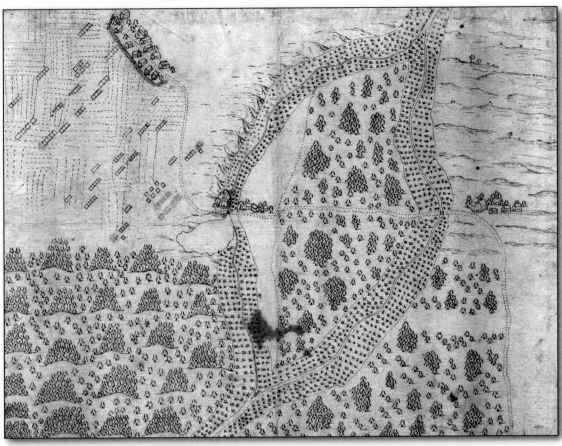

Battle at Górzno, 12
February 1629. (Krigsarkivet,
Stockholm)

Prince Zbaraski's Discurs[31] was not presented in the *Sejm*'s forum but seems to be well known by representatives of the nobility. Zbaraski planned a large army that was to take the initiative in the war against Swedes:

Formation	Strength
Hussars	2,000
Korycarze	2,000
Cossack cavalry	500
Polish infantry	4,000
Hungarian infantry	2,000
Dragoons	1,500
Foreign infantry	6,000
Zaporozhian Cossacks	3,000
Wybraniecka infantry	2,000
Total	23,000

What he suggested could be easily called revolution, no surprise then that also this project was not put into motion. Again we can see here an

---

31   National Library of Russia in St. Petersburg, Sobranije P. P. Dubrowskiego, no 166. Text courtesy of Radosław Sikora.

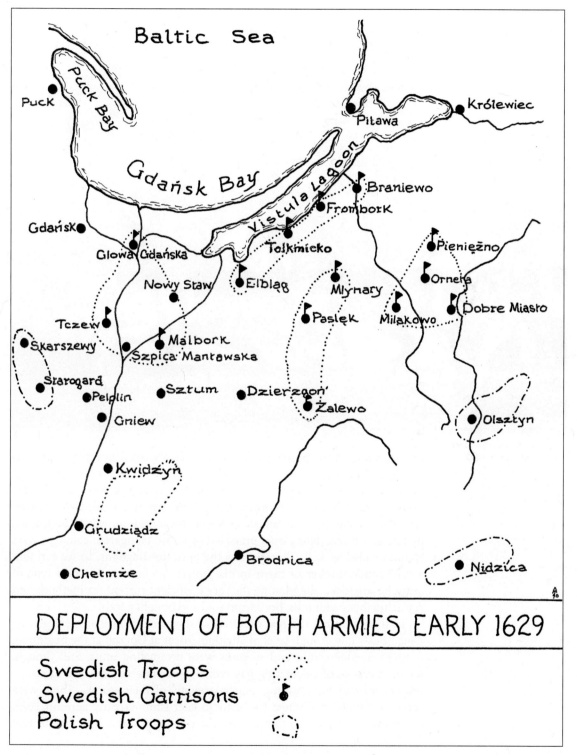

Baltic Sea

Puck
Puck Bay
Gdańsk Bay
Vistula Lagoon
Piława
Królewiec
Braniewo
Frombork
Gdańsk
Głowa Gdańska
Tolkmicko
Pieniężno
Nowy Staw
Elbląg
Młynary
Orneta
Dobre Miasto
Tczew
Pasłęk
Miłakowo
Skarszewy
Malbork
Szpica Mątawska
Starogard
Sztum
Dzierzgoń
Zalewo
Pelplin
Gniew
Olsztyn
Kwidzyn
Grudziądz
Brodnica
Nidzica
Chełmże

DEPLOYMENT OF BOTH ARMIES EARLY 1629

Swedish Troops

Swedish Garrisons

Polish Troops

Source: Polska Kriget.

53

Polish troops drawn by Abraham Booth in 1627. Top, left to right: hussar, cossack in chainmail and with carbine, bow-armed cossack. Bottom left to right: Polish haiduk, hussar, cossack. (Author's archive)

idea of reducing the number of cavalry, he also wanted to replace Western reiters and the vast majority of cossack cavalry with a new formation that he called *korycarze*.[32] There were many interesting suggestions regarding the infantry: the Polish infantry was to have higher pay and be supplemented by recruitment amongst the nobles, however this formation was to be trained by foreign officers. Hungarian units, led by native Hungarian colonels, were recommended as well. Zbaraski saw the need for dragoons, so we can find a substantial number of them in his project. To finance this new type of army, he suggested abandoning the very inefficient current tax methods and replacing them with tolls, both from sold and bought goods.

In the meantime the real numbers of the army in Prussia were getting dangerously low. A high level of attrition, losses at Górzno at the beginning of 1629, and desertion and sickness were decimating units. Still though, for the purpose of calculating pay (which was massively delayed anyway), officers insisted on counting 'paper strength' of their troops. There were some new units that joined the army in later summer/early autumn 1629, so we can safely assume that at least their strength was fairly close to that

---

32   See Chapter 3, section describing cossack cavalry, for more details.

recommended in recruitment letters. Let us try to estimate what the army 'on paper' was, under command of Hetman Koniecpolski in 1629:[33]

Formation	Strength of old units (already in service)	Strength of new units (beginning of service in summer/autumn 1629)	Total strength (old + new units)
Hussars	2,345	650	2,995
Reiters	1,197	–	1,197
Arkabuzeria	–	150	150
Cossack cavalry	3,600	–	3,600
Polish infantry	1,900	1,400	3,300
Foreign infantry and dragoons	7,765[34]	1,400[35]	9,165
Wybraniecka infantry	420	Unknown	420
Total	17,227	3,600	20,827

Of course real numbers were much lower and this shows how big the difference was between theory and practice. A muster of the greater part of the army, which took place on 15 September 1629, draws a rather sad picture of the Polish troops. Unlike many similar musters recorded in the seventeenth century, this one mentions both the paper and real strength of the units. It clearly shows how badly decimated some of the units were:[36]

Hetman Stanisław Koniecpolski's Regiment

Rotmistrz	Formation	Paper strength	Muster strength	Notes
Royal Prince Władysław	hussars	200	100	
Hetman Stanisław Koniecpolski	hussars	232	50	
Łukasz Żółkiewski	hussars	150	81	
Adam Kalinowski	hussars	150	68	
Samuel Żaliński	hussars	150	88	
Andrzej Jeżewski	cossacks	150	80	
Mikołaj Herburt	cossacks	150	–	Unit was not present on muster, as it was serving sentry duty. Paper strength – 150 horses
Aleksander Cetner	cossacks	150	115	
Borzysławski	cossacks	150	110	
Prince Aleksander Pruński	reiters	200	60	Independent unit, ad hoc attached to the regiment
Gothard Bodembroch	reiters	100	60	Independent unit, ad hoc attached to the regiment
Total:		1,632 (+150)	812 (+?)	Only units that were present. In brackets Herburt's cossack banner

---

33   Based on Riksarkivet Stockholm, Extranea IX Polen, 80, *Comput Woyska J.K.M.*; Ferdynand Bostel (ed.), *Rachunek skarbu koronnego z r. 1629* (Kraków: Akad. Umiejętn., 1891), pp.29–35.

34   *Comput Woyska…* does not mention the strength of three companies of infantry. At least 800 portions from the overall number were dragoons.

35   1,000 infantry and 400 dragoons.

36   Archiwum Główne Akt Dawnych w Warszawie (AGAD), AZ, 3116, pp.10–12, no title. The author would like to thank to Radosław Sikora for sharing this document.

Stanisław Potocki's Regiment

Rotmistrz	Formation	Paper strength	Muster strength	Notes
Stanisław Potocki	hussars	100	60	
Stefan Potocki	hussars	150	100	
Zbigniew Oleśnicki	hussars	150	100	
Mikołaj Łysakowski	cossacks	100	–	Muster strength not provided
Struś	cossacks	100	54	
Total:		600	314 (+?)	

Marcin Kazanowski's Regiment

Rotmistrz	Formation	Paper strength	Muster strength	Notes
Marcin Kazanowski	hussars	100	81	
Władysław Myszkowski	hussars	100	75	
Władysław Lipnicki	cossacks	100	87	
Jerzy Budziszewski	cossacks	100	80	
Andrzej Syrakowski (Serakowski)	cossacks	100	72	
Total:		500	390	Only units that were present

Mikołaj Potocki's Regiment

Rotmistrz	Formation	Paper strength	Muster strength	Notes
Mikołaj Potocki	hussars	100	50	
Tomasz Zamoyski	hussars	150	72	
Jan Działyński	hussars	100	56	
Jan Bąk-Lanckoroński	cossacks	100	68	
Firlej?	? (probably cossacks)	50	50	Unit cannot be identified
Jan Odrzywolski	cossacks	150	85	
Samuel Łaszcz	cossacks	150	80	
Stefan Wieruski	cossacks	150	80	
Stefan Nadarzycki	cossacks	100	40	
Total:		1,050	581	

Mikołaj Kossakowski's Regiment

Rotmistrz	Formation	Paper strength	Muster strength	Notes
Mikołaj Kossakowski	hussars	100	62	
Andrzej Kossakowski	hussars	100	57	
Mikołaj Gniewosz	hussars	100	56	
Andrzej Śladkowski (Ślądkowski)	cossacks	100	50	
Total:		400	225	

Former Regiment of Stefan Koniecpolski[37]

Rotmistrz	Formation	Paper strength	Muster strength	Notes
Andrzej Sapieha	hussars	150	71	
Mikołaj Krzyczowski	hussars	100	74	
Balcer (Baltazar) Męciński (Męczyński)	cossacks	200	80	
Hermolus Przyłęcki	cossacks	100	70	
Total:		550	295	

Additional Cavalry Units

Rotmistrz	Formation	Paper strength	Muster strength	Notes
Mikołaj Abramowicz	reiters	600	205	Regiment
Ernest Denhoff	reiters	400	120	Regiment

In total, all cavalry units present in the camp[38] had paper strength of 5,732 horses but only 2,942 were counted at the muster. Additionally the document mentioned, without naming any units, that 400 dragoons were present. It was a far cry from the paper strength of 1,200–1,300 portions that should be in all dragoon companies. It is also another proof to the claims of officials such as Prince Zbaraski, who criticised the lack of control over the real size of the army. It clearly shows that the Polish army in Prussia was really exhausted by the conflict and the conditions in which it had to fight against the Swedes.

---

37 After Stefan Koniecpolski's death in summer 1629, Stefan Żaliński took his place in command of the regiment. Surprisingly enough, though, Żaliński's hussar banner is mentioned as part of the Hetman's regiment during this muster.

38 The document mentioned that other cavalry units did not take part in the muster, being 'away from the camp'.

Chapter 3

Formations, Organisation and Equipment

In this chapter we will look into more details of each formation of the Polish army fighting in Prussia. We will focus on their organisation, equipment and tactics, while additional information about pay, clothing and flags of such units is described in Chapter 4.

Hussars (*husaria*)

Officer of hussars from the beginning of the seventeenth century. 'Stockholm Roll'. (Author's archive)

The famous 'winged hussars', known in Poland as *husaria*,[1] are the most iconic Polish army formation of all time, easily recognisable thanks to the combination of wings, pelts, armour and plenty of deadly weapons carried by each horseman. In the second part of the sixteenth and throughout the seventeenth centuries they were present on practically every battlefield where Polish and Lithuanian armies were fighting against enemies such as Swedes, Muscovites, Turks, Tatars and Cossacks. They were always seen as the elite of the army, with the best soldiers, equipment and horses. Service in hussar banners was seen as a matter of prestige, as it could open the door to a career for nobles from less famous and not so wealthy families. For the purpose of this book, we will be using term 'hussars' to describe both the formation and its soldiers. Of course there is enough evidence, both from written sources and iconography, to support the claim

---

1   *Husaria* as a name of formation, *husarz* (singular) and *husarze* (plural) to describe soldiers. Some older primary sources sometimes use form *usaria/usarze*.

that during their long history hussars on some occasions, including battles, were equipped with their famous wings. The problem is that during the 1626–1629 war such situations were rare and most likely reduced only to occasions when they had to 'show off' to foreign ambassadors and Swedish negotiators.

Hussars were shock cavalry, relying on a fearsome charge where they could use their *kopia* lances to break both cavalry and infantry. Once the lance was shattered on impact or had to be for some reason abandoned, soldiers would switch to 'secondary' weapons, depending on the situation and the enemy they were fighting against. It could be an estoc or heavy pallasch, kept under the saddle,[2] or the most important weapon for each noble – the sabre. In 1623 during the *Sejm* it was suggested that each hussar be equipped with two pistols, preferably good quality Dutch ones.[3] By 1626 a pistol or brace of pistols was most likely the norm, especially when we are talking about companions' equipment. Often used also were the horseman-pick (*nadziak*) and hammer-axe (*czekan*), ideal for both fighting from horseback and drunken brawls in the camp. Such weapons had a special place in Polish history. On 15 November 1620 one was wielded by Michał Piekarski, in an attempted assassination of King Sigismund. He managed to wound the monarch but was stopped by the royal retinue.[4] Therefore all nobles were forbidden from carrying such weapons in public, and those caught with one would be fined 200 zl. When issuing this ban, the *Sejm* made exception for soldiers, as 'we allow use of the *czekan* and other weapons during war against enemies of the Crown'.[5] The hussar retinue could also be equipped with long firearms, such as calivers, harquebuses or muskets, often used during sieges or when defending the tabor wagon.

Hussars from the beginning of the seventeenth century. 'Stockholm Roll'. (Author's archive)

Hussars' weapons and equipment were always a very interesting topic for foreigners, so we have plenty of sources from the period describing soldiers, their weapons and their horses. We chose three sources from visitors to Prussia, from 1627, 1629 and 1635. Abraham Booth, who in 1627 was deputy secretary of the Dutch envoys attempting to negotiate peace between Poland

---

2 Sometimes hussars had both, with estoc on the left and pallasch on the right side of the saddle.

3 *Acta historia*, volume I, p.281.

4 After a short investigation (including torture) he was sentenced to death and then 'drawn by four horses into pieces' in Warsaw on 27 November 1620.

5 *Volumina Legum*, volume III (Petersburg, 1859), p.185.

Drawing of a hussar by Abraham Booth. It clearly shows all armament: pistol, estoc, sabre and lance. (Author's archive)

and Sweden, left very interesting descriptions and drawings from his stay in Prussia. Here is what he wrote about the elite Polish cavalry:

The Hussars of Lancers, on whose force they trust the most, are usually of the highest Nobles of the Land, are beautifully clothed and horsed, have a Harquebusiers Armour and below a mail suit and on the arms up to over the elbows long plates to block the hit of a sabre: besides their sabre, which they carry on the side, they have a pallasch under the saddle of the horse, which is almost as long as a rapier,[6] some also have pistols, and around their neck hangs a leopard or panther skin, with wings on the back, and other strange embellishments; their lances have sometimes been as long as those used here in our Land, which is carried not under the arm but in a certain leather connected to the saddle.[7]

Sir Thomas Roe arrived in Prussia in summer 1629 in order to support another Polish–Swedish peace negotiation. As with the Dutch envoys two years prior, here also the Poles tried to make a large impression on the English embassy. At the beginning of September 1629 Roe wrote about hussars welcoming him and his party:

Another hussar by Abraham Booth. This time no wing and no feathers attached to the helmet. (Author's archive)

Arrived at the Polish campe and was mett by Zolkefsky Lieutenant Generall[8] three English mile [from the camp] and most of the officers of the Army with Coaches attended with 1,000 men at Armes compleat, all their lances paynted and guilt [gilded] with penans [pennants] of silke at the head, according to the Colours of their troupes, on their helmets a crest of eagles wings, upon their armes coates of Lions or Leopards skinnes, in so brave an order, and glory, that a supposed I was entering rather into some triumph, then a camp, that had been long in field. There was warlike musicke of all sorts, kettle-drummes, trumpets and Hoboyes [oboes], the nobility bravely mounted, their bitts and reynes of silver, so gallant a show I never saw out of India,[9] nor found better welcome and reception.[10]

---

6   Booth is using the old word *steeck-kade*, which was used to describe rapiers and similar weapons used for stabbing. Thanks to Mats Elzinga for providing an explanation of this term.

7   Abraham Booth, *Journael van de Legatie in Jaren 1627 en 1628*, pp.12–13.

8   *Rotmistrz* Łukasz Żółkiewski, in charge of the Hetman's cavalry regiment.

9   Between 1615 and 1618 Roe was ambassador at the Mughal emperor Jahangir's court in Agra.

10   National Archive, Kew, SP/88/5/163, *Roe's account of his negotiations*, pp.167–168.

Frenchman Charles Ogier, who was part of the French embassy in 1635, had many occasions to see the hussars and they seem to have left a lasting impression, as he wrote about them in a few parts of his diary. We will quote the two most detailed examples, to see how closely they match Booth's description.

Hussars during the Smolensk War, 1632–1634. Wilhelm Hondius, 1636. (Author's archive)

> The hussar banner rode from the camp to meet us; I have never seen more graceful sight. All of them were Polish nobles, riding beautiful horses, wearing splendid and shining armour, with pelts of panthers, lions and tigers on their backs; they have long lances [*kopie*] supported by leather straps at the saddle, with silken ribbons or pennants just below the spear tip, that flutter on the wind, misleading the enemies' eyes. It is all grand but it is hard not to laugh seeing long wings attached to their backs, which, they believe, also cause to scare the enemies' horses and force them to flee. Bridles on horses are silver and gilded, with silver pendants and roundels at their necks. [Hussars] Have sabres at their sides and at the saddle pistols, maces, hammers, axes and estocs [*koncerze*]. In the battle only the first or second rank can use the lances; for the next ranks they are next to useless, so they use other weapons. Those that do not have expensive pelts, cover their shoulders with carpets, used both as a decoration and as to cover gaps in armour.[11]

> We then stopped at the village, where we have seen a horse banner of so-called hussars. They are all nobles, armed with long lances, empty inside, reinforced with hemp fibre glued around it, they put their end in a small strap attached to the saddle; at their side they have a sable, at the saddle pistols and a second sword, which is an estoc; they also have helmets, plate and other armour from the best iron. Each of them have 20 or 30 horses, five of them are most important, used by hussars in battle; the others for their retinue and their numerous tabor, as they are carrying all their food with them.[12]

As we can see their descriptions are very closely matching, with lances, wings and pelts mentioned as a very specific part of the hussars' equipment. We cannot ignore the description written by the soldiers as well. Samuel Hutor Szymanowski, who in 1633 and 1634 served as a hussar fighting against the Turks, wrote a very interesting poem called *Mars sauromatski…* in which he described many details of the equipment of Polish soldiers fighting under the command of Hetman Koniecpolski. Due to the short passage of time from

11   *Karola Ogiera dziennik podróży do Polski 1635–1636*, part I (Gdańsk: Biblioteka Miejska: Towarzystwo Przyjaciół Nauki i Sztuki, 1950), pp.171–173.
12   *Ibidem*, p.143.

Lobster-tailed pot helmet, known in Poland as *szyszak*, used by hussars. (Muzeum Narodowe, Kraków)

the end of the Prussian war there were no changes in soldiers' attire, therefore we can look into it as an additional source for the description of the elite of the Polish army during the war against the Swedes. We can see soldiers with 'iron armour, cuirass',[13] covered with a variety of pelts: bears, tigers and leopards.[14] What is especially interesting – Szymanowski mentioned wings. There are large ones with vulture feathers,[15] other units had eagle feathers.[16] Helmets were decorated with a crest of feathers, called *forga*.[17] Another example from the period very close to the war in Prussia comes from 1636, with the description of equipment belonging to hussar companion Marek Łahodowski. Amongst his war gear we can find three sets of iron armour and helmets (*szyszak*) plus additional 'polished aureate armour and blackened aureate vambraces'. Finally something that hussars were famous for: four leopard pelts, worth in total 200 zl.[18] Even their saddles could be very expensive and made from good quality materials, especially those that were used by wealthy officers.

In 1616 in the register of belongings of the powerful Ostrogski's family, we can find two fine hussar saddles. One was covered with green and red velvet, with silver ornaments and precious stones, while the second was covered with blue and white velvet, also with some silver and precious stones. On the same list there were a few gilded hussar's stirrups, some of them covered with mother-of-pearl.[19] It appears that the armour worn by the hussars provided them with solid protection, there are some cases of them being hit by small cannonballs and surviving even through serious wounds. Albrycht Stanisław Radziwiłł, who was present at the battle of Gniew (Mewe) in 1626, mentioned that a standard bearer from Niewiarowski's hussar banner was 'shot with bullet through his whole body, so he bled from front and from the back [of the body] and his breath was stopped but [staying] a whole year in

Breast- and backplate from hussar's armour, end of the sixteenth century. (Author's archive)

13 Samuel Hutor Szymanowski, *Mars sauromatski i inne poematy*, edited by Piotr Borek (Kraków: Collegium Columbinum, 2009), pp.92, 98
14 *Ibidem*, pp.98, 100.
15 *Ibidem*, p.92.
16 *Ibidem*, p.98.
17 *Ibidem*, pp.98, 100.
18 Władysław Łoziński, *Prawem i lewem. Obyczaje na czerwonej Rusi za panowania Zygmunta III* (Lwów: nakładem W. Webera, 1903), p.212.
19 Tadeusz Lubomirski, 'Regestra skarbca książąt Ostrogskich w Dubnie', *Historya Sztuki w Polsce*, volume VI, parts 2 and 3 (Kraków, 1898), p.210.

Examples of hussars from the early 1620s. Decoration from Hetman Stanisław Żółkiewski's sarcophagus, circa 1621. (Muzeum Narodowe, Kraków)

Gdańsk he recovered'.[20] Of course not all hussars could afford expensive high quality armour, exotic pelts or feathers. Many, especially amongst the retainers, had wolf pelts, or instead of them covered their armour with *delia* or *kilim*/*welens* (one-coloured or striped) capes, usually woollen. It is possible that during a long conflict, like the one in Prussia, more expensive pieces of equipment were used only on special occasions (musters, the arrival of the king or ambassadors) and during 'normal' activities more common (and cheap) items were used. It is interesting to note that none of the Swedish relations mentioned hussars using wings during the fight but we can read of them during Polish–Swedish negotiations, when Dutch, French and English envoys were present.

Battles usually took a heavy toll in killed and wounded horses, however, especially as hussars were always in the thick of the fight. For example the initial casualty muster after the battle of Kłuszyn (Klushino) in 1610, where the majority of Polish cavalry was composed of hussars, shows 61 killed, 96 wounded and nine missing companions and retainers, while losses amongst horses were noted as 188 killed, 181 wounded

20 Albrycht Stanisław Radziwiłł, *Rys panowania*, p.121.

and at least 20 missing.[21] In 1637, during the battle of Kumejki against mutinied Zaporozhian Cossacks, nine banners of hussars lost 12 killed and 40 wounded companions, 27 killed and 53 wounded retainers, while at the same time losing 68 killed and 121 wounded horses.[22] The next year, between May and August, again fighting against mutinied Cossacks, 13 banners of hussars that we have detailed information about[23] lost 41 killed and 93 wounded companions, 78 killed and 90 wounded retainers, 122 killed and 158 wounded horses, with a further 46 horses noted together as 'killed and wounded'.[24]

Unfortunately not many of the Polish banners' muster rolls from that period have survived, so in order to look into details of organisation of the units we have to rely mostly on Lithuanian rolls from the same period, as the number and strength of retinues should be very similar. It gives some idea of the composition of the banners, especially when compared with their strength. Luckily there is one very detailed Polish example from 1630, that can provide a further point of reference.

Polish Hussar Banner of Ludwik Weyher in 1630[25]

Number of horses in retinue	Number of retinues of that type in banner	Additional comments
12	1	*Rotmistrz* retine
5	1 (see comments)	Lieutenant's retinue
1	1 (see comments)	Ensign's retinue
6	1	
5	2	
4	6	
3	7	
2	8	
1	5	
Total: 32 retinues with 100 horses		

21 Radosław Sikora, *Kłuszyn 1610* (Warszawa: Instytut Wydawniczy Erica, 2010), p.113.
22 Szymon Okolski, *Dyaryusz transakcyi wojennej między wojskiem koronnem a zaporoskiem w r. 1637* (Kraków, Wyd. Biblioteki Polskiej, 1858), pp.57–58.
23 There was one more banner in the army but its losses are described only as 'Lieutenant Belina killed and many more companions and retainers'.
24 'Rejestr wielmożnych mężów w potrzebie z Kozakami pozabijanych, postrzelonych, także i czeladzi ich i koni, ab 8 Mai ad 7 Aug. w roku 1638', Szymon Okolski, *Kontynuacja dyaryusza wojennego* (Kraków, Wyd. Biblioteki Polskiej, 1858), pp.196–198.
25 AGAD, Archiwum Warszawskie Radziwiłłów, dz. II, 1034, pp.1–4, Rejestr popisowy chorągwi husarii Ludwika Wejhera.

Lithuanian "Yellow" Hussar Banner of Lithuanian Field Hetman Krzysztof II Radziwiłł in 1625[26]

Number of horses in retinue	Number of retinues of that type in banner	Additional comments
12	1	*Rotmistrz* retinue
3	1 (see comments)	Lieutenant's retinue
5	1 (see comments)	Ensign's retinue
5	5	
4	10	
3	11	
2	7	
1	1	
Total: 37 retinues with 133 horses		

Lithuanian Hussar Banner from Samogitia (Żmudź) District Under Andrzej Radzimiński in 1625[27]

Number of horses in retinue	Number of retinues of that type in banner	Additional comments
12	1	*Rotmistrz* retinue
7	1 (see comments)	Lieutenant's retinue
5	1 (see comments)	Ensign's retinue
6	1	
5	4	
4	11	
3	27	
2	17	
1	2	
Total: 65 retinues with 211 horses		

Lithuanian Hussar Banner of Mikołaj Korff in 1622[28]

Number of horses in retinue	Number of retinues of that type in banner	Additional comments
5	1 (see comments)	Lieutenant's retinue[29]
4	1 (see comments)	Ensign's retinue
4	6	
3	18	
2	4	
1	3	
2	1 (see comments)	Trumpeter's retinue
1	1 (see comments)	Drummer's retinue[30]
Total: 35 retinues with 101 horses		

---

26 National Library of Russia in St. Petersburg, F 321, op. 2, manuscript 67, pp.1–2, *Comput woiska za pieniądze Xcia Je Msci Pana Hetmana Polnego…*

27 Henryk Wisner, 'Wojsko litewskie I połowy XVII wieku', p.89.

28 Leonid Arbusow, 'Aus dem Handbuch des Wojewoden Nicolaus von Korff auf Kreuzburg', *Jahrbuch für Genealogie, Heraldik und Sphragistik*, 1911–1913 (Mitau: Kurländische Gesellschaft für Literatur und Kunst, 1914), pp.437–438.

29 The banner did not have a *rotmistrz* retinue.

30 The presence of trumpeters' and drummers' retinues is very unusual. It is most likely result of the lack of a *rotmistrz* retinue, which would normally include any musicians.

Hussars armour and helmet
from the beginning of
the seventeenth century.
(Skokloster Castle)

Thanks to the detailed muster of Weyher's banner in 1630, we can also describe a very interesting structure of the *rotmistrz's* retinue. While often a large part of it was composed of 'blind portions', where soldiers were not present and their pay was used as extra money either for the *rotmistrz* or his lieutenant, in this case a Polish officer presented a 12-horse retinue as: himself, two additional spare horses for himself, two mounted grooms, three mounted pages, three mounted trumpeters and one mounted drummer. Of course the exact composition of such retinue, if it was present at all, could vary from banner to banner. There was no specific rules that a *rotmistrz* was obliged to follow, it all depended on his own idea and the contents of his purse (plus his willingness to spend additional money on musicians, pages, a surgeon and a chaplain).

The core of hussars during the 1626–1629 war were 'quarter' army banners, that arrived in Prussia with Hetman Koniecpolski in November 1626 (name of nominal *rotmistrz*, followed by paper strength of the unit): Hetman Stanisław Koniecpolski (250 horses), Tomasz Zamoyski (150), Marcin Kazanowski (100), Stefan Potocki (150), Stanisław Potocki (100), Adam Kalinowski (100), Mikołaj Potocki (100), Mikołaj Kossakowski (100), Łukasz Żółkiewski (100), Stefan Koniecpolski (100), Tomasz Szkliński (100) and Jan Potocki (150). These 12 banners were supported by a few enlisted units which were left from the army initially gathered and led by Sigismund III: Royal Prince Władysław, under Mikołaj Stogniew (200), Andrzej Stanisław Sapieha (150), and Mikołaj Krzyczowski (100).

The *Sejm* of 1626 decided to create one more banner, under Jan Działyński, with 100 horses that started its service in June 1627. Throughout the whole war there were only minor changes in the organisation of the hussars' 'corps'. In 1627 Działyński's and another new unit – under Władysław Myszkowski – joined the army but Tomasz Szkliński's banner was disbanded. The *arkabuzeria* of Mikołaj Gniewosz and reiters of Andrzej Kossakowski were converted into hussar banners, most likely in 1627. Władysław Lipnicki's banner joined Koniecpolski's army in July 1629 but surprisingly it was not part of the group of new banners (four of hussars and one of *arkabuzeria*) that were raised in spring/summer of 1629 and arrived in Prussia prior to the end of the campaign. His banner was kept in service after the end of the war and marched with the Hetman's army to Ukraine, while all other units raised in 1629 were very short-lived and were disbanded after the end of the conflict with Sweden. Below are the numbers and sizes of all banners serving as part of the regular army during the war, we can see minor changes in their 'paper strength' throughout those years:

Rotmistrz	Summer–Autumn 1626[31]	Dec. 1626–Feb. 1627[32]	March–May 1627	June–August 1627	Sept.–Nov. 1627	Dec. 1627–Feb. 1628	March–May 1628	June–August 1628	Sept.–Nov. 1628	1629[33]
Royal Prince Władysław	200	198	188	200	183	193	190	200	200	200
Hetman Stanisław Koniecpolski	226	226	224	224	220	218	203	220	224	225
Łukasz Żółkiewski	150	150	150	150	150	150	150	150	150	150
Adam Kalinowski		100	100	95	100	100	99	100	100	100
Marcin Kazanowski	100	100	98	94	92	91	94	100	100	100
Tomasz Szkliński	100	100	100	100[34]	–	–	–	–	–	–
Władysław Myszkowski	–	–	–	100	100	100	100	100	100	100
Stanisław Potocki	100	100	100	100	100	100	100	100	100	100
Jan Działyński	–	–	–	100	100	99	98	100	100	100
Stefan Potocki	150	150	143	143	138	138	138	150	150	150
Jan Potocki/Zbigniew Oleśnicki	150	150	139	146	126	136	148	150	150	150
Mikołaj Potocki	100	100	100	100	100	100	100	100	100	120
Tomasz Zamoyski	150	132	120	149	150	150	150	150	150	150
Stefan Koniecpolski/ Samuel Żyliński[35]	100	89	89	99	100	100	100	100	100	150
Andrzej Sapieha	150	150	147	146	146	149	145	150	150	150
Mikołaj Kossakowski	100	100	100	90	95	100	100	100	100	100
Andrzej Kossakowski[36]	100	100	95	95	99	97	98	100	100	100
Mikołaj Krzyczowski	100	85	96	96	100	100	100	100	100	100
Mikołaj Gniewosz[37]	125	125	80	89	85	93	100	100	100	100
Władysław Lipnicki	–	–	–	–	–	–	–	–	–	100[38]

Hussars were designated as the main shock troops of the Polish and Lithuanian armies, proving their power and skills on many battlefields and against different types of enemies. During its long history, the formation fought against Turkish *sipahi* and janissaries, Swedish reiters and infantry, Zaporozhian Cossacks *moloitsy* in their fortified tabor wagons, Tatar light horsemen and Muscovite boyars, *streltsy* and 'new type' troops. The Swedes knew very well how fearsome and devastating a hussars' charge could be. They witnessed that during bloody defeats in Livonia during 1600–1611, especially at Kieś (Wenden) in 1601, Kokenhausen (Koknese) in 1601, Biały Kamień (Weisstenstein, Paide) in 1604 and Kircholm in 1605. So it is not a surprise that during new conflicts in Livonia in 1621–1622 and 1625–1629, then later in Prussia in 1626–1629, Swedish commanders were always very

---

31 Riksarkivet Stockholm, Extranea IX Polen, 82, *Comput Woyjska K.J.M. Koronnego.*
32 Strength between December 1626 and November 1628 based on: Biblioteka ks. Czartoryskich w Krakowie, 1772, *Regestrum rationis thesauri Regni in Conventu anni MDCXXIX expeditae.*
33 Riksarkivet Stockholm, Extranea IX Polen, 80, *Comput Woyska J.K.M.*
34 The unit was disbanded at the end of August 1627.
35 Żyliński took over the banner after Koniecpolski's death in June or July 1629.
36 Initially a reiters banner, converted into hussars (1627?).
37 Banner of *arkabuzeria*, treated as hussars.
38 Centralnyj derżawnyj istorycznyj archiw Ukrainy in Lviv (CDIAUL), f.9, op.1, 381, p.1650.

Szyszak helmet, typical for hussars. Part of King Władysław IV's armour, circa 1635. (Livrustkammaren)

Breastplate, part of King Władysław IV's armour, circa 1635. (Livrustkammaren)

Backplate, part of King Władysław IV's armour, circa 1635. (Livrustkammaren)

Late sixteenth-century hussar helmets. (Author's archive)

wary of the hussars' presence and potential effect on the battlefield, taking extra precautions to protect their troops against them. Therefore most of the charges would be rather small-scale actions, with just a few banners attacking on a certain part of the battlefield. They often had to operate in difficult terrain (Gniew in 1626, Tczew in 1627), that to some extent limited their ability for a successful charge. The most effective and efficient use of hussars can be seen during the battle of Trzcianą (Honigfelde) on 27 June 1629. While the cossacks tied up the Swedish rearguard, Hetman Koniecpolski took two hussar banners – his own and Royal Prince Władysław's – to flank the enemy. The charge of the lance-armed horsemen was devastating, capturing a battery of 10 leather cannons and 'mightily breaking lances' crushing Swedish cornets.[39] There were at least eight banners of hussars that took part in this battle, all of them 'a few times bravely engaging the enemy' and 'breaking all the lances'.[40]

Hussars were also used as camp guards, most likely as a reserve force that could on short notice be thrown into a fight to support cossacks deployed as a first line of defence. On 11 July 1627,[41] when a Swedish reconnaissance force was engaged near the Polish camp by the cossack banner of Aleksander Cetner, it was two hussar banners that initially joined the fight. Stefan Koniecpolski's banner had

---

39   'Relacja bitwy trzciańskiej posłana od P. Hetmana', p.430.
40   Od Pana Hetmana do Króla Jego Mości, z pod Nowejwsi na pobojowisku, dnia 28 czerwca 1629, pp.155–156.
41   Description of the skirmish based on 'Diariusz albo Summa', pp.31–32.

just finished 'night guard [duty], without their armour' and it was to be replaced as 'day guard' by Mikołaj Krzyczowski's banner – instead both of them crossed the dike in front of the Polish camp and charged at the Swedish cavalry. The Poles became victims of their own success however, as chasing the retreating reiters they met a stronger Swedish reserve. The Polish main army was not ready for a protracted engagement, as 'all their horses were still in the field [pasture]'. The only unit that managed to prepare at short notice was Łukasz Żółkiewski's hussar banner but it deployed only a token force of 35 men 'that were ready'. It provided welcome relief for the three banners that were engaging the Swedes but paid a heavy price for it. Żółkiewski's banner took massive losses: four companions were killed, a further eight were 'all shot, and of them four later died [of wounds] and four recovered'. We need to remember that all eight killed were companions, the best equipped and trained soldiers in the unit.

A very interesting Polish point of view regarding hussars and the lessons they could take from the wars against Sweden comes from Stefan Pac (1587–1640), who in 1624 and 1625 was part of Royal Prince Władysław's entourage during a visit in Western Europe. In September 1624 the Poles were present in the camp of the Spanish army besieging Breda. Here they had the chance to discuss many aspects of military matters with Spanish officers. Pac wrote in his journal:[42]

Examples of different equipment of Polish hussars, from Pieter Snayers' painting depicting battle of Kircholm in 1605 (painted circa 1630). Some have pelts over armour, others *kilim/welens* or *delia*. We can also see a mix of helmets and fur caps. (Photo courtesy of Tomasz Ratyński)

We always sat at the table with [Ambrogio] Spinola and [his] other important men, where we had many conversations; they encourage it by asking about Polish knights [and] ways of warfare. As well it happened that they asked about our hussar, lancer, [and the] way he is mounted. We explained it to them. So Spinola said to Count Hendrich van den Bergh, how he would fight against such powerful cavalry. The Count answered that he would face the lancers with horsemen armed with long carbines and as soon as the lancers would start their charge he would order [his soldiers] to shoot and he understands that such [fire] would break the lancers. I laughed when I heard that, so they asked me why is that. I answered that not long ago we have been with His Majesty the Royal Prince as guests of the Prince of Bavaria [Elector Maximilian I] who hosted for us an expensive hunt,

---

42 *Obraz dworów europejskich na początku XVII wieku przedstawiony w Dzienniku Podróży Królewicza Władysława syna Zygmunta III do Niemiec, Austryi, Belgii, Szwajcaryi i Włoch, w roku 1624–1625. Skreślony przez Stefana Paca* (Wrocław: Z. Schletter, 1854), pp.71–72.

as few hundred deer and does were gathered together and many of us were then shooting [at them] from the hunting huts; and despite such serious fire from such a large group only a few [killed] were left on the ground; the rest, despite some of them being wounded, managed to flee. A lancer in the fight is not as easy a target as an animal to the shooter; if during the hunt from 200 such small damage is made from shooting, then what those carbines can do to armoured [men] on good horses; they may probably unsaddle some and kill some horses from the whole crowd but they will not break whole banner [company] and will not stop the impetus [of the attackers] with which [our] lancers not only broke [Swedish] cavalry but also pikemen (as proved by recent actions in Livonia).[43] And all agreed that I am speaking the truth. But now, after the Prussian expedition,[44] I would not dare to safely make such a claim.

On one hand we can see here the initial belief of the Poles and Lithuanians about the skill and power of their hussars in a fight against both cavalry and infantry. Pac took part in the 1621–1622 war in Livonia, so in 1624 he was speaking from the experience of fighting with a fairly new army led by Gustav II Adolf. However as he edited his journal around 1630, he was already much wiser due to his vast experience of the Polish army in Prussia, where the Swedes were better trained and adjusted their tactics to counter the hussars. It clearly shows that the Poles and Lithuanians noticed both improvement in their enemy's army and fewer opportunities for hussars to make a major impact on the battlefield.

Cossack/light horseman, equipped with bow, sabre and horseman's pick. 'Stockholm Roll'. (Author's archive)

Cossack Cavalry (Including Lisowski's cossacks)

Before we look into detailed description of this formation, we need to first of all clarify some misunderstandings in regards to its name: both in Polish and in English. Originally this cavalry was called *jazda kozacka* (cossack cavalry), with its soldiers being known as *kozacy* (written with lower case). It was a term used to describe free men, 'serving for money' and was adopted for both military use and to describe household servants, often mounted. In the sixteenth century the word started to be used to describe free men settled in Ukraine near the Dnieper river but they were called *Kozacy* (written with upper case). As such, in the original Polish text one could find both *kozacy* and *Kozacy* serving together in one army. Obviously it made it very confusing when translating it into English, when normally always one form – Cossacks – is being used, leading to

---

43 The 1621–1622 war in Livonia.
44 The 1626–1629 war in Prussia.

many errors in identifying who is in fact described in the text and attributing many military features of Polish cossack cavalry to Zaporozhian Cossacks. As such, in this book we will be using the term cossack cavalry or cossacks[45] to describe regular cavalry in the Polish army and Cossacks to describe Zaporozhian Cossacks.

We also mentioned so-called Lisowski's cossacks (*lisowczycy*). It was a volunteer formation, created by Colonel Aleksander Lisowski in 1614, during campaigns in Muscovy. *Lisowczycy* were known as very good light cavalry, masters of 'small war' but had the same bad reputation as the Imperial Croats, of being ruthless pillagers. Many of their units served without pay, living on what they could capture during their operations. After 1618 their banners served as mercenaries, fighting as part of the Imperial army against Protestant armies in the opening phase of the Thirty Years' War. They also supported Polish armies against Turks and Tatars in 1620–1621 and fought (without much success) against the Swedes in Livonia in 1622. Finally a few banners of *lisowczycy* also took part in the campaign in Prussia in 1626, showing great skills during reconnaissance missions and skirmishes against the Swedes. At the end of 1626 two of their banners were disbanded, with officers and many companions discharged from the army for disciplinary matters[46] while the rest became part of Koniecpolski's army as regular troops. The equipment and weapons of the *lisowczycy* were the same as other cossack cavalry units, also the organisation of their banners followed the normal Polish pattern, with retinues being led by their companions.

Next to hussars, cossacks were the most common cavalry type in both the Polish and Lithuanian armies. They had the dual purpose of both medium cavalry, providing fire support for the hussars but also of light cavalry, able to skirmish, taking part in reconnaissance and foraging missions. They were the main force used in the 'quarter army' to fight against Tatars,

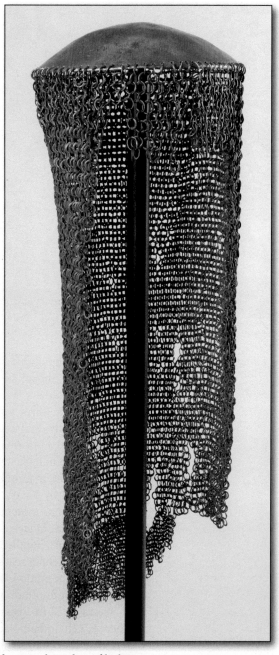

Misiurka helmet, commonly used by cossack cavalry. (Muzeum Narodowe, Kraków)

45 For the purpose of translation into English wargaming rules of the 'By Fire and Sword' wargame, the author of this book used the term 'cossack style cavalry'. While technically not as accurate, such a translation was used to make it much easier to differentiate between the Cossacks and mounted Cossacks also present in the game's setting.

46 Due to breaking royal decrees earlier and serving without his permission in the Imperial army.

Cossack equipped with bow and sabre. Abraham Booth, 1627. (Author's archive)

Different equipment of cossack cavalry by Abraham Booth. (Author's archive)

perfect for hit and run tactics but also employing black powder weapons, which tended to affect the Tatars' morale. Recruitment letters issued to *rotmistrzs* of cossack banners usually mentioned that both companions and retainers should have 'good horse and equipment required for [those] serving as cossacks'[47] but sometimes information was added that soldiers should have a 'good gun' (that is, harquebus/carbine)[48] or specify that 'three guns' (two pistols and a long firearm) were required.[49] Sabres, as individual weapons of all soldiers, were not mentioned – there was no need for that information, as it was after all a symbol of status and privilege of each noble to have it. While bows were also not part of 'official' weaponry, they were often employed, especially by companions (again, as status symbol) and by Tatars serving in cossack banners. There is no indication that spears and/or lances were employed by this type of cavalry during the war in Prussia. 'Quarter army' cossacks in 1623 were to be equipped with two pistols, carbine, light helmet and armour,[50] which should always be included as a requirement in recruitment letters.[51] As we will see, it was just theory and in practice the equipment used by those soldiers could vary.

Abraham Booth drew a few very different cossacks, that he had a chance to see in 1627 in Prussia, indicating a mix of equipment within banners. There is a chainmail-clad (but wearing fur cap) soldier, armed with sabre and bow. Another chainmail-equipped cossack, this time with a *misiurka* helmet, is armed with sabre and harquebus. Further drawings show a lighter version

---

47 Archiwum Państwowe w Łodzi; Archiwum rodziny Bartoszewiczów; Dokumenty, uniwersały, przywileje; document 3, List przypowiedni dla Stanisława Kosubudzkiego.

48 Archiwum Państwowe w Łodzi; Archiwum rodziny Bartoszewiczów; Dokumenty, uniwersały, przywileje; document 8, List zapowiedni Zygmunta III króla Polski, etc. dla rotmistrza Hieronima Dembińskiego na zaciąg do roty kozackiej, Warszawa 1627.

49 AGAD, Teki Naruszewicza, volume 121, no 17 and 19.

50 The text indicates that the author meant chainmail.

51 *Acta historia*, volume I, p.281.

of cossack cavalry, without any armour, equipped with bows. One shows a peculiar-looking shield, probably an odd attempt to draw a wicker *kałkan* shield. His written description is rather odd, as it seems that he confused cossack cavalry with Zaporozhian Cossacks, nonetheless it provides a very interesting insight into the equipment of this cavalry:

> Others, who are mostly used against the Tatars, have no weapons but bow and arrow, and some also a pistol in their belt: the third manner of horsemen are the Cossacks (*Zborofsche Cosacken*), who come from the Turkish border and the Black Sea, who have no armour (*Wapen*) except a mail suit (*Casacque de Mailles*), an iron disc on their head and a carbine (*Carabijn-Roer*) on their back, some also have arm plates (*Arm-schijven*) just like the hussars.[52]

Polish-Hungarian sabres, end of the sixteenth/beginning of the seventeenth century. (Author's archive)

Szymon Starowolski described such cavalry in 1628 as 'some of them with a coat of mail, and two pistols and one long firearm, all with sabres'[53] and in 1632 'some have harquebus, other have bows and short lances, both [types] are covered with a coat of mail and are called cossacks'.[54] Very similar is a description of cossacks by Charles Ogier, who saw them in Prussia in 1635: 'a third type [of cavalry] – are cossacks, wearing iron shirts [chainmails]; [some] have handguns, while others have bow and quiver'.[55] On another occasion he wrote that 'light horse, called cossacks, came closer and rode in front of us, which was a nice sight. They are good looking and lithe men, wearing iron armour;[56] with handguns on their backs'.[57] When 400 horses of *lisowczycy* led by Idzi Kalinowski on 26August 1626 joined the royal army in Prussia, eyewitnesses mentioned that they were well equipped with 'shot' – indicating different types of 'carbines'.[58] This source also described the same good level of available firepower with another *lisowczycy* banner – 300 horses under Władysław Śleszyński.[59] It appears that lack of armour was the problem that affected cossack banners throughout the war though, for example Moczarski's *lisowczycy* fighting at Gniew in 1626 are mentioned as 'naked', which in this context means unarmoured.[60]

---

52 Abraham Booth, *Journael van de Legatie*, p.13. The author would like to thank E.J. Blaauw for his enormous help in translation from Dutch.

53 Szymon Starowolski, *Eques Polonus* (Venice, 1628), p.39

54 Szymon Starowolski, *Polska albo opisanie Królestwa Polskiego*. Translation from Latin by Antoni Piskadło (Warszawa: Wyd. Literackie, 1976), p.113.

55 *Karola Ogiera dziennik podróży do Polski 1635–1636*, part I (Gdańsk: Biblioteka Miejska: Towarzystwo Przyjaciół Nauki i Sztuki,, 1950), p.271.

56 In this case: chainmail.

57 *Karola Ogiera dziennik podróży do Polski 1635–1636*, part I, p.161.

58 *Diariusz Wojny Pruskiej z roku 1626*, p.349.

59 *Ibidem*, p.350.

60 *Ibidem*, p.367.

As we already mentioned regarding hussars, we do not have many surviving Polish banners' muster rolls for this part of the seventeenth century, but again we can use Lithuanian ones from the same period, as the organisation of the units would be very similar. Luckily Ludwik Weyher and his muster comes with help again, as next to his hussar banner he also had a small cossack banner in the Polish army. Here are a few examples of both regular army and district troops:

Polish banner of Ludwik Weyher in 1630[61]

Number of horses in retinue	Number of retinues of that type in banner	Additional comments
2	1	*Rotmistrz* retinue
5	1	Lieutenant's retinue
1	1	Ensign's retinue
1	1	Trumpeter's retinue
3	4	
2	12	
1	5	
Total: 25 retinues with 50 horses. Additionally the *rotmistrz* strengthened the unit with 17 more horses, paid from his own pocket but they were not part of the official roster of the banner or his retinue.		

Krzysztof Pior Kleczkowski's (Lithuanian) cossack banner in 1625[62]

Number of horses in retinue	Number of retinues of that type in banner	Additional comments
12	1	*Rotmistrz* retinue
7	1	Lieutenant's retinue
5	1	Ensign's retinue
5	3	
4	6	
3	6	
2	15	
1	6	
Total: 39 retinues with 115 horses		

61 AGAD, Archiwum Warszawskie Radziwiłłów, dz. II, 1034, pp.5–6, Rejestr popisowy chorągwi husarii Ludwika Wejhera.
62 Henryk Wisner, 'Wojsko litewskie I połowy XVII wieku', p.104.

Banner from Lithuanian Kowno District in 1625[63]

Number of horses in retinue	Number of retinues of that type in banner	Additional comments
12	1	*Rotmistrz* retinue
4	1	Lieutenant's retinue
4	1	Ensign's retinue
5	1	
4	1	
3	6	
2	25	
1	3	
Total: 39 retinues with 100 horses		

Banner from Lithuanian Wiłkomierz District in 1625[64]

Number of horses in retinue	Number of retinues of that type in banner	Additional comments
6	1	Deputy's retinue[65]
5	1	Lieutenant's retinue
3	1	Ensign's retinue
4	2	
3	12	
2	7	
1	3	
Total: 30 retinues with 84 horses		

We can identify the following banners serving as part of the regular army in Prussia between late autumn 1626 and summer 1629. There were also at least four units that appeared in the army during summer 1627, under *rotmistrz* Dembiński, Rogawski, Górski and Plecki.[66] They seem to have been very short lived, however, as none of them appeared on army muster rolls in 1628 and 1629.

---

63   *Ibidem*, p.104.
64   *Ibidem*, p.104.
65   The deputy (*namiestnik*) was a companion assigned to lead the banner when both the *rotmistrz* and lieutenant were not present.
66   'Diariusz albo Summa', p.37.

Rotmistrz	Summer–Autumn 1626[67]	Dec. 1626–Feb. 1627[68]	March–May 1627	June–August 1627	Sept.–Nov. 1627	Dec. 1627–Feb. 1628	March–May 1628	June–August 1628	Sept.–Nov. 1628	1629[69]
Stanisław Suliszowski/Borzysławski[70]	150	150	136	150	150	145	150	150	150	150
Mikołaj Herburt	150	150	150	148	148	150	150	150	150	150
Aleksander Cetner	150	150	128	150	150	150	150	150	150	150
Mikołaj Małyński/Andrzej Jeżewski/	150	144	144	137	144	144	144	150	150	150
Walerian Włodek	100	83	87	96	93	95	96	100	100	100
Jerzy Budziszewski	100	100	100	100	100	100	100	100	100	100
Mikołaj Annibal Strocy	100	100	100	100	100	100	100	100	100	100
Piotr Łabęcki	100	100	100	99	98	100	91	100	100	100[71]
Samuel Łaszcz	150	150	124	123	147	146	146	150	150	150
Jan Odrzywolski	150	139	109	129	149	145	145	150	150	150
Jan Bogusz/Stefan Wieruski	150	125	144	150	141	150	145	150	150	150
Samuel Temruk	100	96	99	100	100	100	100	100	100	100
Gabriel Kuliczkowski/Stefan Nadarzycki	100	100	96	95	100	100	100	100	100	100
Michał (Adam?) Stanisławski/Andrzej Sierakowski	100	100	92	99	97	99	99	100	100	100
Baltazar Męciński (Męczyński)	200	200	198	198	195	194	198	200	200	200
Hermolus Aleksander Przyłęcki	100	88	97	96	100	100	100	100	100	100
Andrzej Śladkowski	100	100	100	100	93	100	93	100	100	100
Jan Boki	100	100	100	100	96	100	100	100	100	100[72]
Mikołaj Łysakowski	100	100	100	100	100	100	100	100	100	100
Albert Roguski (Rogulski)	100	100	97	90	95	98	100	100	100	100
Rożniatowski/Jerzy Łowczycki	100	99	98	98	96	98	98	100	100	100
Władysław Lipnicki	100	100	93	94	98	97	99	100	100	100
Jan Bąk-Lanckoroński	100	100	150	150	150	144	150	150	150	150
Piotr Bujalski	200	150	103	139	135	131	150	150	150	100[73]
Krzysztof Faliński/Paweł Karpiński	200	150	149	150	149	149	150	150	150	150
Paweł Czarniecki	100	100	83	95	98	98	91	100	100	100

---

67   Riksarkivet Stockholm, Extranea IX Polen, 82, *Comput Woyjska K.J.M. Koronnego*.
68   Strength between December 1626 and November 1628 based on: Biblioteka ks. Czartoryskich w Krakowie, 1772, *Regestrum rationis thesauri Regni in Conventu anni MDCXXIX expeditae*.
69   Riksarkivet Stockholm, Extranea IX Polen, 80, *Comput Woyska J.K.M.*
70   Suliszowski died in a skirmish near Rypin in September 1628. Borzysławski (first name unknown), possibly his former lieutenant, took over the unit and led it until the end of the war.
71   Under Lieutenant Struś.
72   Under Lieutenant Minor, as Boki died at the beginning of 1629 during the battle at Górzno.
73   Under Lieutenant Górski.

Rotmistrz	Summer –Autumn 1626[67]	Dec. 1626– Feb. 1627[68]	March– May 1627	June– August 1627	Sept. –Nov. 1627	Dec. 1627 –Feb. 1628	March– May 1628	June– August 1628	Sept.– Nov. 1628	1629[69]
Mikołaj Moczarski	200[74]	200	175	200	193	188	188	200	200	200
Jerzy Kruszyński	100	100	93	95	91	100	91	100	100	100
Jan Maliński	100	100	100	100	100	100	100	100	100	100

Prince Jerzy Zbaraski in his *Discurs* from the beginning of 1629[75] did complain that cossack cavalry could not really stand against Swedish cavalry. His main issues were that cossacks were 'naked' and that they relied so much on bows that even retainers, not trained to use this weapon, were now equipped with it. That is why he suggested the creation of new formation, that he called *korycarze*. It was to be an 'upgraded' version of the cossack cavalry, equipped with helmet, 'armour',[76] a brace of pistols and a sword, making it similar to Swedish reiters or Imperial cuirassiers (although without full armour). Such a formation could be still as mobile as cossacks – as would be recruited from the same soldiers – but would fight more in the style of Western troops. The idea was never put into practice. It is interesting to see, though, that based on the experience of war against Sweden and improvements in the organisation and tactics of Gustav Adolf's cavalry, Zbaraski suggested the introduction of such a new formation. The Prince even claims, that as pistols are weapons 'short and light', they will not require as much training as other equipment and cavalry equipped with them will be able to fight the Swedes on their own terms. While the whole *Discurs* was just a theoretical project, it could indicate that in the one and a half years since Booth had a chance to see cossack cavalry in Prussia, their units lost (and were unable to replace) much of their equipment and were now much 'lighter' cavalry than in 1627.

It could be possible, though, that Zbaraski exaggerated as he wanted to make his point. Sources from the war mentioned many times that cossacks, especially during their raids, were able to fight on even terms against Swedish reiters. Hetman Koniecpolski in his description of the battle of Trzcianą in 1629 mentioned that cossacks 'fought bravely', engaging Swedes as the vanguard of the Polish-Imperial forces. The anonymous author of a diary from July 1629[77] wrote that (allegedly) Gustav Adolf himself highly praised one of the cossack banners, that surrounded by four Swedish cornets managed to break through so fast that barely any of the reiters had a chance to discharge their pistols. Polish mastery in sabre duelling was also in evidence, as 'pistols of other [Swedish] reiters shot only when falling down on the ground with cut off hands'. To support this story, the diarist mentioned that

---

74 At a muster dated 4 November 1626 the unit had 228 horses but on official records presented to the *Sejm* in November 1626 we can find the figure of 200 horses. It was originally a *lisowczycy* banner, that arrived in Prussia with 400 horses. Most likely it was divided into two banners, one under Moczarski, with a second *rotmistrz* unknown.

75 National Library of Russia in St. Petersburg, Sobranije PP. Dubrowskiego, no. 166.

76 Most likely he meant breast- and backplate.

77 Probably someone from amongst Royal Prince Władysław's courtiers.

Polish cossack cavalry (left) and haiduk infantry (right) during the Smolensk War, 1632–1634. Wilhelm Hondius, 1636. (Author's archive)

during inspection of the battlefield, the Poles found 'in this place many [cut off] hands with pistols'.[78]

Polish sources do not give us much detail regarding the tactics used by cossacks during their fights. We usually read about 'hitting the enemy', 'giving fire' but also 'retreating while fighting', which could indicate that feigned flight was often used. After all it was a tactic commonly used by Turks and Tatars, the main opponent of the 'quarter army' and it was very often used by Polish units as well. Cossack cavalry was also ideal for skirmishing, especially during the initial phases of combat, when so-called 'single combat' (*harce*) between individual cavalrymen was fairly common. During pitched battles they would often accompany hussars' charges, providing fire support and looking for a chance to chase broken or retreating enemies. During 1626–1629 war they were the main participant in 'small war', attacking Swedish foragers, convoys and small garrisons. Operating in small groups of a few banners, they were 'eyes and ears' of Koniecpolski's army, capturing prisoners and serving as an initial line of defence. Prince Zbaraski in his project from 1629 mentioned that there are certain tasks that cossacks were useful for, like reconnaissance, 'capturing prisoners, and all quick and sudden needs'. We can see that during the war they played the dual role of medium cavalry, supporting hussars, and that of typical light cavalry, in the later part of the seventeenth century taken over by more 'specialised' banners of Tatars and Wallachians.

Reiters

The Western-type cavalry were normally known in the Polish–Lithuanian Commonwealth as *rajtaria/rajtarzy* (reiters), from the German word *Reiter*, meaning horsemen. It was a very universal term, used to describe any type of

---

78 'Kontynuacja Diariusza', p.432.

Harquebusiers. Johann Jacobi von Wallhausen, Ritterkunst, 1616. (Author's archive)

cavalry: cuirassiers, harquebusiers and a later version, *Schwarze Reiter* (Black Riders), being a sort of hybrid of two previous formations. There were of course some other terms used in the Commonwealth. For example official letters or documents written in Latin called them *sclopetarii*, usually dividing them between *sclopetarii poloni* (in theory composed of Poles) and the much more popular *sclopetarii germani* (where German would just mean non-Polish, as reiters could be recruiting amongst French or Walloons as well). Swedish sources for both Polish and Lithuanian reiters, tend to use different versions of 'German riders': *Tyske rytter*, *Tyske ryttere* or *Deutsche Reuter*.

Both weapons and equipment could help us to answer the question of whether Polish reiters were closer in their attire to cuirassiers or harquebusiers. The problem, as always, is with the rather vague descriptions that we can find in primary sources. The usual term is that reiters were 'armoured', without much of the details of what such armour could look like. Charles Ogier in 1635 mentioned that Polish reiters were fully armoured.[79] We do not know, though, if he meant three-quarter cuirassier's armour or a set of breast- and backplate. The very high cost of the first type gives basis for the assumption that typical 'reiter armour' would be the latter, accompanied by a *szyszak* helmet. A Swedish relation from 1625 describes Lithuanian reiters as '1/2 cuirassiers', which could indicate a unit equipped as Western harquebusiers, but fighting as cuirassiers. Hussars fighting without their *kopia* lance were known as fighting 'in reiter style', which indicates that in the first few decades of the seventeenth-century Commonwealth reiters were expected as a norm to use some sort of armour. In 1625 French *rotmistrz* Gabriel Ceridon, recruiting in Lithuania, was complaining that he managed to enlist 30 men but none of them had armour. The required standard of the equipment meant that units of reiters were difficult and expensive to raise, generating many complaints from the officers that received recruitment letters. While sword or sabre was of course the standard weapon of each horseman, the biggest

---

79   *Karola Ogiera dziennik…*, p.271.

Polish reiters during the Smolensk War, 1632–1634. Painter unknown. (Muzeum Narodowe, Kraków)

emphasis was placed on firearms. The standard requirement was a set of 'three firearms': a brace of pistols and a long weapon (harquebus, musketoon, carbine, etc.), as reiters were often used on garrison duties. We can see it as early as in 1600, when such a set is mentioned in the recruitment letter for reiters that were to serve in Livonia against the Swedes.[80] Again, many problems with acquiring the required weapons generated complaints from both recruiters and commanders in the field, as a lack of firearms negatively affected the reiters' performance. In December 1628, when a new unit of cavalry was to be raised in Royal Prussia, it was decided that it would not be (as usual) a banner of reiters, 'because it is a very difficult task to tell [Polish reiters] apart from the German cavalry [of] the enemy'. A banner of hussars was to be created instead.[81]

It is very interesting to see where such troops were recruited, to better understand why they were seen in the Commonwealth as *sclopetarii germani*. Generally reiters were raised in Prussia, Livonia and Courland, also in German-speaking neighbouring countries. When in 1597 the Bishop of Cracow, Józef Wereszczyński, suggested at the *Sejm* raising a large army against Turks, he mentioned that Prussian, Livonian and Courland lands should prepare '1 horse from each 10 houses, as we really need reiters'. He also insisted that the Polish vassals, the Duke of Courland and Elector of Brandenburg, should send reinforcements equipped as reiters as well. It is not surprising that German-speaking nobles from the Baltic area were predominant amongst the officers of this formation, with names like Denhoff, Korff, Sey (Sej), Szmeling or Tyzenhauz appearing in the army throughout the seventeenth century. A very interesting example is Mikołaj (Nicholaus) Korff, serving as reiter *rotmistrz* in the Lithuanian army in 1611, 1617, 1621–1622 (when he ended up as colonel), 1626–1629 (again as colonel in charge of the whole regiment) and finally in 1635. We are very lucky that a few muster rolls of Lithuanian reiters from the period 1617–1635 have survived to our time, as it gives us great insight into the structure of the units.[82] As some Lithuanian units transferred from Livonia to Prussia in 1626, it helps us with insight into Polish reiters as well. All officers in those units were recruited from Livonian and Courland nobles of German origin, with many private reiters also having German names. At the same time Polish and Lithuanian names, such as Rogowski, Rusinowski, Mogilnicki or Sokołowski

80   BK 1400, *Akta i korespondencja z lata 1597–1602*, document no 4, p.39.
81   Gottfried Lengnich, *Geschichte der Preußischen Lande königlisch-polnischen Antheils*, volume V (Gdańsk, 1727), p.158.
82   Leonid Arbusow, 'Aus dem Handbuch', pp.433–442.

are present as well, indicating that the recruitment net was thrown much further, especially when the unit had to be raised in a relatively short period of time. Of course recruitment – of both full units and experienced officers – was not just limited to German-speaking areas. When in 1621 Tomasz Zamoyski received a recruitment letter for 400 hussars and 500 reiters, Crown chancellor Andrzej Lipski mentioned to him in the letter that '[they shouldn't be] some poor local ones but [instead] some good foreigners or Walloons, experienced and well equipped'.[83] Zamoyski found some captains that were eager to serve under his command and they were sent out 'both to Livonia … and to Silesia, near the Hungarian and German border, where those troops can be gathered'.[84] French officers were always welcome, a few of them were particularly linked with the Lithuanian army: Ceridon, de la Barre, Holazur (Olazur) and Samsony (Samosin). Poles and Lithuanians were usually only nominal *rotmistrz*, relying on experienced foreigners. A notorious exception to this rule was Mikołaj Abramowicz (Abrahamowicz), protégé of Hetman Krzysztof II Radziwiłł, who between 1626 and 1629 with great distinction led his reiter regiment in Prussia. Interestingly enough, when his unit arrived from Livonia, it was described as '400 reiters, good Livonians'. An additional source of recruits was prisoners of war. In April 1627, after the battle of Czarne (Hammerstein), approximately 400 Swedish mercenary horse, initially recruited in Mecklenburg, Brandenburg and Pomerania, were enlisted into the Polish army, strengthening Abramowicz's and Denhoff's regiments. They may not have been as reliable as those directly recruited by Polish officers, however. In mid August 1627 50 reiters from Abramowicz's regiment and 25 'from the company of the other captain' deserted and joined the Swedish army, it is very probable that a large part of this group was composed of ex-Swedish soldiers who decided to rejoin their original employer.[85]

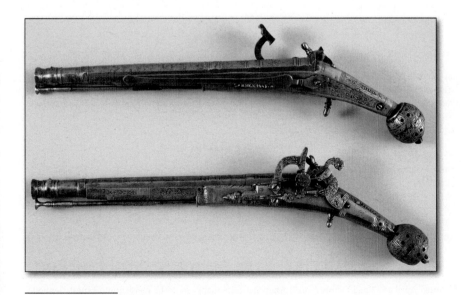

A brace of flintlock pistols, circa 1635. (Muzeum Narodowe, Kraków)

---

83   Stanisław Żurkowski, *Żywot Tomasza Zamoyskiego*, p.70.

84   *Ibidem*, p 74.

85   AGAD, AR V, 17961/III, p.63

Reiters were usually recruited as independent banners/companies, that were gradually combined into small regiments. An unusual feature of Polish and Lithuanian reiters was that they utilised retinues, typical for 'national' cavalry but additionally grouped them into corporalships. As with hussars, a *rotmistrz* retinue was usually 12 horses strong. Lieutenants' retinues varied between four and six horses, with an ensign's retinue normally being smaller, of three or four horses. Corporals, not present in the 'national' cavalry, also usually had three or four horses. Privates had a wide range of retinue sizes, from four horses down to just one (so just a reiter, without a retainer), although two-horse retinues were the most common. Sometimes we can also find separate retinues for a drummer (one horse) and trumpeter (one or two). A banner/company was divided into three corporalships, with the first led by a *rotmistrz*, the second by a lieutenant or ensign,[86] and the third by the senior corporal.

We can identify the following banners and regiments serving in Prussia between late autumn 1626 and summer 1629:

Rotmistrz	Summer–Autumn 1626[87]	Dec. 1626–Feb. 1627[88]	March–May 1627	June–August 1627	Sept.–Nov. 1627	Dec. 1627–Feb. 1628	March–May 1628	June–August 1628	Sept.–Nov. 1628	1629[89]
Mikołaj Abramowicz[90]	400	357	371	415	600	377	377	377	600	597
Ernest Denhoff	200[91]	194	194	194	194	400	400	400	400	300
Andrzej Kossakowski[92]	100	100	95	95	99	97	98	100	100	100
Prince Aleksander Pruński					200	200	200	200	130	200
Zbigniew Oleśnicki/ Gothard Bodembroch				100[93]	100	100	100	100	100	100
Carol Sey[94]						57	57	57		
Johan Brynk[95]						68	68	68		
Johan Denhoff[96]		120	120	120						
Theodor Denhoff[97]				100	100					
Wilhelm Johan Merfeldt[98]			75	75	75					
Johan Georg Gablens[99]				84	84					

---

86   In such cases, the lieutenant was part of the first corporalship.

87   Riksarkivet Stockholm, Extranea IX Polen, 82, *Comput Woyjska K.J.M. Koronnego.*

88   Strength between December 1626 and November 1628 based on: Biblioteka ks. Czartoryskich w Krakowie, 1772, *Regestrum rationis thesauri Regni in Conventu anni MDCXXIX expeditae.*

89   Riksarkivet Stockholm, Extranea IX Polen, 80, *Comput Woyska J.K.M.*

90   Regiment.

91   Banner that since 1628 appears to be called a regiment.

92   Initially a reiters banner, converted into hussars (1627?)

93   Started service on 1 August 1627.

94   The unit was only in service between November 1627 and August 1628. After that time it appears to be merged into Abramowicz's regiment.

95   As above.

96   The unit was only in service between April 1627 and October 1627. After that time it appears to be merged into Ernest Denhoff's regiment.

97   The unit was only in service between August 1627 and October 1627. After that time it appears to be merged into Ernest Denhoff's regiment.

98   Unit was only in service between April 1627 and October 1627. After that time it appears to be merged into Ernest Denhoff's regiment.

99   Unit was only in service between August 1627 and October 1627. After that time it appears to be merged into Ernest Denhoff's regiment.

We do not know much about the tactics used by Polish and Lithuanian reiters. They were often used as fire support for hussars and cossacks, but it appears that were not shy of 'getting their hands dirty' and if needed could join the melee. A Swedish drawing of the battle of Walmozja in 1626 shows Lithuanian reiters deployed, in the same way as hussars, in two ranks, which could indicate that they were used in a more aggressive way, just like Eastern cavalry. During the late stages of the battle of Gniew, on 1 October 1626, Henryk Szmeling's banner of 200 reiters 'struck mightily on the enemy, five times retreating and attacking again, finally forcing the enemy to retreat'. While it could indicate that the unit was employing a caracole (retreating and attacking again), it appears that the reiters were also engaged in hand-to-hand combat.

Arkabuzeria

This is a type of formation was unique to Poland, a rather unusual blend of 'Eastern' and 'Western' influences. Documents written in Latin usually use for it term *Equitibus harkabuseris* or *Arcabuseros*. It was normally fielded as heavy cavalry, well armoured in the way of Western European 'full' cuirassiers but recruited in the same way as native Polish cavalry. Curiously enough though, they were also equipped with harquebuses/carbines, just like lighter Western harquebusiers.[100] Szymon Starowolski described them as equipped with 'iron armour and helmets'[101] and 'armoured as good as hussars'.[102] We can think about them as some sort of hussars without lances (and wings), they were definitely treated by Polish nobles as an elite formation. In August 1627 the *Sejmik* of Poznań and Kalisz' Voivodship, announcing that nobles from this area should prepare themselves to defend their land from ex-Danish soldiers, mentioned that 'we, the citizens, should be all ready to fight, those [serving] as hussars with horse, armour, lance, pallasch, caliver [*rusznica*] and sabre; [while] those [serving] as *arkabuzeria* [with] brace of pistols, musket or carbine, pallasch and sabre'. Strangely enough armour is not mentioned, but at the same time neither is the horse…

During 1626–1629 we can find only rather small representation of such troops in the Polish army. In 1626 Mikołaj Gniewosz served in Prussia with a banner of *arkabuzeria*, taking part in the battle of Gniew. His unit was initially 200 horses strong but in December 1626 dropped to 125 horses and in 1627 even to 80 horses. It served throughout the rest of the war, with strength varying between 90 and 100 horses. In fact at some point in 1627 it began to be treated as a hussar unit, so we can see how the difference between those two formations could easily be crossed. The next unit of *arkabuzeria* did not arrive in Prussia until the summer of 1629, when a 150-horse banner of Prince Jerzy Zasławski joined the main army as part of new reinforcements. It is very probable that Zasławski's troops did not even have a chance to fight against the Swedes at all.

---

100 Hence the similarity in the name of formation.
101 Szymon Starowolski, *Polska albo opisanie Królestwa Polskiego*, p.112.
102 Szymon Starowolski, *Eques Polonus* (Venice, 1628), p.39.

Foreign Infantry and Dragoons

The main part of the infantry 'arm' of the army was based on so-called foreign infantry, sometimes also called German infantry, and dragoons.[103] The Commonwealth had a long history of employing such mercenaries, which were normally recruited in German-speaking parts of the country and in neighbouring states. During the first three decades of the seventeenth-century soldiers from the British Isles, especially Scots, were also a fairly common sight in Polish and Lithuanian armies, while French and Dutch usually appeared only as officers and specialists such as engineers or gunners.

The largest part of the officers' corps was composed of German-speaking nobles, usually from Courland, Livonia or Prussia. Many of them came from families with a long tradition of military service in both the Polish and Lithuanian armies – like Dönhoff (Denhoff), Rosen, Puttkamer, Fittinghoff and Tysenhaus. Despite the fact that we can find the names of all officers ranked captain and higher, we cannot identify the place of origin of many other 'German' officers – although we know for example that Johan Storch came from Gdańsk (Danzig) and Johan Albrecht von Lesgewang from Prussia. It was somehow more natural for such officers to be in charge of the foreign infantry, where most of the soldiers were also German-speaking, often recruited locally or in neighbouring countries. The British Isles seems to have provided a good percentage of Hetman Koniecpolski's foreign officers, both in the infantry and the dragoons. At least three Butlers (James, Walter the Older and Walter the Younger) and Hugo O'Reilly came from Ireland. The Scottish contingent included James Murray, Andrew and William Keith, Patrick Gordon and one Gryma (perhaps Grime or Graham? His first name is unknown). Finally England was represented by Arthur Aston Junior and one Owen (also first name unknown). We can also find a strong French group: Barbier, Ceridon, Duplesis/du Plessis, Forde, de Mareul, de La Crotade and Montaigne. The Dutch were represented by Wilhelm Appelman and Wilhelm Winter/Winteroy. There was even a Swedish officer, one of King Sigismund's

Foreign infantry in Polish service during the Smolensk War, 1632–1634. Wilhelm Hondius, 1636. (Author's archive)

---

103 This section included revised and updated article 'Notes on organisation of the foreign infantry and dragoons in the Polish army during 1626–1629', published in *Arquebusier*, Volume XXXVII/I (Witney, 2020).

loyalists, Gustav Sparre. We have only a few Poles – Bazyli Judycki, Jan Wojsław Żółtowski and Stanisław Janikowski – curiously usually in charge of dragoons. Such a small number of the latter is not surprising though, as the majority of Polish officers were commanding Polish-Hungarian and *wybraniecka* infantry, and were not associated with 'German' troops.

While it is difficult to identify the nationality of the officers, it is even more difficult to do so with the common soldiers. None of the detailed muster rolls have survived to our time, so we have to rely on bits of information scattered in different sources. Aston's company in 1626 is called 'Scottish' but it is most probable that his unit was a rather mixed group, with some Englishmen and Irishmen adding a more British flavour. Butlers' and Keith's companies could also initially in 1626 have had some British contingents but there is no hard evidence to support this theory. Silesia, which at that time was part of Holy Roman Empire – a natural ally of the Commonwealth – was next to Prussia (both Ducal and Royal) and Saxony was the most common recruitment ground for officers of the Polish Crown. Private units raised in 1626 by Bazyli Judycki were recruited there, which led to some problems though. In 1627 Judycki wrote that a 'high number of Silesian rogues, not wanting to fight against Swedes, deserted from the unit'.[104] It was Saxony, however, where two Polish colonels – Gerhard and Magnus Ernest Dönhoff – were sent in January 1627 to raise two foot regiments (3,000 men each). Elector John George I allowed them to recruit in his country, under the condition that they would not enlist miners and Saxonian soldiers. When King Sigismund III issued in March and April 1627 decrees to the nobility of Wielkopolska, ordering them to allow newly recruited soldiers access to provisions and free passage through their land, he mentioned that they were from regiments raised 'in Moravia, Bohemia, Silesia and Germany'.[105] Prior to the outbreak of war in 1626, when the Poles already realised that Gustav Adolf was planning to land in Prussia, recruitment was also organised in Duchy of Pomerania, where Duke Bogislaw XIV allowed a few hundred men to be raised amongst his subjects. In 1627 he had a change of heart though – when one of the Polish officers arrived in the Duchy to raise more troops, he was banned from doing so and had to return to Prussia empty handed. As the war progressed, due to the large demand for soldiers in German-speaking countries, it was more and more difficult to recruit new troops there. Therefore in 1629 a regiment

Both sides of a musketeer's powder flask, dated between 1589 and 1620. (Muzeum Narodowe, Kraków)

104 AGAD, AR V, no 6171, Kawaler Judycki do Zygmunta Karola Radziwiłła, 2 III 1627 obóz pod Tczewem, p.2.
105 Włodzimierz Dworzaczek (ed.), *Akta Sejmikowe województw poznańskiego i kaliskiego*, volume I part 2 (Poznań: Państwowe Wydawn. Naukowe, 1962), p.229.

Dragoons in Polish service during the Smolensk War, 1632–1634. Wilhelm Hondius, 1636. (Author's archive)

led by Colonel Reinhold Rosen became some sort of experiment, as it was the first unit of 'German' infantry, recruited in Poland proper, where only the officers and NCOs were foreigners, with the rest of the regiment Polish 'trained in the German manner'. While Rosen's regiment arrived in Prussia too late to take part in the fight against Sweden, the experiment as whole was deemed to be a success. When a new war against Muscovy broke out in 1632, the majority of 'German' infantry and dragoons units raised for the Commonwealth's army were recruited in the same way as Rosen's regiment three years earlier.

As mentioned, an additional source of new troops was the enlistment of prisoners of war. We can identify two larger groups of infantry that joined Polish army that way, both from 1627. First, when Puck (Putzig) surrendered to Koniecpolski on 2 April, the garrison was allowed to march to Swedish-held Piława (Pillau). Some of its soldiers decided to change sides, and between 120 and 200 infantrymen and 65 horsemen were enlisted in the Polish army. The main part of the garrison was composed of a Swedish national regiment from Norrländ, which could indicate that all of a sudden there was a company-sized group of native Swedes in Polish service. As we read in a relation written at that time in Danzig, 'when the Swedes were leaving Putzig, one of their [national] companies, [numbering] close to 200 [men], in which you could not find a single German, gave their oath to serve His Royal Majesty [Sigismund III]'.[106] Unfortunately it is impossible to trace their further fate, most likely they were divided between different companies of 'German' infantry. Second, a much larger group joined on 17 April, after the battle of Czarne (Hammerstein). When the Swedish contingent under colonels Teuffel and Streiff was forced to surrender, majority of its troops – approximately 800 infantry – switched sides. They 'swear faithful service to His Majesty [King Sigismund III] and were spread between different banners

---

106 AGAD, TK 118, 147, *Nowiny z Gdańska*

[companies] of our infantry'. This group was composed of German-speaking soldiers, recruited mostly in Mecklenburg but also in Brandenburg and Duchy of Pomerania.

The most striking feature of the foreign infantry and dragoons in the Polish army was the way that their units were organised on a regimental level – something we will now look into in more detail. By 1626 many countries already had a well-established organisation of their infantry units: Spanish *tercios* and foreign regiments, United Provinces infantry (including many foreign troops), Imperial and Catholic League regiments or Swedish national and *värvade*[107] regiments, to name just a few. When we are looking into similar structures in Polish armies we see a much more complicated picture. As mentioned in Chapter 1, the ordinarily Polish standing army – the so-called 'quarter army'(*wojsko kwarciane*) – was composed of the cavalry (hussars and cossacks), with only some small units of Polish infantry to support and provide garrison duties. The reason for it was rather simple, as it was the cavalry that was the most useful in protecting the vast border from the Tatar raids. German infantry was normally only appearing in larger numbers when the army was being expanded due to some longer conflict, such as Stephen Bathory's wars waged against Muscovy in 1577–1582. Such troops were usually enlisted for one campaign, after which they were disbanded. The beginning of the seventeenth century brought wars against Sweden, waged in Livonia and Courland. In the Polish and Lithuanian armies that fought there we can find some units of German and Scottish infantry – rather small (no more than 200 men-strong) independent companies, which were often called *freikompanie*, which means 'free companies'. On the battlefield they could be grouped together in some sort of 'brigade' but it was always done ad hoc and without any regimental-level structure (like regimental command, a specific number of same/similar size companies).

Of course that does not mean that in the first two and a half decades of the seventeenth century Poland did not raise any larger unit of Western-type infantry. When between the summer of 1609 and the summer of 1611 King Sigismund III besieged Smolensk, defended by Muscovite forces, an important part of his infantry was Jan Weyher's regiment of German foot. The unit was divided into seven companies, 200 men each, for a total strength of 1,400 men. In 1621, when the large Polish–Lithuanian army was raised to fight against the Ottomans at Chocim (Khotyn), it also had a strong

Matchlock musket, early seventeenth century. (Muzeum Narodowe, Kraków)

---

107 The word used to describe those units of the Swedish army (both infantry and cavalry), which were not formed on the basis of domestic conscription. While *värvade* were mostly enlisted outside of Sweden and Finland (for example in German states, the United Provinces or Scotland), it should be remembered that sometimes they were also formed locally, from Swedes, Finns and the inhabitants of the Baltic provinces.

contingent of German infantry. The sources are rather confusing and often contradict each other but we can safely assume that there were at least two stronger (between 2,000 and 2,300 men each) and one weaker (900-man) regiment, though unfortunately we do not know how many companies were in each of those. There were also a few small free companies, numbering between 150 and 200 men. As we can see there was a rather loose approach to the way that such troops were organised – it is a common motif which we will encounter yet again in 1626, when a new army was raised to fight in Prussia against invading Swedes.

The Polish army gathered to repel Gustav Adolf's invasion in 1626 was raised in various different ways. We can find amongst them private troops (organised by the King and wealthy magnates), district troops (raised by different Polish lands), the local levy of nobility, regular Polish troops from the 'quarter army' diverted from marching to Podole[108] and regular Lithuanian troops, ordered to relocate to Prussia from the Livonian theatre of war.[109] A very important part of such peculiar assembly were 'German' (foreign[110]) infantry and dragoons, as it was expected that musket-equipped troops will be essential part of the struggle against Swedes. As early as in 1625 recruiting officers, especially those commissioned by the King himself, were trying to raise as many units as possible. Unfortunately, with many competitors to enlist available soldiers, their efforts were often far worse than expected. It led to the situation that in the early stage of the war the Polish army contained many independent units, which really varied in strength. There were between 20 and 25 of such free companies[111] serving in the period between June and November 1626, with their individual strength between 76 and 500 men. Most of them were initially paid from the Royal Treasury but gradually became part of the standing army in Prussia (the so-called *komput*) and were therefore paid, like other troops, from taxes. Additionally, when in November 1626 Hetman Koniecpolski arrived with the main part of 'quarter army', he brought with him 1,000 dragoons, divided into two small regiments (400 men each) and one company of 200 men. War attrition and the end of initial contracted service quickly led to a change in the number and strength of the units. When the *Sejm* in Toruń discussed, between November and December 1626, the composition of the Polish army in Prussia, it seems that only 12 free companies of 'German' infantry were left in service. Their total strength was 2,509 men, with units varying between 119 and 350 men.[112] There were also six units[113] of dragoons, varying between 76 and 400 men, for a total of 1,152 dragoons.

---

108 Where at that time Hetman Stanisław Koniecpolski and the main 'quarter army' were preparing to fight against an expected Tatar raid.

109 Three banners of winged hussars, one regiment and one banner of reiters (Western-type cavalry), two banners of Polish infantry.

110 Both names are used in period sources.

111 The exact number is rather difficult to confirm, as some of the units were very short-lived, serving just two or three months.

112 Interesting fact: each of those 12 units have different strength.

113 The three bigger ones were sometimes called regiments, while some sources still call them companies or banners.

It is important to remember, though, that all the above numbers refer only to 'paper strength'. The system of 'dead pays' (*ślepe porcje*)[114] was present here, with officers and NCOs receiving extra pay in so-called 'portions' (*porcje*). In theory between 10 and 15 percent of unit strength was to be used for those. Such a system led to frequent cases of fraud, when officers kept their units purposely understrength, filling the ranks only for (very infrequent) musters and in the meantime still taking full pay for the 'paper strength' of the unit. Prince Jerzy Zbaraski, castellan of Cracow, wrote in a letter to King Sigismund:

Musketeer from Friedrich Jungermann's *Paraten Schlachtordung*, dated between 1617–1625. (Biblioteka Cyfrowa Uniwersytetu Wrocławskiego)

> Who are those captains, that gathered troops for His Majesty, I do not know but I know what my servant told me under an oath, on his return from Danzig (and he is good man and I trust his words), that instead of soldiers those captains took raftsmen[115] [fleeing] from boats and only put German clothes on them, so they can pretend to be soldiers, and even from my own boats 30 raftsmen fled to them that way.[116]

Additionally the local *Sejmiki*, when sending their representatives to each *Sejm*, were very vocal in their protests against the high number of foreign troops, the huge cost connected with them and the non-patriotic attitude of such mercenaries.

The *Sejm* held in 1626 agreed, though, that the large increase in the number of 'German' infantry was needed, as it was a must-have to fight against the Swedes in Prussia. Three newly promoted colonels – Denhoff, Magnust Ernest Denhoff and Gustav Sparre – received a royal commission to raise one 3,000-man regiment each. It appears that such units were planned to be organised in the same way as the Catholic League's regiments, with 10 companies, 300 men each. Denhoff's were sent to Saxony, while Sparre was to create his unit in Prussia, based mostly on the free companies already present there. Such an idea was met with fierce opposition from the captains of those units, who did not want themselves and their troops ending up under the command of newly assigned colonels. When on 4 May 1627 envoys of the Polish army – demanding mostly better conditions of service and overdue pay – presented their petition to Sigismund III, one of their points was:

---

114 Which literally means 'blind portions'.
115 In Polish *flisacy*, working on timber rafting (in this case on the Vistula river) from all over the country to Danzig.
116 Prince Jan Zbaraski to King Sigismund III, Kraków, 18 July 1626. *Listy księcia Jerzego Zbaraskiego, kasztelana krakowskiego, z lat 1621–1631* (Kraków: nakł. Akademii Umiejętności, 1878), p.106.

what captains of His Royal Majesty's foreign troops are asking, to have mercy and look into their services [in this war], as they are faithful subjects and servants of HRM and lead the free companies, so please can HRM not demote them but allow them to keep their [current] ranks and not be placed in the regiments under [command of] different colonels.

Musketeer from Friedrich Jungermann's *Paraten Schlachtordung*, dated between 1617–1625. (Biblioteka Cyfrowa Uniwersytetu Wrocławskiego)

One of the other officers, Polish Captain Bazyli Judycki, made an even stronger case, when facing his unit being merged into Sparre's regiment. In a rather blunt way he wrote that, 'as a citizen of this country I do not want to serve in the regiment under a Swedish commander'.[117] We can only wonder what Sigismund III thought about such a response. Nonetheless, it worked, as Judycki managed to keep his unit of dragoons as an independent company until the end of the war in 1629. It is possible that the King appreciated his justification though, as the officer wrote that 'I received [initial] orders to raise a free company, besides, as a Knight of Malta, I am much more experienced than Colonel Sparre in the military craft and [I] do not want to serve under him.'[118]

Recruitment in Saxony proved to be rather difficult and it was impossible for Denhoff to recruit 6,000 men. On 20 July 1627, near Piotrków in central Poland, royal commissioners witnessed the muster of Gerhard Denhoff's regiment, en route to Koniecpolski's army in Prussia. The regiment (which officially entered the service on 1 June 1627) had only 1,042 men from 3,000 planned. The commissars wrote that these were all experienced and very good men, except 'up to 30, that we did not like but the colonel assured us, that they will improve while training during the march'. Of course the biggest problem was that the unit was so understrength compared to the letter of commission. Interestingly enough, Denhoff enlisted enough officers to fill vacancies in all 10 planned companies, even though he was able to muster only six companies of soldiers. It led to a clash with the commissioners, as they did not want him to pay for nonexistent companies. Finally they had to give up, as Denhoff advised that he would not continue with his march to Prussia until the full amount was paid off.[119] Magnus Ernest Denhoff was even less successful, as on 2 August 1627 his regiment mustered only 767 men. It appears that sometime by the end of 1627 both regiments were merged into one, with Gerhard as colonel, and at least two independent units (Winteroy's dragoons and Fittinghoff's infantry) were added to it as well.

117 AGAD, AR, V, no 6171, Kawaler Judycki do Zygmunta Karola Radziwiłła, 2 III 1627 obóz pod Tczewem, p.2.

118 *Ibidem*, p.2.

119 'Relacja z inspekcji pułku piechoty z 1627 r', Zdzisław Spieralski, Jan Wimmer (ed.), *Wypisy źródłowe do historii polskiej sztuki wojennej*, volume V (Warszawa, 1961), pp.143–144.

When talking about the organisation of both foreign ('German') infantry and dragoons of the Polish army in Prussia during the war we have to discuss two quite distinct periods. The first will be summer 1626 to late autumn 1627, when practically all the units in service were independent free companies (*freikompanie*), with some of them even called regiments, despite being fairly small in size. In summer 1627, after the battle of Tczew (Dirschau) two larger regiments, recruited in Saxony, arrived in Prussia, which started the process of gradual incorporation of almost all free companies into those regiments. As such, from approximately late winter 1627/beginning of 1628 we move into the second period, with a more formal structure of infantry and dragoons under Koniecpolski's command, where most troops were grouped into two, then three regiments, supported by a few independent units. Luckily there are quite a few sources that have survived to our time, that allow us to draw a rather complicated picture of foreign troops and dragoons serving in Polish army during the period 1626–1629.

Let us first have a look into the situation starting from the beginning of the war until the end of 1627. The list below includes only enlisted units paid by the National Treasury (so no private units), also all 'quarter army' troops that arrived in Prussia. The research is mostly based on *Comput Woyjska K.J.M. Koronnego*,[120] showing units serving in 1626 and those planned for 1627 (including their paper strength) and *Comput Woyska K.J.M. Zaciągu do prus, w służbie będąceo i wiele sie mu winno*,[121] describing units serving until the end of 1627. Additional information is based on army muster rolls from the end of 1628[122] and from summer 1629.[123]

Commander's name	Formation [foot or dragoons]	Beginning of service	End of service[124]	Paper strength[125]	
Ernest Fittinghof	foot	July 1626	December 1627	269	
Gabriel Ceridon	foot[126]	July 1626	October 1626	193	Disbanded after 4 months of service
Friedrich Denhoff	foot	July 1626	December 1627	316/289	
Otton Fittinghof	foot	July 1626	September 1626	204	Fittinghoff left the service in September 1626, his company was reduced and taken over by Gerhard Friedrichson (see below)
Gerhard Friedrichson	foot	September 1626	December 1627	155	Ex-Otton Fittinghof's unit

---

120 Riksarkivet Stockholm, Extranea IX Polen, 82, *Comput Woyjska K.J.M. Koronnego*.

121 Riksarkivet Stockholm, Skoklostersamlingen, E 8600, *Comput Woyska K.J.M. Zaciągu do prus, w służbie będąceo i wiele sie mu winno*.

122 Biblioteka ks. Czartoryskich w Krakowie, 1772, *Regestrum rationis thesauri Regni in Conventu anni MDCXXIX expeditae*.

123 Riksarkivet Stockholm, Extranea IX Polen, 80, *Comput Woyjska J.K.M.*

124 For those units that were kept in Prussia, either as part of new regiments or as independent companies, December 1627 is mentioned as the 'border date', as it was start of the new 'quarter' of service.

125 If two different numbers are present, the first is taken from Skoklostersamlingen E 8600, the second from *Extranea 82*.

126 Although Hoppe in his chronicle mentioned that Captain Zeridongo (a very odd version of Ceridon's name) led unit of dragoons: Israel Hoppe, *Geschichte des ersten*, p.57. The unit was also mustered as dragoons in November 1626, see Appendix II.

Commander's name	Formation [foot or dragoons]	Beginning of service	End of service[124]	Paper strength[125]	
Guillam (Wilhelm) Kit (Keith)	foot	July 1626	December 1627	119	
Balthasar Rotenstein	foot	July 1626	December 1627	134	
Tomasz (Thomas) Duplesis (du Plessis)	foot	July 1626	December 1627	108/103	
Adrian Kit (Keith) and his Lt. Dangelew(?)	foot	July 1626	?	?	
Johan (Jan) Storch	foot	November 1626	December 1627	110/174	
Jan Forde	foot	July 1626	September 1626	?	Disbanded after 3 months of service
Wilhelm Appelman	foot	July 1626	December 1627	335/304	Unit in 1628 to be incorporated into Sparre's regiment but later musters show it as independent company
Walter Butler Older	foot	July 1626	December 1627	300	
Walter Butler Younger	foot	July 1626	December 1627	300	
Arthur Aston	foot	August 1626	December 1627	350	A large part of the unit, including Aston, captured at Kiezmark in July 1627. Later incorporated into Sparre's regiment
Reginald Kisk	foot	October 1626	March 1627	?	
James (Jacob) Murray	foot	January 1627	December 1627	200	
Andrzej Kit (Andrew Keith)	foot	September 1626	March 1627	76	
Andrzej Kit (Andrew Keith)	dragoons	September 1626	March 1627	76	
Magnus Ernest Denhoff	foot	August 1627	Until end of war	Unit for planned for 3,000 soldiers, he was able to enlist 767	In late 1627 the regiment was merged with Gerhard Denhoff's, and Magnus Ernest left the army, focusing on diplomatic duties
Gerhard Denhoff	foot	July 1627	Until end of war	Unit was planned for 3,000 soldiers, he was able to enlist 1,047	The regiment was strengthened in late 1627 by merging with Magnus Ernest Denhoff's regiment and some free companies.
Andrzej Retkier (Radke)	foot	April 1627	December 1627	100	
Paul Magno	foot	April 1627	December 1627	160	
Alexander Hoffen	foot	April 1627	December 1627	160	
Gustav Sparre	foot	-	-	600	Sparre received money to enlist a 600-man regiment but the unit was never raised. Instead he took over the command of a new regiment, composed of previously independent companies.
Walter Butler Older	Foot [second unit]	?	?	300	He is mentioned in Skl E 8,600 as receiving money for gathering another 300 men but in Extranea IX Polen, 82, a 300-men strong unit of the voivod of Malbork is mentioned. It is most probable that Butler led this new unit
Bazyli Judycki	dragoons	July 1626	Until end of war	330/300	Originally a private unit raised by Judycki, from summer 1626 it became part of the standing army in Prussia.

Commander's name	Formation [foot or dragoons]	Beginning of service	End of service[124]	Paper strength[125]	
James (Jakub/Jacob) Butler	dragoons[127]	October 1626	Until end of war	432/400	Originally a 'quarter army' regiment, in service since 1625, in 1628 it reformed into a regiment of foot (with at least two companies of dragoons) by adding independent companies
Florian Winter (Winteroy)	dragoons[128]	October 1626	December 1627	470/400	Originally a 'quarter army' regiment, in service since 1625, in 1627/1628 it was incorporated into Gerhard Denhoff's regiment of foot
Guillam (Wilhelm) Lesse	dragoons	September 1626	December 1627	200	Originally a 'quarter army' regiment, in service since 1625, in 1628 it was incorporated into James Butler's regiment of foot
Michał Moler	dragoons	?	?	76	Mentioned only in Extranea IX Polen, 82
Adrian Fuldrops	infantry	?	?	172	Unit only present at the muster of the Royal Army in November 1626, no other information about its service

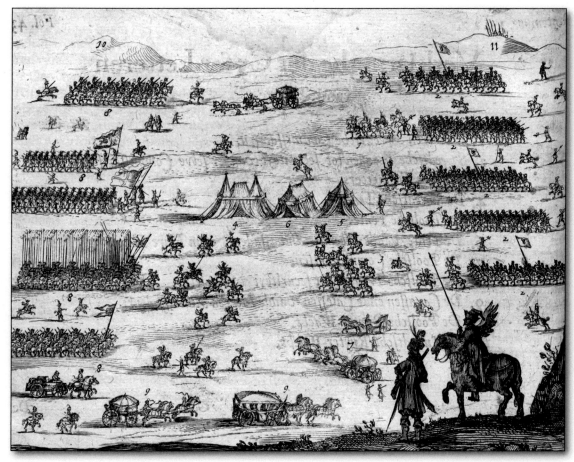

Polish–Swedish negotiations in summer 1627. Polish troops can be seen on the left side of the drawing, also haiduk and either a winged cossack or unarmoured hussar are present the bottom right. Drawing by Abraham Booth. (Author's archive)

127 In 1625, when stationed in Podolia, the unit was described in some sources as 'German infantry'. It is very probable that it was converted into dragoons prior to deployment in Prussia or even en route from Podolia.

128 Same as Butler's unit above.

Despite the previously mentioned opposition of the captains, Sparre's regiment seems to be organised by the end of 1627/beginning of 1628 by merging many of the free companies serving since summer/autumn 1626. Finally, a third regiment – under command of James Butler – was to be created by the end of 1628 but it appears that it was de facto confirmation of his colonelship over a few already existing units of dragoons and 'German' infantry.

Gustav Sparre's Regiment – the strength of each company is based on 'paper strength' from May 1628[129]

Name[130]	Strength	Notes
Colonel Gustav Sparre	334	
Lieutenant Colonel Fridrich Denhoff	316	
Fridrich Denhoff's dragoon company, under Phillippe de Mareul (de Marevil)	200	
Major Arthur Aston	200	Infantry initially raised to fight on ships
Alexander Hoffen	160	Ex-Swedish soldiers, who switched sides after the battle of Hammerstein (Czarne). At the time of the muster the officer was noted as deceased, no information about the replacement.
Baltazar Rotenstein	134	
Wilhelm Keith	121	
Tomas Duplesis	189	
Dittloff Tyzenhauz	130	Former company of Johan Stork, who died during sea battle at Oliwa in 1627
James (Jacob) Murray	207	
Gerhard Friedrichson	149	Former company of Otton Fittinghof, who left the service in autumn 1626
Jakub Lesgewang	391	
Hugo Orelly (O'Reilly)	124	
Former company of Walter Butler the Older	308	At the time of the muster officer noted as deceased, no information about the replacement
In total 14 companies (including one dragoon company) with 2,963 men (including 200 dragoons)		

Jacob Butler's Regiment – strength of each company is based on 'paper strength' from May 1628[131]

Name	Strength	Notes
Colonel Jacob Butler	437	Former dragoons
Wilhelm Lesse	200	Former dragoons
Walter Butler the Younger	300	Unit initially raised in 1626 by Bishop of Warmia
Wilhelm Gall	147	
Richard Welsz (?)	149	
In total five companies with 1,233 men		

---

129 Biblioteka ks. Czartoryskich w Krakowie, 1772, *Regestrum rationis thesauri Regni in Conventu anni MDCXXIX expeditae.*
130 If no rank is mentioned next to an officer's name, it indicates that he was a captain.
131 Biblioteka ks. Czartoryskich w Krakowie, 1772, *Regestrum rationis thesauri Regni in Conventu anni MDCXXIX expeditae.*

Gerhard Denhoff's Regiment – strength of each company based on muster from 2 October 1627[132]

Name[133]	Strength	Notes
Colonel Gerhard Denhoff	289	
Florian Winteroy	470	Former dragoons
Ernest Fittinghoff	335	
Adersbach	164	
La Montaigne	139	Captain was court-martialled and executed on Koniecpolski's order in October 1628 for surrendering Brodnica (Strasburg) to the Swedes
Nisimeifeld	134	
Ley	166	
Dominici	151	
Puttkamer	201	
Henrich Denhoff	204	
Szaff Hansen	160	
Brynk	130	
In total 12 companies with 2,543 men		

Independent Units – strength of each company (except Keith's) is based on 'paper strength' from May 1628[134]

Name	Strength	Notes
Bazyli Judycki	320	Dragoons
Wilhelm Appelman	364	Infantry initially raised to fight on ships
Andrzej Radke	91	Dragoons. Ex-Swedish soldiers, who switched sides after the battle of Hammerstein (Czarne).
Paulus Magnus/David Rotkier[135]	168	Ex-Swedish soldiers, who switched sides after the battle of Hammerstein (Czarne).
Patrick Gordon	200	Dragoons
Andrew Keith	76	Dragoons. The unit seems to be disbanded in April or May 1627, the remaining soldiers joining Wilhelm Keith's company in Gustav Sparre's regiment

When in autumn 1628 the war commissioners visited the army to organise the units' musters and discuss overdue pay, they did not have a chance to properly inspect the foreign troops. As Hetman Koniecpolski required his troops in the field, to fight against the Swedish offensive, the commissioners suggested to him to organise, when time allowed, a general muster. For the time being they simply accepted unit strength as per the documents delivered to them by their commanders, which of course did not have much to do with reality. The commissioners prepared a document listing all foreign units, where they mentioned their new 'paper strength', as per agreement from the *Sejm* from summer 1628. This so-called *Comput Piechoty Cudzoziemskiej* looks as follows:[136]

---

132 *Ibidem.*

133 Unfortunately the first names of the majority of the officers are not mentioned.

134 Biblioteka ks. Czartoryskich w Krakowie, 1772, *Regestrum rationis thesauri Regni in Conventu anni MDCXXIX expeditae.*

135 Magnus was in charge of the company in 1627, Rotkier took over at some point in 1628.

136 Biblioteka Jagiellońska w Krakowie, manuscript 7, pp.621–622.

Unit	Old strength	New strength
Gustav Sparre's regiment	2,763	3,004
James Butler's regiment	1,223	1,453
Gerhard Denhoff's regiment	2,500	2,676
Patrick Gordon's company	-	202[137]
Wilhelm Appelman's company	364	376
Bazyli Judycki's company	320	443
Andrzej Radke's company	91	91
David Rotkier's company	168	168
Total:	7,429	8,413

Of course for many Polish nobles it sounded impossible, that all of the sudden those units would increase in size. As Prince Jerzy Zbaraski wrote in one of his letters, 'you mentioned to me, that German infantry [officers] claim that there are more than 900 of them now than before [above 'paper strength'], but I'll be damned if in fact there were not 2,000 or 3,000 less of them present that they claim. After all from where could they take the reinforcements?'[138] Unfortunately it became the norm during the war that officers demanded (and received) pay for full strength of their units, no matter their actual size.

In 1629 we can notice further changes in the organisation of the regiments, with some companies being disbanded and their soldiers being used to strengthen the others. A muster[139] dated in late summer of this year[140] shows the following structure of the regiments:

Ex-Gustav Sparre's Regiment

Name	Strength	Notes
Gustav Sparre	335	Sparre died in Gniew on 18 July 1629, probably from plague
Fridrich Denhoff	343	Former lieutenant colonel, took over as colonel after Sparre's death
Arthur Aston	360	
Baltazar Rotenstein	333	
James Murray	301	
Dittloff Tyzenhauz	205	
Von Rosen	145	
Jakub Lesgewang	375	
Stessel	174	

---

137 Treated as a new unit, created in spring 1628.

138 Prince Jan Zbaraski to Marchockiego starosty Czchowskiego, Kraków, 22 November 1628. *Listy księcia Jerzego Zbaraskiego*, pp.145–146.

139 Riksarkivet Stockholm, Extranea IX Polen, 80, *Comput Woyska J.K.M.*

140 While the document is not dated, we can make some educated guesses to locate it within the timeline. It mentioned Sparre as deceased and that he died in Gniew (Mewe) on 18 July. We can also find some of the newly raised units, that arrived in Prussia in the same month. As such I would estimate it as written down in either August or September 1629.

Plate 1
Winged Hussar
(Illustration by Sergey Shamenkov, © Helion & Company)
See Colour Plate Commentaries for further information.

Plate 2
Cossack Cavalry
(Illustration by Sergey Shamenkov, © Helion & Company)
See Colour Plate Commentaries for further information.

Plate 3
3.1 Foreign Musketeer; 3.2 Reiter in Polish service
(Illustrations by Sergey Shamenkov, © Helion & Company)
See Colour Plate Commentaries for further information.

Plate 4
4.1 Polish-Hungarian infantryman (haiduk); 4.2 *Wybraniecka* infantryman
(Illustrations by Sergey Shamenkov, © Helion & Company)
See Colour Plate Commentaries for further information.

Plate 5
5.1 High-ranking commander in hussar's attire; 5.2 Foreign infantry officer
(Illustrations by Sergey Shamenkov, © Helion & Company)
See Colour Plate Commentaries for further information.

Plate 6
6.1 Winged hussar's retainer; 6.2 Cossack cavalry retainer
(Illustrations by Sergey Shamenkov, © Helion & Company).
See Colour Plate Commentaries for further information.

Plate 7
Engineer in Polish service
(Illustration by Sergey Shamenkov, © Helion & Company)
See Colour Plate Commentaries for further information.

Plate 8
8.1, Imperial cuirassier; 8.2, Imperial/Prussian/Brandenburg pikeman
(Illustrations by Sergey Shamenkov, © Helion & Company)
See Colour Plate Commentaries for further information.

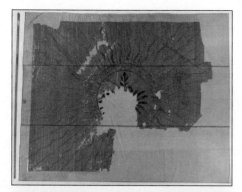

Plate 9
9.1, Colour of Arthur Aston's or Friedrich Denhoff's infantry company;
9.2, Seventeenth-century drawing based on the original;
9.3, Polish cavalry banner, probably cossack cavalry; 9.4, Seventeenth-century
painting based on the original flag; 9.5, Polish infantry colour
(All from Armémuseum, Stockholm)

Plate 10
10.1 and 10.2, Polish cavalry standard;
10.3, 10.4, Drawings based on the original flag
(All from Armémuseum, Stockholm)

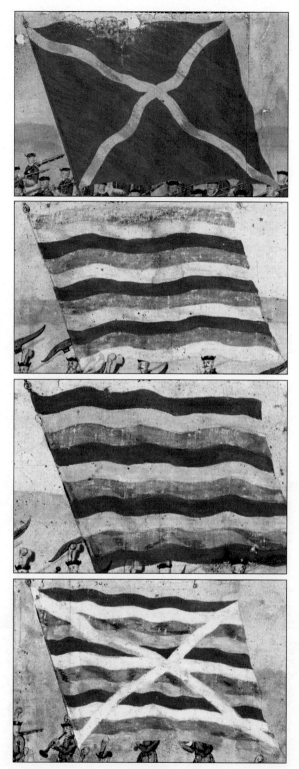

Plate 11
11.1, Typical motif seen on colours of the Polish-Hungarian infantry;
11.2, 11.3 and 11.4, Flags of town militia
(All from Michał Paradowkski's archive)

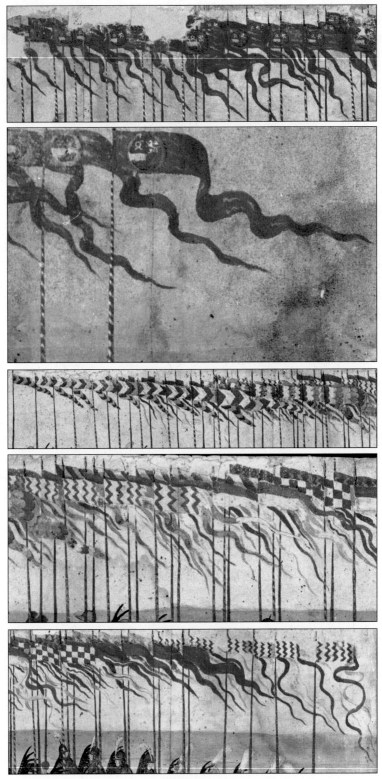

Plate 12
Winged hussars' pennants from 'Stockholm Roll'
(All from Michał Paradowkski's archive)

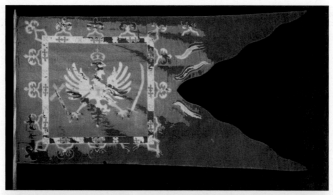

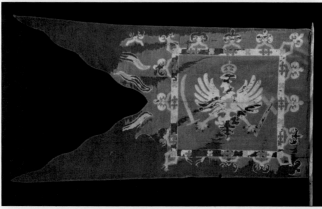

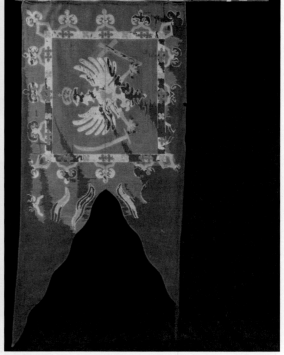

Plate 13
Standards of a Polish cavalry banner, probably hussar
(Armémuseum, Stockholm)

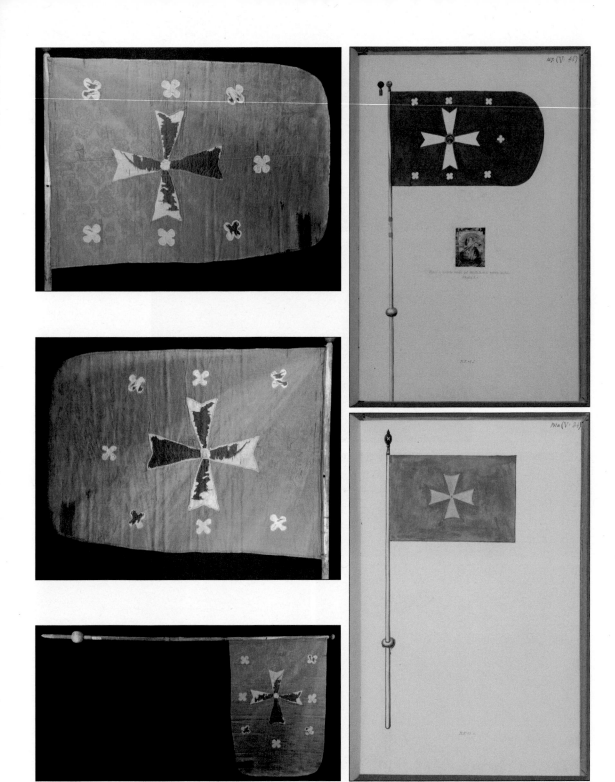

Plate 14
14.1, 14.2., 14.3., 14.4 Cossack cavalry standard;
14.5, Polish cavalry or dragoon standard
(All from Armémuseum, Stockholm)

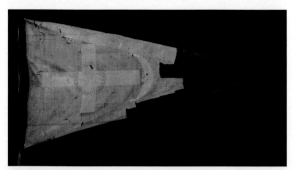

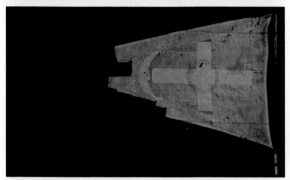

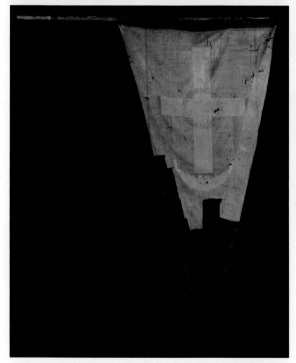

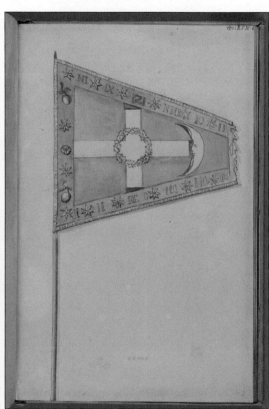

Plate 15
Cossack cavalry standard
(Armémuseum, Stockholm)

Plate 16
**Flags of town militia from Cracow
from the 'Stockholm Roll'**
(Michał Paradowkski's archive)

Name	Strength	Notes
Wilhelm Appelman	–	No strength of those three companies given in the text, possibly not present at the muster.
Gerhard Friedrichson	–	
Thomas Duplessis	–	
In total nine companies with 2,517 men + three companies without their strength		

Gerhard Denhoff's Regiment

Name	Strength	Notes
Colonel Gerhard Denhoff	430	
Lieutenant Colonel Ernest Fittinghoff	393	
Major Puttkamer	306	
Henrich Denhoff	269	
Florian Winteroy	303	
Joachim Blan	300	
Albrecht Waizer	310	
Morelle/Korelle?	323	
Georgius Firck	–	No strength given
In total nine companies with 3,073 men which indicates that Firck's company was in fact 339 men		

Jacob Butler's Regiment

Name	Strength	Notes
Colonel Jacob Butler	265	Dragoons
Lieutenant Colonel[141]	188	
Patrick Gordon	250	
Wilhelm Lesse	222	Mentioned as 'foot company'
Wilhelm Gall	382	
In total five companies with 1,307 men		

Independent Units

Name	Strength	Notes
Bazyli Judycki	461	It appears that by that time the unit was no longer classified as dragoons
David Rotkier	207	
Andrzej Ratke	100	Dragoons

---

141 No name mentioned, but most likely Walter Butler the Younger.

Newly Raised Units, that Arrived in Prussia in July 1629

Name	Strength	Notes
Reinhold Rosen's regiment	1,100	All other documents mentioned this regiment as 1,000 men, so 1,100 seems to be just an error by the clerk writing down the numbers.
Stanisław Janikowski	200	Dragoons
Jan Wojsław Żółtowski	200	Dragoons

Employing such a large number of foreign troops led to many voices of discontent amongst Polish nobles. The main issues were high cost combined with often controversial effectiveness during the campaign. Many times it was suggested that Polish recruits should be trained 'in the foreign manner' and used as replacements for expensive mercenaries. The *Sejmik* of the Ruthenian Voivodship was a good example of how local nobles would discuss the problem. On 31 August 1627 the *Sejmik*'s resolution was 'We would like the *milicya pedestris*[142] in our own country to be trained and well drilled … as once it is ready we could deal without foreign troops.'[143] On 5 June 1628 the Ruthenian nobles wrote 'to wage war against Gustavus there is a need for large number of infantry but [to hire] so many foreigners it is both very expensive and dangerous for the Commonwealth, so our envoys [at the *Sejm*] will suggest raising [national] infantry from lands [owned] by clergy, nobles and from towns.'[144] It was many such voices that finally led to a military experiment. In 1629 Colonel Reinhold Rosen was tasked with raising a new infantry regiment, recruited amongst the Poles, with foreigners serving only as officers and NCOs. The unit arrived to Prussia in summer 1629 and it is highly unlikely that it saw much combat action. Nonetheless it shows that Poles were able to create Western-type units themselves. Already on 4 September 1630 the *Sejmik* of Ruthenian Voivodship mentioned '… as we can see that in the Polish nation, with its innate bravery, [men] are *ad quavies genera armorum*[145] and can be quickly trained, as we have seen in the Prussian Expedition in Rosen's infantry [regiment], what was confirmed even [at that time] by foreigners'.[146] In was during the Smolensk War of 1632–1634 that such a way of recruitment was widely used, and it provided King Władysław IV with a large force of infantry and dragoons.

It may sound odd, but we have very scarce information about the weapons, equipment and tactics employed by both foreign infantry and dragoons during the 1626–1629 war. There's no indication that pikemen were used at all, it is highly likely that all units were composed of musketeers only. It may sound very unusual but according to Polish battle tactics their own cavalry – especially hussars and cossacks – should be enough to protect the infantry from opposing cavalry, so the infantry should focus on their

---

142 Infantry.
143 *Akta grodzkie i ziemskie z czasów Rzeczypospolitej Polskiej*, p.246.
144 *Ibidem*, p.285.
145 (Latin) Able to carry any arms (fight in any formation).
146 *Akta grodzkie*, p.286.

role as fire support. When Prince Krzysztof Zbaraski presented, during the *Sejm* of autumn 1626, his proposal for a new Polish army in Prussia, he specified that 13,000 foreign infantry should be composed solely from musketeers.[147] In previous years muskets were normally purchased from German and Dutch manufacturers, via merchants in Gdańsk and Toruń, so most likely the same channels were used prior to 1626 war as well. One of the Polish sources[148] mentioned that Aston's and Judycki's infantry at the battle of Gniew were using heavy muskets,[149] possibly of Dutch origin. On most occasions only 'musket' is mentioned, without any further details. Officers seemed to be, as their Swedish counterparts, equipped with partisans as both additional weapons and a symbol of the rank. During the fight at Czarne (Hammerstein) in 1627 Lieutenant Owen from Winteroy's dragoon regiment mortally wounded a Swedish reiter corporal with his *szefelin*, which is a word used to described different sorts of polearms, in this case most likely an officer's partisan.[150] Tactics are never mentioned in any details in the Polish sources, so we can only make an educated guess that they fought in a similar manner to musketeers in the Imperial army, while at the same time Dutch and Swedish influence could already have affected at least those units whose officers had some dealings with them in the past.

Polish-Hungarian infantry

The Polish and Hungarian infantry[151] was organised into banners (*chorągwie*), that could vary between 100 and 400 men. The unit was led by *rotmistrz*, just like cavalry. He had a small staff to support him, usually consisting of a lieutenant, ensign and some musicians (a drummer was the norm, additionally sometimes pipers and fifers), often also a clerk. Larger

Details of sabres and swords of the Polish infantry from the beginning of the seventeenth century. 'Stockholm Roll'. (Author's archive)

---

147 'Komput wojska z 1626 r.', p.142.
148 *Diariusz Wojny Pruskiej, passim.*
149 The word that is used is *kobyła*, a common Polish name for mare.
150 'Diariusz albo Summa', p.23.
151 Period sources tend to call them Polish infantry; later secondary sources, based on how formations evolved mid century, tend to use the term Polish-Hungarian infantry or haiduks. As even in 1626 differences between such formations were very small, we will be using all those terms interchangeably.

Details of a drawing of a
haiduk by Abraham Booth.
(Author's archive)

units would normally be divided into 'hundreds' or 'wings', so their staff was larger to command such sub-units. As such a banner of 200 men would have two lieutenants, two ensigns and at least two musicians, with two drummers being a standard set-up; banner of 400 (which was the largest size of the unit) would have four lieutenants, four ensigns, etc.[152] Such formations could often lead to confusion amongst foreign observers and enemies, as they would perform a 'unit count' as per the number of flags they could see, not knowing the real tactical organisation. NCOs in this type of infantry were called *dziesiętnicy*, which means 'tenth man' – as they would be in charge of nine privates. Polish infantry was typically a shot unit, in this period still using calivers (which were gradually replaced by muskets), alongside the sabre and small axe. Instead of handguns, 'tenth men' were instead equipped with halberds, called *darda*.

Based on available sources we can try to identify the majority of units that served in Prussia since November 1626, after private and Royal Guards units were withdrawn.

Rotmistrz	Summer–Autumn 1626[153]	September 1628[154]	1629[155]
Samuel Nadolski	200	400	400
Palcewicz[156]	200		
Mikołaj Bobiatyński	200	200	200
Miękiński[157]	200		
Florian Uleniecki	200	200	200
Stanisław Biedrzycki	100	100	100
Maciej Jeliński	200		
Aleksander Czopowski		200	200
Albert Pepłowski		200[158]	200

---

152 Teodor Wierzbowski, *Matieraly k istorii Moskovskago gosudarstva v XVI i XVII stoletiiakh*, volume II (Warszawa, 1898), pp.17–27.
153 Riksarkivet Stockholm, Extranea IX Polen, 82, *Comput Woyjska K.J.M. Koronnego*.
154 Biblioteka ks. Czartoryskich w Krakowie, 1772, *Regestrum rationis thesauri Regni in Conventu anni MDCXXIX expeditae*.
155 Riksarkivet Stockholm, Extranea IX Polen, 80, *Comput Woyska J.K M*.
156 First name unknown.
157 First name unknown.
158 In service since 1 March 1627.

Rotmistrz	Summer–Autumn 1626[153]	September 1628[154]	1629[155]
Piotr Kurecki		200[159]	200
Kacper Śliwnicki		200[160]	200
Adam Rybiński, after his death Jakub Bukowiecki		150	150
Mikołaj Sadowski[161]			200
Jan Dąbrowski			200
Jakub Chorzelski			200
Dobek,[162] replaced by Maciej Jarocki			200
Prince Jerzy Zasławski			200
Feliks Psarski			100
Andrzej Wybicki			100
Jan Gratiani			100
Szymon Czwelina			100

Additionally three more banners were to start their service in March 1627: 400 men under Tryzna, 200 men under Otwinowski and 200 men under Orwitowski. Tryzna's banner arrived in camp in late August 1627 but it is probably that served only for one quarter and was then disbanded, which would explain its absence on the muster rolls in 1628. Two other planned banners probably never entered the service. The reason for the disappearance of three banners between late 1626 and late 1628 could be possibly found in a petition sent by the army in Prussia to the King in May 1627. It mentioned that 'as pay for His Royal Majesty's [Polish] infantry *rotmistrz*[s] was put on hold, many of the infantrymen deserted, [especially] from new command [units].'[163] Older banners were continuously kept in service only due to the sacrifice of their officers, who paid soldiers from their own pocket, hoping for the arrival of the delayed money.[164]

There is always a problem with describing tactics used by the Polish infantry in the seventeenth century. As a pure 'shot' unit, it had to utilise some sort of shooting drill, unfortunately period sources tend to just laconically mention Polish haiduks as 'giving fire' without any detailed description. Modern Polish researchers tend to claim that this infantry was shooting by ranks starting from the last one (unit was normally deployed in 10 ranks), while the remaining ranks were kneeling and stood up to shoot once the one behind them gave fire.[165] The main problem here comes from the fact that there is no basis for such a theory in the period sources. Crown Grand

159 As above.
160 As above.
161 This and eight following banners were raised in spring/summer 1629 and were very late to arrive in Prussia.
162 First name unknown.
163 'Petitia do Króla J.M. od wojska w Prusiech na służbie J.K.M. będącego, przy oddawaniu oberszterów z chorągwiami wojska Sudermańskiego Xiążęcia z victoriej Amersztyńskiej', *Pamiętniki o Koniecpolskich*, p.52.
164 *Ibidem*, p.52.
165 Jerzy Teodorczyk, 'Bitwa pod Gniewem', p.103.

Polish infantry from the beginning of the seventeenth century, 'Stockholm Roll'. (Author's archive)

Hetman Jan Tarnowski in his military treaty *Consillium rationis bellicae*, published in 1558, wrote:

> if in battle, when the first rank will give fire, they should kneel and reload, while the second rank behind them [give] fire [and] then in the same way kneel [to reload] and all the other ranks to do it in such order, so in the same way all [ranks] will fire and reload as it was described here.[166]

We can see here a much more rational idea, but we are unable to confirm if it was still in use in 1620s. The main problem with applying Tarnowski's idea to the early seventeenth century would be due to the weapons used. During his time soldiers were using fairly short *rusznica* calivers, which would be much easier to reload while kneeling. During Sigismund's reign, however, infantrymen were equipped with longer and heavier calivers or harquebuses, making the whole exercise much more difficult. Iconography is not much help here either. On Pieter Snayers' painting of the battle of Kircholm we can see the Polish infantry deployed in nine to 10 ranks, with few of the them shooting at the same time and none of them are kneeling to shoot or reload. There are no tenth men armed with halberds though, and they tended to form the first rank of the unit, as some sort of quasi-pikemen. Written sources from the war itself do not provide any insight, as authors of diaries and letters probably saw infantry tactics as obvious things that did not require further description. The Polish infantry was not shy of engaging in hand-to-hand combat though, even though it did not have the support of pikemen. On the first day of the battle of Gniew (Mewe), on 22 September 1626, private banners of Polish infantry and Hungarian haiduks of the Royal Guard were to take a heavy toll on the Swedish infantry, during fighting in close quarters in one of the woods. As a Polish

---

166 Jan Tarnowski, *Consillium rationis bellicae* (Tarnów, 1558), p.19v.

Polish haiduk infantry from Pieter Snayers' painting depicting battle of Kircholm in 1605 (painted circa 1630). It is a very interesting example of a 10 rank-deep formation of this infantry, although few ranks shooting at the same time could be only Snayers' way to present them in combat. (Photo courtesy of Tomasz Ratyński)

diarist described it, 'in the fight many Swedes died from [our] hand weapons, as they are not used to fighting this way'.[167] It seems that both sabres and short axes in the hands of haiduks were much more lethal than their calivers.

Wybraniecka Infantry

The unit organisation of the *wybraniecka* would normally follow the already described pattern of the Polish and Hungarian infantry, with *rotmistrz*, lieutenant, ensign and some musicians composing the banner's staff and rest of the units divided into 10-men files, led by NCOs. In Chapter 1 we mentioned how the *wybraniecka* infantry was recruited and how it should be equipped. Lack of proper training meant that by the 1620s this formation was not highly valued as proper infantry, in fact many nobles preferred to use them as support troops. In 1627, complaining that the army in Prussia lacked engineers and sappers, Tomasz Zamoyski mentioned that 'it would be good to make diggers from those *wybrańcy*. They are [already] more familiar with [such work], as an untrained peasant is closer to the plough than to the musket'.[168] Two years later Prince Zbaraski also wrote about their lack of training but added that past experience during the war in Prussia made them at least dependable, as 'they can guard the camp, dig [fortifications] and give proper shot [when] defending earthworks'.[169] It seems that even the Swedes shared such sentiments of the Polish nobility, as on a battle diagram representing orders of battle of the Polish army in Prussia in 1628, units of *wybraniecka* are mentioned as *Schantzgrabers*.[170]

---

167 *Diariusz Wojny Pruskiej z roku 1626*, pp.358–359.
168 Stanisław Żurkowski, *Żywot Tomasza Zamoyskiego*, p.264.
169 National Library of Russia in St. Petersburg, Sobranije P. P. Dubrowskiego, no 166.
170 Krigsarkivet, Stockholm, Erik Dahlbergh, Ordres de Bataille 1600–1679, diagram no 56.

Polish infantry officer. Abraham de Bruyn, 1580–1581. (Rijksmuseum)

Polish infantry standard bearer. Abraham de Bruyn, 1580–1581. (Rijksmuseum)

At the beginning of the war in 1626 only a small number of *wybraniecka* from Northern Poland and Prussia could take part in the fight, as a majority of the raised units were serving in Podolia, in support of the 'quarter army'. Summer 1627 brought a much larger number of this infantry into Prussia. Formed into eight banners, they could be used as garrison troops and as support to the artillery train, but we lack sources to confirm if any of their units were at any point used as the part of the field army. The organisation of this infantry looks as follows:

Lands/districts where infantry was organised	Rotmistrz	Strength
Cracow and Sandomierz	Adam Rybiński[171]	204
Wielkopolska	Wiadrowski	158
Masovia	Paweł Pilichowski	190
Podlasie	Andrzej Taczanowski	190
Prussia	Adam Pągowski	226
Podole, Kiev and Bracław	Głuchowski	100
Lublin, Wołyń and Bełż	Krzysztof Kwiliński	107
Ruskie	Mikołaj Zaćwilichowski	200

In 1628, after the effort taken previous year, a much smaller number of *wybraniecka* were raised in Poland. We know the strength of three banners, it is most likely, though, that they were not even sent to Prussia but served in Podolia instead.

Lands/districts where infantry was organised	Rotmistrz	Strength
Cracow and Sandomierz	Adam Pągowski	200
Lublin, Wołyń and Bełż	Aleksander Stocki	100
Podlasie	Andrzej Baranowski, later Mikołaj Łoknicki	200
Masovia	Tomasz Wołkowicki	Number unknown
Prussia	?	Number unknown

By 1629 the number of *wybraniecka* diminished further, and only three Polish regions still had their troops in Prussia:

Lands/districts where infantry was organised	Rotmistrz	Strength
Wielkopolska	Krzysztof Kwiliński	100
Masovia	Tomasz Wołkowicki	160
Podlasie	Mikołaj Łoknicki	160

171 Killed in November 1628 during the attack on Brodnica, but it seems that at that point he was already *rotmistrz* of a Polish-Hungarian infantry banner.

In all, the *wybraniecka* infantry had a very low impact on the operations of the Polish army during the war. Poorly trained and undermanned, it was used as an auxiliary force and was not seen as a viable military unit. It is not surprising then, that during the next major conflict, the 1632–1634 Smolensk War, they were supposed to serve 'without muskets and uniforms' and be used as sappers 'with spade, hoe and axe'.

Artillery

In 1902 researcher Konstanty Górski wrote in his book about Polish artillery that 'we lack archival documents regarding the war against the Swedes in 1626–1629'.[172] As such it is very difficult to draw a full picture of the way that artillery was used by Sigismund's and Koniecpolski's forces during the war. Based of surviving documents and notes from different primary sources, we can at least attempt to gather some information.

During Sigismund's reign we can find three main type of ownership of artillery in Poland: royal, town and private. The first, kept in arsenals in Malbork, Kraków and Puck, was used during the war as field artillery in support of the Polish army. Wealthy towns like Gdańsk, Kraków or Toruń had their own arsenals and artillery, used to defend city walls. Rich magnate families – for example Zamoyski, Wiśniowiecki, Potocki – were also in possession of artillery which was used to support their private armies.

During the initial Swedish attack on Prussia in summer 1626 two royal arsenals, in Malbork and Puck, were captured by Gustav Adolf's forces. It limited the numbers of cannon and amount of engineering equipment that could be used by the Polish army in the first year of the war. Modern historian Jerzy Teodorczyk wrote that the royal army marching at Gniew was supported by 20 cannons: seven heavy, two medium and 11 light,[173] however it has not been possible to confirm on which sources he based such detailed numbers. Eleven cannons were used during the siege of Gniew, directing their fire on the Swedish-held castle,[174] at least four of them were heavy siege pieces.[175] Despite more than 70 shots, the wall defending the city was not damaged. Soon the Poles were short on cannonballs and powder.[176] It appears that it was due to an error of an unnamed Master of the Ordnance (*starszy nad armatą*),[177] who ordered delivery of the wrong cannonballs, not suitable for the available cannons.[178] It took three days to bring correct ammunition, which further delayed the siege of Gniew. On 22 September cannons placed in a sconce manned by Judycki's musketeers played an important role in stopping the Swedish attempt to move reinforcements to Gniew. Between 22

---

172 Konstanty Górski, *Historya artylerii polskiej* (Warszawa: Wende E. i Spółka, 1902), p.92.
173 Jerzy Teodorczyk, 'Bitwa pod Gniewem (22 IX–29 IX–1X 1626). Pierwsza porażka husarii', *Studia i Materiały do Historii Wojskowości*, volume XII, part 2 (Warszawa, 1966), p.95.
174 *Diariusz Wojny Pruskiej z roku 1626*, p.356.
175 *Polska kriget*, p.280.
176 Stanisław Żurkowski, *Żywot Tomasza Zamoyskiego*, pp.108–109.
177 He was in charge of the artillery train in the Polish army.
178 Albrycht Stanisław Radziwiłł, *Rys panowania Zygmunta III*, p.119.

Polish artillery during the siege of Smolensk, 1609–1611. Workshop of Frans Hogenberg, 1610–1612. (Rijksmuseum)

and 29 September the Polish artillery continued its fusillade against the castle. According to Albrycht Stanisław Radziwiłł, Grand Chancellor of Lithuania, who was present during the siege, the Polish gunners did an abysmal job, 'their shots never reached the castle and their work in preparation of the cannons was very poor'; however once Radziwiłł intervened and gave them some advice, 'they improved their aim and managed to destroy the tower, from which enemy was shooting at us'.[179] Hook guns (*hakownice*) and cannons were used against the Swedish infantry during the battle on 29 September.[180] Also on 1 October a few cannons were successfully used to support Polish troops defending Ciepłe farm.[181] The unlucky Master of the Ordnance, whose name is strangely omitted in the sources, died in some meaningless skirmish with the Swedes at the end of November or beginning of December.[182]

Another document that provides us with some glimpse of the information regarding the Polish artillery is the army list (*komput*) from the *Sejm* that held its proceedings between October and December 1626. We can find there some details regarding the costs of equipment and gunners' pay planned for the army in Prussia.

> For cannons, mortars, powder, bullets, match, lead, spades, hoes, hot shots [it will be] give or take 200,000 zl.
> Gunners that arrived with Hetman from Ukraine [pay of] 150 zl/per month, so for six months [it] makes 900 zl.
> Gunners that stayed with the Artillery Train in the Camp[183] [pay of] 435 zl, so [for six months] it will be 2,610 zl.
> Total pay for gunners – 3,510 zl.[184]

179   *Ibidem*, p.120.
180   *Diariusz Wojny Pruskiej z roku 1626*, pp.367–368.
181   *Ibidem*, p.370.
182   Albrycht Stanisław Radziwiłł, *Rys panowania Zygmunta III*, p.122.
183   Remaining from the army led initially by the King himself.
184   Riksarkivet Stockholm, Extranea IX Polen, 82, *Comput Wojska K.J.M. Koronnego* [1626].

Additionally the document mentioned 295 horses with their drivers (*furmani*) which were hired for 'permanent service with the artillery train' and that further drivers were hired to bring more guns to the camp. Sadly the document does not mention the type and numbers of cannons available for Koniecpolski in Prussia. It seems, though, that the Poles were desperately looking for ways to obtain more artillery. Sigismund III even wrote to John George I, Elector of Saxony, asking him for the loan of cannons and muskets, promising to pay for them in cash. However, the Saxons did not appear to help.[185]

At the beginning of November 1626 Polish troops led by Marcin Kazanowski surrounded and, after two days, captured Orneta. According to the accounts of Gdańsk's envoys, the Poles had three cannons with them during this operation.[186]

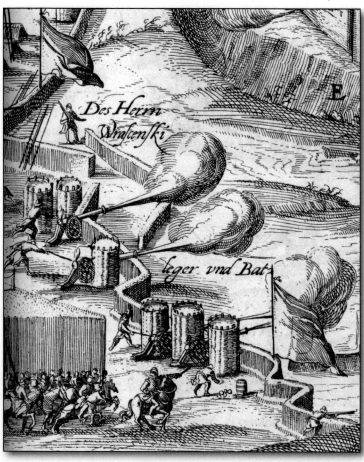

Polish artillery during the siege of Smolensk, 1609–1611. Workshop of Frans Hogenberg, 1610–1612. (Rijksmuseum)

We know that the Polish army employed their cannons during the siege of Puck in 1626/1627, sadly we lack the details of the number and type of guns.[187] It seems though that Koniecpolski's forces lacked proper heavy siege cannons, as Gdańsk had to send four of their heavy guns to support the Poles in November 1626. Besides trained artillerymen, the city provided them with 200 cannonballs and a supply of powder.[188] When Puck surrendered on 2 April 1627, the Polish army captured 31 cannons, including six bronze 3-pounders, eight bronze 2-pounders and five iron 6-pounders.[189] Some of them could be later used by the field army but most likely the majority were left in Puck. Koniecpolski was very concerned regarding specialists and their equipment, writing to the King in February 1627 that the army lacked engineers, diggers, gunners, cannons, mortars, petards, cannonballs, black

---

185 Adam Szelągowski, *O ujście Wisły*, p.84.

186 *Polska kriget*, p.301.

187 'Diariusz albo Summa', p.20.

188 Archiwum Państwowe w Gdańsku, 300/29, no 105, p.59. Rada Miasta Gdańska do Zygmunta III, Gdańsk 9 października 1626

189 Stanisław Koniecpolski do Zygmunta III, Puck, 3 kwietnia 1627 roku, *Pamiętniki o Koniecpolskich*, p.47.

Polish–Lithuanian field artillery from Pieter Snayers' painting depicting the battle of Kircholm in 1605 (painted circa 1630). (Photo courtesy of Tomasz Ratyński)

powder, grenades and musket match, asking Sigismund to hire men, purchase equipment and send both to Prussia.[190]

Sources sometimes mentioned the number of cannons used by the Poles in later campaigns. What is frustrating, though, is the lack of further information about the type of those guns. During the battle of Czarne in 1627 the Poles used eight cannons when they surrounded Swedes in Czarne itself.[191] In the same year at least six cannons were deployed during the Polish siege of Gniew, with Hetman Koniecpolski mentioning setting up three batteries, including one next to the river (to stop possible Swedish reinforcements).[192] At Kiezmark (Käsemark) in July the Swedes captured 12 or 13 cannons, although some of them probably belonged to Gdańsk's mercenaries.[193] On the second day of the battle of Tczew in 1627, Koniecpolski's troops used at least 12 cannons, placing them, alongside dragoons and infantry, in fortifications hastily erected during the night of 17 to 18 August. Throughout 18 August the Polish artillery exchanged very intense fire with its Swedish counterpart.[194]

We can see Polish cannons again in action during summer 1628, initially supporting infantry in their fortifications near Gniew.[195] Hetman Koniecpolski, in the official relation from the campaign, mentioned that 'His Royal Highness' artillery was not idle, doing their job, continuing to fire at the enemy [when he marched away] half a mile [from the Polish positions] and causing him serious harm'.[196] The Swedes estimated that the Poles had between 14 and 22 cannons with their field army.[197] Some of them were also deployed during the autumn campaign of the same year, but this time the artillery train was rather a hindrance than a help. The Hetman wrote that both his artillery and infantry slowed down the march of his army, so he could not follow the Swedes fast enough.[198]

In November the Polish troops were unable to recapture the town of Ostróda, as due to heavy rain the artillery could not move along the road, 'as

190 Adam Szelągowski, *O ujście Wisły*, p.83.
191 'Diariusz albo Summa', p.23.
192 Od Pana Hetmana do Xiędza Biskupa Chełmińskiego (Jakuba Zadzika), z obozu pod Gniewem, dnia 3. Lipca 1627, *Pamiętniki o Koniecpolskich*, p.57.
193 *Polska kriget*, pp.348–349.
194 *Wahrhafte und ausfürliche Warhaffte und aussfuerliche Erzehlung dess ernstlichen Treffens, welches sich unlangst in Preussen zwischen dem Koenig in Polen und Schweden nit weit von Dyrschaw begeben* (Gdańsk, 1627). Thanks to Kuba Pokojski for sharing this particular source.
195 'Diariusz albo Summa', p.39; Od Pana Hetman do Króla Jego Mości, w obozie pod Gniewem, dnia 28 czerwca 1628, *Pamiętniki o Koniecpolskich*, p.85.
196 'Relacja IMP. Wojewody Sendomirskiego', pp.421–422.
197 *Polska kriget*, p.413.
198 'Relacja IMP. Wojewody Sendomirskiego', p.426.

we could not move neither cannons nor mortars'.[199] While yet again we do not have number of pieces, at least we can find important information about use of the siege mortars by the Polish army.

In 1629, during the battle of Górzno, the Swedes captured all the deployed Polish cannons, four 6-pounders,[200] with at least one Polish source confirming that number and naming them as 'smaller cannons'.[201] The Master of Ordnance during this battle, and throughout the rest of the 1629 campaign, was Bazyli Judycki. He was in charge of the Polish artillery during the fighting around Malbork in July, where also Imperial guns of von Arnim's corps were present. It is possible that he served in this capacity even earlier (maybe from 1627), while at the same time Jan Waxman seemed to fulfil the role of Master of Ordnance in the Royal Arsenal in Warsaw, dealing with equipment that was purchased or repaired and sent to Prussia. During the final month of the campaign, Polish cannons were exchanging fire with the Swedes, focusing on the outer fortification of the Swedish camp near Malbork.[202]

While artillery played some role in the operations of the Polish army, especially during different sieges, it was not deployed on the scale of its counterpart in the Swedish army. It was troubled with many problems, due to lack of sufficient guns, crews and supplies. Yet it clearly showed to Polish field commanders how important it was to field a modern and well-prepared artillery train. Modernisation of that part of Polish warfare would later become one of the main reforms during King Władysław IV's reign.

Engineers

Finding properly educated and experienced engineers who could provide their expertise during siege operations, and while defending army camps, was always a big problem. Dutch, French, Spanish and German specialists were always sought, but it was not easy to secure their services. The Polish army, facing many Swedish-held towns, was in desperate need of such engineers. Tomasz Zamoyski was complaining in 1627 that '[while in Prussia] I did not see at the side of His Royal Highness nor next to Hetman [Koniecpolski] even one trained [as an engineer], who could understand where [and how] to build an earthwork'.[203] Some foreign infantry officers had experience with engineering works, so they had opportunity to use it during their time in Prussia. For example Wilhelm Appelman, who in 1621 helped with fortification of the Polish–Lithuanian camp in Chocim (Khotyn), in 1626 was initially in charge of siegeworks around Puck. In fact at the start of the war he was in the service of Gdańsk and only on Sigismund's request

199 Od Pana Hetmana do Króla Jego Mości, w Grudziądzu, dnia 25 listopada 1628, *Pamiętniki o Koniecpolskich*, p.152.
200 *Polska kriget*, p.447.
201 *Kronika Pawła Piaseckiego biskupa przemyślskiego*, p.338.
202 *Ibidem*, p.438.
203 Stanisław Żurkowski, *Żywot Tomasza Zamoyskiego*, p.264.

did the city council send him to the Polish army.[204] The siege of Puck took a heavy toll on Koniecpolski's specialists: an engineer named Hernek was wounded, while Paul Rudel a 'good and skilful young man', another 'loaned' to the Hetman by Gdańsk's city council, died during one of the attacks. No surprise then that the Hetman in his letters to the King often mentioned that he need more engineers, as considering how dangerous their work was, such specialists needed to be well prepared for their role.[205] In 1629 in his *Discurs*, Prince Zbaraski also highlighted need to employ 'good and skilled engineers', as they were badly needed in Prussia. His suggestion was to employ four or five specialists from Ambrogio Spinola's Spanish army in Flanders, 'despite the fact that they will require high pay'. Their experience would be especially useful during siege operations and all kinds of 'ruses of war'.

The Fleet

King Sigismund understood that he would not be able to realise his dream of reclaiming the Swedish Crown without a strong enough fleet, that would allow him to safely transport troops to his former kingdom. The main problem was that he could not rely on the support of the Polish *Sejm*, as the nobles were not interested in spending taxes on ships. Therefore he had to use his own private funds to pay for naval specialists, crews and ships. In 1620 he appointed Scotsman James (Jacob) Murray as a 'trusted royal servant, with good knowledge of naval architecture' to work as *servitor architectus navalis* (senior naval architect) in the port of Gdańsk and Puck.[206] His annual pay was due to be 420 florins and the first ship built under his supervision – *Gelbe Löw* – was ready in 1622. Another document, this time from April 1626, confirmed that his appointment was still in place and raised his pay to 500 florins.[207] When King Sigismund arrived in Gdańsk in November 1626, he decided to establish the Royal Naval Commission, which was to control and coordinate the actions and activities of the Royal Fleet. It was composed of nine commissioners, led by Royal Chamberlain, Swede Gabriel Posse,[208] and it was officially created on 9 November 1626.[209] It was a very peculiar form of admiralty, with representatives of the Royal Court and city council of Gdańsk but without any officers. The main roles of the Royal Fleet were to disrupt Swedish sea transports to Prussia, support coastal actions of the Polish army (for example during the recapture of Puck) and attempt to stop and check merchant ships arriving in Gdańsk, to prevent any contraband.

---

204 Archiwum Państwowe w Gdańsku, 300/29, no 105, p.60. Rada Miasta Gdańska do Zygmunta III, Gdańsk 9 października 1626

205 Stanisław Koniecpolski do Zygmunta III, Puck, 3 kwietnia 1627 roku, *Pamiętniki o Koniecpolskich*, p.47.

206 AGAD, Metryka Koronna, MK166, p.210.

207 AGAD, Metryka Koronna, MK 174, p.153.

208 Other commissioners were: Wolfgang von der Olsnitz, Albert Ghiese, Hermann von der Becke, Henrich Kemmerer, Johann Wendt, Christian Strobandt and Daniel Riediger.

209 Wiktor Fenrych (ed.), *Akta i Diariusz Królewskiej Komisji Okrętowej Zygmunta III z lat 1627–1628* (Gdańsk-Gdynia: Gdańskie Towarzystwo Naukowe, 2001), p.6.

Sea battle of Oliwa, 28 November 1627. Painting by Adolf Boy, from so-called *Sztambuch gdański* of Heinrich Böhme. (Biblioteka Kórnicka)

While in theory it was an independent force, it was supposed to work very closely with Hetman Koniecpolski, in order to provide support to his army. The main problem was strained relations with Gdańsk, where burghers saw the Royal Fleet as a hindrance and the way to royal control over the wealthy town.

Captains and crews were mostly recruited in German-speaking coastal towns but also as far as the United Provinces (Arendt Dickmann) or even Scotland (James Murray). It is interesting to note that in Gdańsk (where the majority of the population were Lutherans) the fleet's crews were known as *Herren Calvinisten*, indicating that a large part of them were composed of Calvinists. It added another religious component to Sigismund III's forces, with the Polish part of the army predominantly Catholic and a large part of the foreign troops being Lutherans. Practically the whole correspondence by the Royal Naval Commission was in German, this was the *lingua franca* between commissioners, captain, crews and officers of foreign infantry supporting the fleet.

We can in fair detail reconstruct the size of the fleet, with enough surviving documents describing the ships and their armaments. It also allows us to trace the fate of practically all ships, up to their inglorious end at Wismar in 1632.

Main Ships of the Polish Royal Fleet 1622–1629[210]

Name[211]	Class	Cannons	Crew	Infantry[212]	Origin	Notes
Ritter Sankt George	Galleon[213]	31	50	100	Joined fleet in 1626[214]	Captured by Swedes in Wismar in 1632
König David	Galleon	31	60	100	Built in Gdańsk in 1623	Captured by city of Lübeck in 1630
Meerman	Galleon	17	45	80	Probably built in Gdańsk in 1623	Captured by Swedes at Wismar in 1632
Fliegende Hirsch	Galleon	20	50	80	Bought in 1626 from Danish captain Michael Martenson	Lost 2 December 1627 near Öland
Tiger	Galleon	22	?	?	Former Swedish *Tigern*, captured at Oliva	Captured by Swedes in Wismar in 1632
Arca Noë	Pinnace	16	35	70	Probably built in Gdańsk in 1625	Captured by Swedes in Wismar in 1632
Meerweib	Pinnace	12	30	50	Probably built in Gdańsk in 1623	Captured by Swedes in Wismar in 1632
Gelbe Löw	Pinnace	10	30	50	Built in Gdańsk in 1622	Lost 6 July 1628 near Wisłoujście
Weisse Löw	Fluyt	8	25	80	Former Dutch or Rostock-based ship, captured in 1626	Captured by Swedes in Wismar in 1632
Schwarze Rabe	Fluyt	16	35	80	Former Dutch or Rostock-based ship, captured in 1626	
Delphin	Krejer[215]	12	50	50	Started service in 1628	Captured by Swedes in Wismar in 1632
Phoenix	Fluyt	14	50	50	Started service in 1628	Captured by Swedes in Wismar in 1632

---

210 Based on: Aleksander Czołowski, *Marynarka w Polsce: szkic historyczny* (Lwów, Warszawa, Kraków: Wydawn. Zakładu Narodowego im. Ossolińskich, 1922), pp.123–153, Marian Huflejt, *Bitwa pod Oliwą 1627, fakty i mity* (Olsztyn: Wydawnictwo Mantis, 2019), *passim*, Eugeniusz Kaczorowski, *Flota polska w latach 1578–1632* (Warszaw: Wyd. MON, 1973), *passim*, Eugeniusz Kaczorowski, *Oliwa 1627* (Warszawa: Bellona, 2002), *passim*, Wiktor Fenrych (ed.), *Akta i Diariusz, passim*.

211 All ships were named in German.

212 The maximum number, mostly based on the information from the battle of Oliwa.

213 We use the term 'galleon' as the closest English equivalent, even though this name was not used in the Baltic area. Instead, such a type of ship was known in German-speaking countries as a *kriegsschiff*.

214 It is probable that it was bought by Gdańsk City Council, as part of their obligation towards the Polish King.

215 A type of small merchant ship.

The sea battle of Oliwa, 28 November 1627. Drawing by Abraham Booth. (Author's archive)

Due to the relatively small size of the Royal Fleet and the local supremacy of the Swedish fleet, Polish activities were initially fairly limited to patrolling Gdańsk Bay. Some Dutch and English merchant ships were stopped, checked and arrested, their captains accused of transporting contraband to Swedes in Prussia. Warships were crucial in supporting the Polish siege of Puck, providing additional firepower during assaults on the town. In May 1627 there were two small encounters of Polish and Swedish squadrons but the Royal Fleet managed to survive them with minimal losses. The biggest success of Sigismund's fleet was the battle of Oliwa (Oliva), that took place on 28 November 1627. The Royal Fleet attacked a small Swedish squadron, with 10 Polish ships against six Swedish. During the fierce and bloody battle the Swedish galleon *Tigern* was captured, while a second ship, *Solen*, was blown up by her own crew on the brink of being captured by the Poles. The Royal Court used this victory as a propaganda tool, ordering broadsheets to be published and sent all over the Europe. It was the biggest historical Polish naval triumph, but in fact it did not have any impact on the war. After all, in each autumn/winter season the Swedes were losing many more ships due to Baltic storms than the activity of the Royal Fleet.

In fact Oliva was the high-water mark of Sigismund's naval project. Subsequently things became worse: at the beginning of December a patrol of four Polish ships was scattered during a storm, with *Fliegende Hirsch* ambushed and sunk by the Swedes near Öland. For the next few months the Royal Fleet was inactive, stuck in its moorings near Wisłoujście (Weichselmünde), with a strong Swedish fleet controlling Gdańsk Bay. Here, during the night of 5 to 6 July 1628, the Poles were surprised by a Swedish attack with troops led by King Gustav Adolf himself, bringing cannons (including leather pieces) through a marshy area and opening fire on the ships. *Gelbe Löw* and *Ritter Sankt George* were sunk, with many others damaged and barely managing to flee towards Gdańsk.

It is interesting to note that the rank of Admiral of the Royal Fleet seems to be the most dangerous officer's post in the whole Polish military establishment during the war. The initial candidate for this post, Wilhelm Appelman, had health problems in autumn 1627 and he was replaced by Arendt Dickmann. The newly nominated admiral led the fleet to victory at Oliwa on 28 November 1627 but died during the battle. His replacement, Herman Witte, was killed in action almost immediately after his nomination, around 2 December 1627,[216] when his ship was ambushed by the Swedes. The next admiral, Gregor Fentross, survived until 6 July 1628, when he died during a Swedish attack on the mooring.

The year 1628 brought an end to the short episode of the Royal Fleet. After some prolonged negotiations with the Habsburgs, Sigismund decided to send his ships to Wismar, to be put under the command of Wallenstein as part of anti-Swedish operations in Baltic. In February 1629 a Polish squadron of nine ships[217] arrived in Wismar, where it became the core of a new Catholic fleet. The Royal Fleet did not see much action there, so as early as mid September 1629 Sigismund asked Wallenstein to sent it back to Poland. The Imperial commander pointed out that the ships were under the control of the Spanish Crown, so in January 1630 Sigismund wrote to Philip IV to intervene.[218] Prolonged negotiations did not bring any success, though, with the inactive ships stuck in Wismar while the crew gradually disbanded and left them. The end of the Polish squadron came in January 1632, when Wismar was captured by Gustav II Adolf's army. A few years later Władysław IV (who also had his own plans to create a fleet) was demanding from Spain a refund for the cost of the Royal Fleet, which he estimated as 1,000,000 florins (zl).[219]

---

216 The exact date is unknown.
217 There is indication that in fact 10 were sent out, although so far researchers were unable to identify the last one.
218 Ryszard Skowron, *Olivares, Wazowie i Bałtyk* (Kraków: Towarzystwo Wydawnicze 'Historia Iagellonica, 2002), pp.242–243.
219 *Ibidem*, p.240.

Chapter 4

To Pay, to Feed, to Clothe

Financial Cost and Awards for Military Service

Every two years there was an ordinary session of the Polish *Sejm* (parliament), which normally took place over six weeks. Each Polish voivodship and land, during their own pre-*Sejm* gathering called a *Sejmik*, was choosing their representatives and preparing for them lists of queries that they should discuss during the *Sejm*. One of the main points was always agreeing new levels of taxes, that should be gathered locally and then delivered to the National Treasury.[1] Next to the main tax, called the *łanowe* (land tax), there were many very specific forms of taxation, for example *czopowe* (from sale of beer, vodka, mead and wine), border tariffs and *pogłówne* (a head tax, collected only from Jews). In special circumstances, normally during the war, a so-called extraordinary *Sejm* could be gather, its session usually just two weeks long. During the 1626–1629 war there were the following sessions:

Type of *Sejm*	Start	End	Place of the proceedings
Ordinary	27/01/1626	10/03/1626	Warsaw
Extraordinary	10/11/1626	29/11/1626	Toruń
Ordinary	12/10/1627	24/11/1627	Warsaw
Extraordinary	27/06/1628	18/07/1628	Warsaw
Ordinary	09/01/1629	20/02/1629	Warsaw
Extraordinary	13/11/1629	28/11/1629	Warsaw

The *Sejm* had the power to agree special higher rates of taxes but usually the main problem here was opposition from the local *Sejmiki*, for example lands from southern Poland were not very eager to spend money from their taxes on war waged in Prussia. There was also always the option to expand certain taxes to other social groups, as in 1613 and 1620, when it was decided that a head tax was to be gathered from Scottish merchants as well. In 1629 a head tax was to be taken from all merchants who were not Polish citizens. Additionally the Polish priesthood sometimes decided on a voluntary tax

---

1   There was also an additional 'Quarter Treasury', used to pay the 'quarter army'. It was kept in the castle of Rawa Mazowiecka.

Officer of hussars from the
beginning of the seventeenth
century. 'Stockholm Roll'.
(Author's archive)

called the *donatywa* but, considering the overall wealth of this group, the money received through such a tax was always very small amounts.

The main issue with the Polish taxation system was that it was very inefficient. Many voivodships were late gathering their quota and often delivered far less than agreed. The treasury was for most of the time in debt, especially during times of war, when it had to issue large sums to the soldiers. Some Polish lands even refused to pay the agreed amount of taxes and opposed any changes proposed during the *Sejm*. It led to a vicious circle, where delay in paying taxes led to an increase in debt owed to the army, which then led to unpaid soldiers starting mutinies and pillaging their own country. Destroyed lands were not able to raise enough of their planned quotas in taxes, leading to a growing difference between planned and received taxes. This was especially visible during 1626–1629 war, with the constant need to keep a large army in the field that required a huge amount of money, of which the National Treasury was not able to deliver either enough of or on time. As money raised through taxes was insufficient, debt towards the army in Prussia was growing with each year. As early as May 1627 Koniecpolski wrote to Crown Chancellor Wacław Leszczyński[2] that the soldiers needed at least 'one quarter of the pay in full', otherwise they could mutiny and even move towards central Poland.[3] He repeated this plea in a letter to Sigismund III, sent on the same day, explaining that he not only asked but practically begged unpaid soldiers to return to his command.[4] In August 1627 he mentioned that 'unpaid soldiers are wretched and starving, due to lack of pay units do not have full strength ... Once the fighting season is over [and] winter starts, I cannot see and find any way to keep troops in service without money.'[5] Between the end of the *Sejm* in 1627 (24 November) and that in 1628 (18 July), troops in Prussia received 1,475,001 zlotys of delayed pay, with another 1,620,270 zlotys still overdue.[6] When Koniecpolski was in Warsaw in early spring of 1628, he received information about the huge delay in gathering planned taxes. The situation was desperate, as only one quarter of the money

---

2   Leszczyński died in May 1628 and Jakub Zadzik replaced him as a Crown Chancellor.

3   Od Pana Hetmana do Pana Kanclerza Koronnego, z obozu pod Brzoznem, dnia 22 Maja 1627, *Pamiętniki o Koniecpolskich*, p.55.

4   Od Pana Hetman do Króla J. Mści, z obozu pod Brzoznem, dnia 22 Maja 1627, *Pamiętniki o Koniecpolskich*, p.56.

5   'List Stanisława Koniecpolskiego, wojewody sandomierskiego i hetmana polnego koronnego, do sejmu przedsejmowego województw poznańskiego i kaliskiego w Środzie 31 sierpnia 1627 r., z obozu pod Libiszowem 25 sierpnia 1627 r.', Włodzimierz Dworzaczek (ed.), *Akta Sejmikowe województw poznańskiego i kaliskiego*, volume I part 2 (Poznań, 1962), p.243.

6   Anna Filipczak-Kocur, *Skarbowość Rzeczpospolitej 1578–1648* (Warszawa, 2006), p.151; Jan Wimmer, 'Wojsko i skarb Rzeczypospolitej u schyłku XVI i w pierwszej połowie XVII wieku', *Studia i Materiały do Historii Wojskowości*, volume XIV (Warszawa, 1968), p.50.

agreed in the *Sejm* was gathered.[7] In May 1628, when the overdue pay was already in arrears of five quarters (so more than one year of service!) soldiers gathered in the camp near Grudziądz received Sigismund's letter, advising that money was not yet available and asking them to continue their faithful service for 'love of the Homeland'. Hetman Koniecpolski often protested that his army was on the brink of mutiny, lacking money and supplies. New taxes agreed at the 1628 *Sejm* were to be used for the current quarter pay of that year (September–November; approximately 930,000 zloty) and any surplus was to be spent on overdue sums.[8] As of 1 December 1628 the debt towards the army was as follows:[9]

Formation	Overdue pay (in zl)
Hussars	316,958
Cossack cavalry	498,363
Reiters	181,087
Foreign infantry and dragoons	408,976
Total[10]	1,405,384

Additionally the tabor wagon's drivers were due 20,000 zl and unpaid bills from the merchants (mostly from Gdańsk and Toruń) for 'powder, bullets, match, etc.' were already at 100,000 zl. The commissioners estimated that they only had 600,000 zl with them. Hetman Koniecpolski managed to convince the mutinous soldiers to not leave Prussia, and the commissioners (see below) managed to pay the equivalent of one quarter 'to replace [lost] equipment'.[11]

Tax and spending reports provided for the *Sejm* in November 1629 show the huge toll that the war was taking on Poland, and at the same time proving how inefficient the Polish taxation system was at that time. Between February and November 1629 2,070,371 zl was received from taxes of all kinds, while 1,747,587 zl was spent on military endeavours (the vast majority on troops in Prussia). Considering some additional, non-military spending, there was only 160,000 zl in cash left in the National Treasury. At that point debt towards soldiers in Prussia was estimated at 2,800,000 zl, with additional payments due to Imperial allies, troops from the 'quarter army', and registered Cossacks.[12] It is not a great surprise, then, that the soldiers had to wait for their overdue pay well after the end of the war. Only by autumn 1630, thanks to additional taxes and some loans (including from Sigismund III's wife, Queen Constance of Austria), did the former 'army in

---

7   Biblioteka Kórnicka, BK 341, *Diariusze z lat 1625–1630 oraz korespondencja dyplomatyczna*, pp.309–310v, *Manifestatio Ie Mci Pana Hetmana Polnego Koronnego cu solennni Protestatione podana do Xiąg Grodzkich Warszawkich y inszych w Koronie*.

8   Jan Wimmer, 'Wojsko i skarb…', p.51.

9   Biblioteka Jagiellońska w Krakowie, manuscript 7, p.623. The author would like to thank Emil Kalinowski for sharing this document.

10   The Polish infantry is not mentioned, which would indicate that at least units of this formation were not overdue with pay.

11   'Relacja IMP. Wojewody Sendomirskiego', pp.420–421.

12   Jan Wimmer, 'Wojsko i skarb', p.55, Anna Filipczak-Kocur, *Skarbowość*, pp.142–143.

Another example of an official/officer from the 'Stockholm Roll'. (Author's archive).

Prussia' receive 2,771,870 zl, with 'just' 34,597 zl still overdue.[13] The cost of the conflict was overwhelming. It is estimated that the National Treasury, between 1626 and 1631, paid between 9,500,000 and 10,426,000 zl to cover all aspects of the war in Prussia.[14] Of course that is not taking into consideration all the 'hidden' costs: soldiers' individual spending; raising, equipping and paying of private and district troops, massive damages to the population and infrastructure in Prussia, etc.

The initial way in which soldiers received their pay was very inefficient and generated many complaints. Each banner and company had to send their envoys to meet officials from the Treasury, those army representatives were then forced to wait a few weeks until the money was released. It led to the situation where they spent more money on their accommodations and supplies, as officials were keeping a safe distance from the theatre of war, usually staying in Toruń. Additionally it severely weakened the army in the field, as each banner sent two companions (with their retinues) and each foreign company despatched officers with at least a few soldiers – which decreased available manpower. In their petition from May 1627 the soldiers suggested that officials should bring money directly to the army camp, as 'they receive their own salaries, they take from soldiers special taxes, why [on top of that] soldiers need to spend their own money [travelling away]'.[15]

This 'voice of the army' was in fact heard and some changes were already introduced in 1627. To control the actual strength of the army, and to ensure that the soldiers were paid the correct amount of money and muster their units at the designated times, the *Sejm* in autumn 1627 nominated 20 war commissioners. They were led by the Primate of Poland, Jan Wężyk; alongside him was a group composed of six senators and 13 representatives (*posłowie*) from the lower house of the *Sejm*, including *Sejm* Marshal Aleksander Chalecki. Alongside financial control, they also received the power to negotiate with the Swedes, if any opportunity for that arose.[16] An extraordinary session of the *Sejm* in summer 1628 confirmed the role of the war commissioners but changed the composition of their group. There were now just three senators and eight representatives. Their main task was to gather by 1 September 1628 in Grudziądz, then proceed to muster the troops in Prussia and pay them the outstanding money.[17] Next a group of commissioners was nominated at the *Sejm* in February 1629, this time with

---

13   Jan Wimmer, 'Wojsko i skarb', p.57.
14   Anna Filipczak-Kocur, *Skarbowość*, p.145.
15   'Petitia do Króla J.M. od wojska w Prusiech', p.52.
16   *Volumina Legum*, volume III (Petersburg, 1859), p.261.
17   *Ibidem*, p.277.

just two senators and four representatives.[18] Finally in November 1629 the last group, of three senators and seven representatives, was to organise checks of final musters of the troops and payment of the outstanding money, so the units could then be disbanded.[19] Each meeting of the commissioners with the army was usually a string of long negotiations, full of excuses regarding lack of money and attempts to convince the soldiers to voluntarily cancel some of the debt owed to them.

The war commissioners and their work were frequently criticised by the Polish nobility, especially for the lack of control of the real size of the army, for not organising musters or even for taking bribes. In November 1628 Prince Jerzy Zbaraski complained to one of the commissioners in Prussia – Paweł Marchocki – about the poor methods of controlling the size of the army. His main point was that no musters of the units were taking place and commissioners just took officers' words for granted, releasing money for soldiers that were not present. Zbaraski mentioned that in 1627 the commissioners provided a local *Sejmiki* with the 'paper strength' of the army and needed to raise money to pay for 17,000 men, while in reality less than half of this number were present under Koniecpolski's command. The same month Marchocki himself complained in a letter to the Crown Grand Treasurer, Hormolaus Ligęza, that there were huge problems in paying the army, as they only received pay for the current quarter (three months) of service, without any outstanding money.[20] During the *Sejm* in autumn 1629, when discussing spending on the army in Prussia, one of the commissioners, Marcin Talibowski, had to explain himself for releasing the large amount of 90,000 zl to Captain Florian Winteroy from Gerhard Denhoff's infantry regiment. Talibowski presented the *Sejm* with a list of spending, but one of the Treasury clerks, named Wojankowski, accused him of taking an 8,000 zl bribe from Winteroy, in order to provide the officer with the rest of the funds for recruitment of troops and engineers in Netherlands (that never took place). Both officials started a huge argument, with Wojankowski finally expelled from the place of proceedings and the whole matter was presented to King Sigismund.[21] Of course it is not surprising that representatives of the Polish

Heavy-armoured hussar and infantryman (possibly officer). Pieter Serwouters, 1627. (Rijksmuseum)

---

18   *Ibidem*, p.289.
19   *Ibidem*, p.310.
20   *Zbiór pamiętników do dziejów polskich*, volume IV (Warszawa, 1859), List starosty cehowskiego, Pawła Marchockiego, do podskarbiego wielkiego koronnego Hermolausa z Bobku Ligenzy, pp.131–132.
21   AGAD, Teki Naruszewicza, volume 121, no 124, p.478.

nobility were so angry with the mismanagement of funds and cases of fraud, after all it was money from their taxes that was spent on the army in Prussia. There were also numerous complaints that the commanding officers – both Polish and foreign – were taking initial payments to raise new units but then not providing their real numbers and delaying the date of their arrival in Prussia.

There was another financial burden that the Poles had to deal with at the end of the war. Despite their rather lacklustre performance, the Imperials demanded very high payment for their services. At the beginning of October 1629, the Polish commissioners in Prussia were presented a bill for the Imperial presence in the campaign against the Swedes. Wallenstein's soldiers demanded pay for five months (despite the fact that the Poles described the actual service as only three months): 161,714 zl/month for cavalry and 131,884/month for infantry, a total of 1,467,990 zl. Additionally the Polish side received further bills for provisions, special gratification for officers and the cost of artillery used during the campaign, for the total amount of 571,696 zl. The final bill, at 2,039,686 zl, was far too high for the Poles, who were willing to pay no more than 800,000 zl for the Imperial help.[22] It led to long negotiations, where the Emperor's envoys finally decided to abandon their claims to a fifth month's pay and have their fourth month based on actual, not 'paper' strength of the units. At that stage the Imperial officers most likely realised that with the Polish National Treasury struggling to pay even their own soldiers, there was little chance of claiming such high amounts for their intervention in Prussia. Further negotiations and delays in payments led to the situation that the overall pay received by the Imperials was spread over the period 1629 and 1631. It is estimated that in all the Poles paid 745,000 zl, with 445,000 provided by the National Treasury and the rest covered by King Sigismund III himself.[23]

Soldiers' pay was normally delivered quarterly to the cavalry and monthly to the infantry. It is interesting to see the level of pay and the way it changed, depending on the formation and period. Based on surviving documents we can create a fairly comprehensive list, for the purpose of the comparison using also rates of pay for Lithuanian troops fighting in Livonia in 1621–1628, and both Polish and Lithuanian troops taking part in the Smolensk War against Muscovy in 1632–1634. Additionally, proposed rates of pay from Prince Zbaraski's project from 1629 have been added as well:

---

22 Jan Seredyka, 'Wypłata żołdu armii cesarskiej w Polsce po rozejmie altmarskim (1629–1631)', *Śląski kwartalnik historyczny Sobótka*, year XXXI, nos 1–4 (Wrocław-Warszawa-Kraków-Gdańsk, 1976), pp.232–233.
23 *Ibidem*, p.236.

Formation[24]	Date	Pay	Additional Notes
Lithuanian hussars	1621–1622	31 zl/quarter	
Lithuanian cossacks	1621–1622	21 zl/quarter	
Lithuanian reiters	1621–1622	31, 41 and 51 zl/quarter	Rate of pay depended on length of service. Paradoxically a new unit, raised in 1622, had the highest pay.
Lithuanian foreign infantry and dragoons	1621–1622	32 zl/quarter	
Lithuanian infantry	1621–1622	14 and 15 zl/quarter	Depended on the unit
Polish hussars	Whole 1626–1629 war	51 zl/quarter	Same pay for one banner of *arkabuzeria* and one banner of reiters from the 'quarter army'[25]
Polish hussars	Zbaraski's project from 1629	50 zl/quarter	
Polish reiters (old units)	December 1626–June 1627	15 zl/quarter	
Polish reiters (new units)	December 1626–June 1627	45 zl/quarter	Additionally a one-off payment of 15 zl of so-called *anritgeld*
Koracarze	Zbaraski's project from 1629	48 zl/quarter	
Polish cossacks	Whole 1626–1629 war	41 zl/quarter	
Polish cossacks	Zbaraski's project from 1629	40 zl/quarter	Same pay for district troops raised in Poznań Voivodship at the end of 1627.
Polish infantry	December 1626–June 1627	Initially 5–7 zl/month, later 14–15 zl/month	Pay depends on the unit
Polish infantry	March–September 1629	6 zl/month	
Polish infantry	Zbaraski's project from 1629	10 zl/month	
Hungarian infantry	Zbaraski's project from 1629	Approximately 4.4 zl/month	Pay was to be 4 Hungarian thalars/month
Polish foreign infantry	December 1626–June 1627	10 zl/month	
Polish foreign infantry	After June 1627	11 zl/month	
Polish foreign infantry	Zbaraski's project from 1629	10 zl/month	
Polish dragoons	December 1626–June 1627	11 and 12 zl/month	Pay depends on the unit
Newly raised units of dragoons	Spring/summer 1629	12 zl/month	Additionally a one-off payment of 10 zl of so-called *laufgelt*
Polish dragoons	Zbaraski's project from 1629	10 zl/month	

24 The term 'Polish' and 'Lithuanian' here means only to which army these units were assigned.
25 Later during the war, both were converted into hussars.

Formation[24]	Date	Pay	Additional Notes
Newly raised unit of *arkabuzeria*	Summer 1629	45 zl/ quarter	
Lithuanian hussars	1628	41 zl/ quarter	
Lithuanian reiters	1628	57 zl/ quarter	
Hussars[26]	1632–1634	41 zl/quarter	
Reiters	1632–1634	41 zl/ quarter	
Cossacks	1632–1634	31 zl/ quarter	
Dragoons	1632–1634	13 zl/month	
Foreign infantry	1632–1634	11 zl/month	Same pay also for 'Polish infantry trained in the German way'
Polish infantry	1632–1634	8 and 1/3 zl/ month	

Drawing of the *nadziak* used by Michał Piekarski during his assassination attempt against King Sigismund III in 1620. (Author's archive)

Of course such a level of pay was inadequate even when paid on time, and during 1626–1629 massive delays affected the Polish military effort in so many ways. But it is interesting to see the prices of different military equipment during that time, to better understand the cost of raising new units and the complaints of unpaid soldiers, who were unable to replace lost and destroyed weapons and other items. In 1627 Lithuanian officers estimated the cost of material for one haiduk: uniform: 'good equipment … with a good and solid musket' was between 42 and 50 zl.[27] In autumn 1627 the *Sejm* set up a special commission, that was to work on preparing a list of prices for items made by artisans locally and imported from other countries. The commission worked until May 1628, when it finally registered this new act in Lublin, as valid for the whole territory of Poland (but not Lithuania). It is worth looking at some of the items and their cost, as it presents us with an interesting source of information about soldiers' and civilians' weapons at that time:[28]

---

26   All figures for the 1632–1634 war are for both Polish and Lithuanian soldiers.

27   Henryk Wisner, 'Wojsko litewskie I połowy XVII wieku', p.104.

28   Jerzy Teodorczyk, 'Broń i oporządzenie polskie w świetle cennika komisji lubelskiej, oblatowanego 22 maja 1628 r.', *Muzealnictwo Wojskowe* (Warszawa, 1964), pp.501–510.

Hand Weapons

Item	Cost	Notes
Haiduk's sabre with scabbard	2 zl and 10 gr	Price given as 70 gr
Estoc (koncerz) with scabbard	5 or 4 zl	Price depended on quality of the leather used for scabbard
Pallasch with scabbard	6 or 5 zl	As above
Sword with scabbard[29]	6 or 5 zl	As above
Kord sword[30]	4 or 3 zl	As above
Simple sabre blade, no ornaments	20 gr	
Good quality sabre blade	1 zl	Price given as 30 gr
Pallasch blade	24 gr	
Kord sword blade	20 gr	
Estoc blade	24 gr	
Sword blade	1 zl 6 gr	
Haiduk's axe	16 gr	
Hussars' lance head	12 gr	For hussars' kopia

Firearms[31] and Associated Equipment

Item	Cost	Notes
Musket	No more than 8 zl	Text mentioned both 'long' and 'short' muskets
Pistol, bandolet, carbine[32]	8 zl	
Cavalry pistol	6 zl	
Holster for long musket[33]	1 zl 15 gr	
Holster for short musket	1 zl 6 gr	
Holster for carbine	1 zl	Probably for harquebus
Holster for long pistol	26 gr	
Holster for short pistol	15 gr	
Holster for pistol 'made in French style'	1 zl 12 gr	Pistol here may mean long firearm
Holster for pistol 'made in simple way'	20 gr	As above

The price of muskets could vary depending on the place and period of time when they were purchased. In May 1634 muskets bought for foreign infantry in Lithuanian army cost 11 zl each when bought in Lithuania,[34] but 17 zl each for those purchased in Toruń in Poland.[35] There is also interesting

---

29 Possibly Western-type weapons, rapier type.
30 Possibly it was some sort of cutlass.
31 The document mentioned that it is hard to establish a manufacturing price for calivers (rusznica) as 'work [for making them] vary in cost and quality'. There is also important information, that 'if someone ordered from the artisan [a weapon] for their [special] liking, they will pay as much as they will agree [with the artisan]', allowing higher prices for better quality weapons.
32 This part seems rather confusing, as it would indicate same price both for pistols and long firearms. Probably the authors of the price list meant here a different type of long firearms (especially those used by cavalry), that were not muskets and calivers.
33 Polish cavalry, especially hussars, could have a musket as an additional weapon, so it would be carried either on a tabor wagon or in a special holster.
34 Urszula Augustyniak, W służbie hetmana i Rzeczypospolitej. Klientela wojskowa Krzysztofa Radziwiłła (1585–1640) (Warszawa: Semper, 2004), p.82.
35 Przemysław Gawron, 'Koszty wystawienia regimentu piechoty cudzoziemskiej w Wielkim Księstwie Litewskim w pierwszej połowie XVII wieku', Rocznik Lituanistyczny, volume 5 (Warszawa, 2019), p.154.

Batorówka sabre, that began to be popular in Poland during Stephen Bathory's reign. (Livrustkammaren)

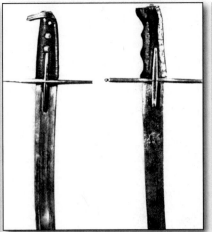

Polish-Hungarian sabres, end of the sixteenth/ beginning of the seventeenth century. (Author's archive)

Different types of *nadziak*, used by Polish cavalry. (Author's archive)

Details of calivers (*rusznica*) and harquebuses used by the Polish infantry from the beginning of the seventeenth century. 'Stockholm Roll'. (Author's archive)

information regarding prices in Wrocław (Breslau),[36] which could shed some light on similar items sold in Poland. Between 1626 and 1634 halberds there cost 1 thaler (between 3 and 4 zlotys),[37] muskets 2 thalers and 18 gr (6 zl 18 gr) and a harquebus 2 thalers (6 zl).[38] Very good quality Turkish bows, seen as luxury items and highly valued by Polish nobles, in 1633 cost between 15 and 30 zl, with cheaper 'simple Turkish bows' being sold for 9 zl.[39]

Of course we cannot forget about a crucial element of Polish armies – horses. Their prices varied depending on the formation, with hussars' mounts the most expensive. The best horses for this formation were either

---

36 Which belonged to the Austrian Habsburgs.
37 By the end of 1626 the price of 1 *thaler* was approximately 88 *groszy*, later it started to increase in value. See: Adam Szelągowski, *Pieniądz i przewrót cen w XVI i XVII wieku w Polsce* (Lwów: Towarz. Wydawn, 1902), pp.182–183.
38 Jerzy Maroń, *Wojna trzydziestoletnia na Śląsku. Aspekty militarne* (Wrocław-Racibórz: Wydawnictwo i Agencja Informacyjna WAW Grzegorz Wawoczny, 2008), p.262.
39 Wilhelm Rolny, 'Dwie taksy towarów cudzoziemskich z r. 1633', *Archiwum Komisyi Prawniczej*, volume V (Kraków, 1897), p.570.

Hussars (drawn in Western-type armour) and cossack cavalry during Smolensk War 1632–1634. Wilhelm Hondius, 1636. (Author's archive)

Polish or Turkish, with their prices often exceeding 1,000 zl. In 1636 the already mentioned hussar companion Marek Łahodowski had three Turkish horses, valued at 2,500, 2,000 and 1,200 z, 1,000–1,500 ducats (approximately 4,000–6,000 zl), while the majority cost 600 or 700 ducats (approximately 2,400–2,800 zl) and the minimal price being 200 ducats (approximately 800 zl).[40] There is also a very interesting pricing list of the Turkish horses sold by merchants in Lwów (Lviv) in 1633: 200, 250, 280, 345, 400, 480, 500, 530, 600, 600, 660, 690, 890, 1,010 and 1,065 zl.[41] Another bit of information about the cost of the horses we can find on the list of the horses killed and wounded during the battle of Kłuszyn (Klushino) in 1610. Their prices varied from 100 zl (a retainer's horse) to 300 zl (most likely a companion's).[42] We have also some more information about average market prices of horses in the main cities of the Commonwealth. Of course such horses would not be used in battle by hussar companions, but rather their retainers and soldiers from other formations.

Town	Year	Price[43]
Cracow[44]	1627	60 zl
	1628	85 zl
	1629	95 zl
Warsaw[45]	1628	45 zl
	1629	60 zl
Lviv[46]	1627	50 zl

---

40 Szymon Starowolski, *Eques Polonus*, pp.37–38.
41 Wilhelm Rolny, 'Dwie taksy towarów', pp.571–572.
42 Radosław Sikora, *Kłuszyn 1610*, p.141.
43 Prices were normally given in *grosze*, here we calculate 30 gr as 1 zl.
44 Edward Tomaszewski, *Ceny w Krakowie 1601–1795* (Lwów, Warszawa: Inst. pop. polsk. twórczości nauk., 1934), p.39
45 Władysław Adamczyk, *Ceny w Warszawie w XVI i XVII wieku* (Lwów, Warszawa: Kasa im. Mianowskiego, 1938), p.20.
46 Stanisław Hoszowski, *Ceny we Lwowie w XVI i XVII wieku* (Lwów, 1928), p.198.

Examples of wings and pelts worn by officer and hussars. 'Stockholm Roll'. (Author's archive)

It is important to remember that even a small retinue required many more than their 'paper strength' horses. A companion would require at least two, with the best one used for battles and the other(s) mounted during marches and even some small-scale actions. Retainers would probably have only one horse each, but there were additional 'spare' horses used by servants (as they were normally sent to obtain food and forage) and harnessed to the tabor wagon. So even a two or three horse retinue could in fact have at least eight horses, all of them paid for from the companion's pocket. It seems that Charles Ogier did not exaggerate, when he wrote in 1635 about Polish hussars who 'each of them have 20 or 30 horses, five of them are most important, used by the hussars in battle; the others for their retinue and their numerous tabor, as they are carrying all their food with them'.[47]

As with many other armies of the period, sometimes soldiers might receive special rewards for their military service. In regard to the 1626–1629 war, we can find two types. The first would be a financial reward for bravery during the battle or siege, usually awarded by a king or hetman, sometimes

---

47   *Karola Ogiera dziennik podróży do Polski 1635–1636*, p.143.

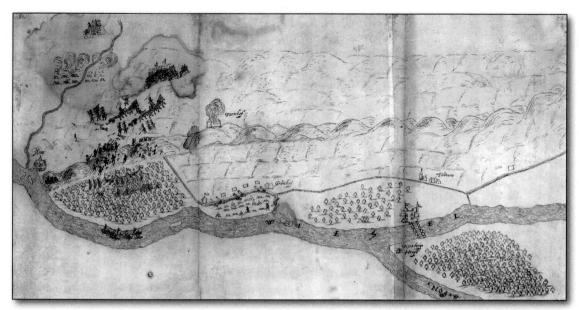

Swedish sketch of the battle of Gniew (Mewe) in 1626. (Krigsarkivet, Stockholm)

by an officer in charge (for example a colonel). Normally it was just a small amount of money but accompanied by some official document, which the soldier could later use to support further claims and have a proof of their service. For example after the capture of Puck in 1627 a few companions from the cossack cavalry are mentioned as being rewarded for their actions during the siege. Their names are noted as lieutenant Jan Dobiecki, standard bearer Jakub Charzyński, Jan Doliński and Jan Marszewski from Jan Bąk-Lanckoroński's banner, standard bearers Mikołaj Szpakowski and Hieronim Strzelecki[48] from Krzysztof Faliński's banner and Jan Rusiński from Jan Bogusz's banner.[49] Additionally Paweł Karpiński, probably serving as lieutenant, was promoted to *rotmistrz* to replace Faliński, who died during one of the unsuccessful assaults.

Much more important were the official rewards given by the King to veterans in recognition of their military service. Sometimes they were given out immediately after (or even during) the campaign but more often the soldiers had to wait years for such an example of royal favour. We have records of some veterans of Jan Karol Chodkiewicz's campaigns in Livonia in 1600–1611, who received their rewards in 1637 and 1638. We can identify 108 cases of the officers and soldiers who between July 1628 and July 1643 received such accolades for their 'military labours' during the war in Prussia.[50] There are at least an additional 50 that were mentioned as 'veteran soldiers' but without naming the campaigns that they took part in, so it is certain that some of them also served in Prussia. The scale of received rewards varied

---

48 It is possible that one of them was wounded, so another companion had to step up and replace him as a unit's standard bearer.

49 Wacław Odyniec, 'Lądowo-morska obrona wybrzeża polskiego w rejonie Pucka w latach 1626–1629', *Studia i Materiały do Historii Wojskowości*, volume I (Warszawa: Wyd. MON, 1954), p.461.

50 AGAD, MK 180–185, Riksarkivet, Skoklostersamlingen E 8636, 1 a.

greatly. It could be the lease of royal land (for example a village) which was normally awarded for the life of the recipient. Commonly some financial awards or goods had been received by the Crown through escheat law (*prawo kaduka*) or through confiscation of belongings of the traitors of the state, especially in Prussia and Livonia. Foreigners could be nominated as royal servitors, courtiers or even receive an *indygenat* (a grant of nobility to a foreign noble). A good example of a recipient of the latter is James Butler, who in November 1627 received it from the *Sejm*:

> Taking under consideration the brave and full of sacrifices services of Iakub Buthler, Irish noble, that he delivered to Us and to the Commonwealth during different military expeditions, [while] serving faithfully and in such good manner; under agreement from all Polish and Lithuanian states, we take him as *indigena*, [which means he is now] the Commonwealth's noble; under condition that he will give Us his oath of allegiance.[51]

We can also partially identify in which formations the rewarded men served. Twenty-four of them were companions in hussar banners, eight were in the cossack cavalry, two were reiters and seven served as infantrymen. Twenty-six were officers, ranking from Hetman Koniecpolski himself to one infantry lieutenant. There were 10 royal courtiers, which could indicate that at least some of them served in 1626 and 1629 in a hussar 'court banner'. Finally the remaining 31 were from unidentified units (they are only mentioned as 'soldiers') but most likely the majority were hussars and cossack companions.

Officer of hussars from the beginning of the seventeenth century. 'Stockholm Roll'. (Author's archive)

It is interesting to see how such royal rewards could be used to pacified unpaid troops and prevent possible mutinies. On 13 August 1627 Hetman Koniecpolski returned from Toruń, where he had met King Sigismund, and brought with him a royal decree rewarding many soldiers in the army. Of course the main prizes went to Koniecpolski's officers, as amongst those that received district offices were Jan Działyński, Andrzej Stanisław Sapieha, Marcin Kazanowski, Stanisław Potocki and Jan Odrzywolski: the first four held the rank of a hussar *rotmistrz*, while Odrzywolski led a cossack banner. There were awards for companions and other soldiers as well though, 'as the hetman obtained [from the King] many [of them] thanks to escheat law'.[52]

---

51   *Volumina Legum*, volume III, p.265.
52   Biblioteka ks. Czartoryskich, TN, part 118, document 176, p.763, *Nowiny z Prus*.

Army Provisions

Considering the size of the Polish–Lithuanian Commonwealth, availability of food depended on the region where the troops were stationed and campaigned. The list below is a quarterly ration for one cavalryman of the 'quarter army', as proposed by Crown Field Hetman Stanisław Żółkiewski in 1616 as a part of his memorandum *O chowaniu żołnierza kwarcianego*.[53]

Item	Measurement	Quantity
Oats	*Trzecinnik*[54]	6
Rye	½ of *trzecinnik*	1
Wheat	¼ of *trzecinnik*	1
Millet	½ of *trzecinnik*	1
Peas	¼ of *trzecinnik*	1
Barley	*Trzecinnik*	1
Buckwheat	*Trzecinnik*	1
Hay	Cart	6
Mutton	–	3
Lamb	–	3
Half a slab of meat[55]	–	1
Goose	–	13
Chicken	–	26
Butter	Quart (*kwarta*)[56]	6
Cheese	–	13

In 1634 a commission gathered in Lwów, led by Hetman Stanisław Koniecpolski, set up regulation of the provision for 'quarter troops' in their winter quarters. Again, it is a quarterly ration per one cavalryman:[57]

Item	Measurement	Quantity
Heifer	–	1
Mutton	–	2
Slab of lard	–	1
Butter	*Faska*[58]	½
Cheese	–	30
Wheat	*Osmaczek*[59]	2
Rye	*Osmaczek*	4
Peas	*Osmaczek*	2
Millet	*Osmaczek*	1½

53 Kazimierz Tyszkowski, 'Problemy organizacyjno-wojskowe z czasów wojny moskiewskiej Zygmunta III', *Przegląd Historyczno-Wojskowy* (Warszawa, 1930), volume II/2, p.291.
54 An old Polish measurement. Depending on the region and type of food it was between 120 and 250 litres of dry capacity.
55 There is no information about the type of meat, most probably it was breast or belly of lamb, or pork belly.
56 One *kwarta* equals approximately 0.9 litre of dry capacity.
57 Władysław Łoziński, *Prawem i Lewem*, pp.139–140.
58 Small wooden vessel, used for keeping butter.
59 Old Polish measurement of dry capacity, approximately 1/24 of *trzecinnik*.

Item	Measurement	Quantity
Barley	*Osmaczek*	4
Oats	*Miarka*[60]	3
Salt	*Tołpa*[61]	1,000
Oil	Quart (*kwarta*)	2
Hay	Cart	4

Such provision was estimated to cost 35 zl, but commissars suggested that it should be sold to soldiers for half its price, 'so they can have some money [from their pay] for other expenses for themselves and their servants'.

Of course that was just theoretical regulations, practice often looks much different and was normally a huge burden for the local population. The cossack banner of Aleksander Piaseczyński,[62] with 'paper strength' of 150 horses, was accused of eating in just two days in 1628 '505 chickens, 275 quarts of butter, 213 maturing cheese, 5,700 eggs, not counting meat for soldiers and oats for horses'.[63] While some of the above numbers, especially in regards to eggs, sounds highly exaggerated, such figures can be often found in primary sources, especially in cases set up in district courts by the locals. It clearly shows the impact that stationed troops had on an area, with soldiers and their associated servants sometimes even clashing with local population over provisions, place to stay and spare horses.

We need to remember though, that these were the soldiers stationed on the southern border of Poland, where certain items (like different types of grains) could be much easier to acquire than in Prussia. Sources from Lithuanian campaigns in Livonia, where the available diet would be much closer to the one that the soldiers had in Prussia, mention wheat, rye, barley, mutton, groat, goose, lard, heifer, cheese, butter and salt as items that should be delivered to the units.[64] Haiduks and cossacks sent to the levy of the nobility by the city of Nowy Sącz in 1621 took with them following supplies:[65]

Item	Measurement	Quantity
Slab of meat	–	5¼
Butter	*Faska*	3
Cheese	–	180
Millet	*Wiertel*[66]	3
Barley	*Wiertel*	2
Salt	*Faska*	2
Biscuits	–	No information
Oats	–	No information

---

60 Old Polish measurement of dry capacity, approximately 15 litres.
61 Old Polish measurement of salt, approximately 40 g.
62 One of the new banners, created in 1627 to supplement the 'quarter army' in Ukraine.
63 Władysław Łoziński, *Prawem i Lewem*, op. cit., p.138.
64 Henryk Wisner, 'Wojsko litewskie I połowy XVIII wieku. Cz. III', p.82.
65 Jan Sygański, *Historya Nowego Sącza*, p.22.
66 An old Polish measurement of dry capacity, depending on region and period it varied between 15 and 120 litres.

However we need to notice that it was food for the whole 'city contingent': four haiduks, two cossacks and three supply wagon drivers, and it should last them for three months service.

However, there is slightly more detailed information regarding food for Royal Fleet crews during the war in Prussia. On 7 June 1628 the royal commissioners issued a regulation regarding victuals that were to be delivered to all ships. As an example, they took the 60-man crew of galleon *König David*, which should have received a monthly ration of:[67]

Item	Measurement	Quantity
Bread	Barrel[68]	16
Meat	Barrel	7
Beer	Barrel	30
Cabin bread[69]	Barrel	1
Cabin beer	Barrel	1
Baltic herring	Barrel	1½
Atlantic herring	Barrel	1
Butter	Barrel	6/8
Millet	*Mały korzec*[70]	3
Peas	*Mały korzec*	4
Stockfish	Barrel	1½
Oat groats	*Mały korzec*	1
Coarse salt	Barrel	¼
Mustard seed	*Miarka*	3
Vinegar	Barrel	½
Table salt	Barrel	1/15

The best area that could supply food and horse forage in Prussia was so-called Żuławy Malborskie (*Marienburger Werden*), between the river Vistula and its right arm, the Nogat. It was under Swedish control though, with a strong garrison in Malbork, also the local population was more keen to sell its supplies to Swedes than to Poles. At the end of 1626/beginning of 1627 a strong Polish force of 1,500 cavalry was sent on a reconnaissance mission in the Malbork area, where they found 'country that looks almost like the promised land, with many riches available [and] goods, horses and cattle in large numbers'.[71] Servants of the Polish cavalry started pillaging and looting the villages, and the whole scattered force was surprised and beaten back by a Swedish counter-attack. Throughout January and February 1627 the Polish cavalry was attacking areas in Żuławy Malborskie, trying to force the peasants to provide them with food. The local population claimed that the Swedes would not allow them to do that, and continued to supply Gustav Adolf's forces in Malbork and Elbląg instead. It led to the situation where the

---

67 'Diarum Commissionis Regiae A tertia Novembris Anni MDCXXVII usque ad ultimam Augusti A[nn]o 1628 Conscriptum per Joannem Heppium Secratarium Commissionis' in Wiktor Fenrych (ed.), *Akta i Diariusz*, p.258.
68 So-called 'small barrel', which was equivalent of approximately 300 litres.
69 A free additional ration, issued to the crew only when the ship was at sea.
70 An old Polish measurement, equal to 60 litres of dry capacity.
71 'Diariusz albo Summa', p.17.

City plan of Malbork (Marienburg) in July–August 1629, with additional drawings of city gates and Swedish fortifications. (Krigsarkivet, Stockholm)

Polish force was practically cut off from any areas in which they could find food. Hetman Koniecpolski, facing increasing desertion and losses during the attrition, sent many letters to King Sigismund, asking for food to be bought in other areas of Poland and then transported via the Vistula river to his forces. At the beginning of March 1627, thanks to the thaw on the Vistula, large food transports were finally despatched. The army was due to receive 333 *łaszty*[72] of rye, 443 *łaszty* of oats, 32 *łaszty* of groat, eight *łaszty* of peas, 60 barrels of butter and a large quantity of lard.[73] The Polish cavalry continued to harass Swedish-held territory, though, trying to gather as much in the way of supplies as possible. For example in April 1627 a Polish raid managed to capture 98 pigs, 132 sheep, 94 head of cattle and 91 horses from the farmsteads between Malbork and Elbląg.[74]

Already in 1626, at the Polish *Sejm*, gathered for an extraordinary session, nobles realised that Prussia alone would not be able to provide enough food to supply the fighting armies. A special commission, led by Krzysztof Ossoliński was created, to ensure that food could be purchased in other Polish regions and then transported to the army (usually via the Vistula). Commissioners were also to set fixed prices which soldiers would then pay for the delivered food.[75] In autumn 1627, at the new *Sejm*, Ossoliński was replaced in this role by Prokop Leśniowski, whose duty was to continue to purchase food 'where it is the cheapest and the easiest, then to send it to our troops [in Prussia]'.[76] Both Ossoliński and Leśniowski were normally called *Prowiant Magister* (provisions officer) and were treated as civilian functionaries working alongside Koniecpolski's officers. In the *Sejm* in February 1629 the

---

72 *Łaszt* (plural: *łaszty*) was old Polish measurements, normally used for grain. It was between 3,000 and 3,840 litres of dry capacity.

73 Jerzy Teodorczyk, 'Wyprawa', p.126

74 Robert Frost, *The Northern Wars: War, State and Society in Northeastern Europe, 1558–1721* (Harlow: Longman, 2000), p.109.

75 *Volumina Legum*, volume III, p.251.

76 *Ibidem*, p.260.

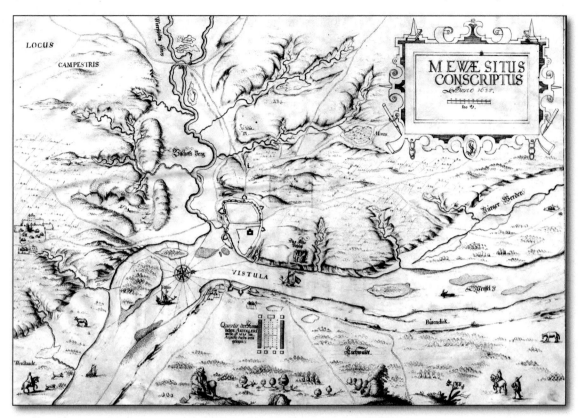

Area of Gniew (Mewe) on the drawing of Fryderyk Getkant from 1635. (Krigsarkivet, Stockholm)

war commissioners (two senators and four deputies)[77] who were dealing with the army's pay were also ordered to ensure that soldiers purchase food according to a fixed price.[78]

Despite the special commission and funds that, at least in theory, were designated for the purchase of provisions, the situation in Prussia was very problematic. The *Sejm* of 1626 assigned 200,000 zl for that aspect of the supplies but only half that amount was spent in 1627.[79] On many occasions Hetman Koniecpolski, in both letters and official documents, complained about the poor state of his army and the difficulties in obtaining supplies. After capturing Puck at the beginning of April 1627, he wrote to Sigismund, 'I will leave Lanckoroński[80] as a governor in Puck; but do not know from where I can take food to supply him with, as I cannot see to find in this such ravaged [by war] country.'[81] There is at least one confirmed account of a nominal *rotmistrz* of a hussar banner, Tomasz Zamoyski, sending both additional money and food to his troops in Prussia. He also despatched trusted servant Andrzej Drwalewski, who managed not only to calm down

77   *Ibidem*, p.289.
78   *Ibidem*, p.292.
79   Jan Wimmer, 'Wojsko i skarb', p.49.
80   Jan Bąk-Lanckoroński, *rotmistrz* of a cossack banner, appointed as commander of Polish troops in Puck area.
81   Hetman Stanisław Koniecpolski to Sigismund III, Puck, 3rd April 1627, *Pamiętniki o Koniecpolskich*, p.46.

unruly companions from the banner but also restored discipline in the unit and convinced all those that had left to return to the ranks.[82] Unfortunately we do not know how widespread such actions were, but many of the officers – both of 'national' and foreign troops – supported troops from their own purse.

In May 1628 one of the main points of the declaration issued by a 'general gathering' of the troops (*koło generalne*) stated that:

> food for the army should be given away equally and proportionally, [in such quantity] that will sustain us [and] that it will not be spoiled [and] provided for free[83] by His Royal Highness. That is a demand issued by both us and our Hetman for the future *Sejm*.[84]

Not only provisions for men were delayed: in July 1628 Koniecpolski complained to Chancellor Jan Zadzik that:

> I wrote many times, both to His Royal Highness and to You, asking you to rebuke the starost of Brańsk [Prokop Leśniowski] to not delay [any further] his arrival with provisions, especially with oats, but those rebukes do not have any effect. And it led not only to inconvenience but also great danger to our army; as normally a soldier could keep [and feed with oats] his horse next to him but now he had to take him two or three miles to get grass.[85]

Things did not improve much though, as in autumn the same year Koniecpolski was writing to the war commissioners who were staying in Toruń, asking them for the promised food deliveries, especially 'to those towns and castles, where he placed garrisons.'[86] The problem was, that they did not know when it would arrive and how much, they only received information that Prokop Leśniowski did not manage to spend all the available money when buying provisions, and by November it was already too late to buy more due to the oncoming winter. Their only hope was that food would be delivered to garrison troops in 'castles that are important to His Royal Highness and the Commonwealth.'[87]

In 1629 a newly arrived Imperial corps added thousands more soldiers and horses that required food from already strained and depleted territories. We know that the city of Toruń sent some supplies to von Arnim's troops, '120 oxen, several dozen of *łaszt* of oats, over the dozen thousands loaves of bread and 200 barrels of beer.'[88] It is no surprise then that Koniecpolski

---

82 Stanisław Żurkowski, *Żywot Tomasza Zamoyskiego*, pp.117–118.
83 As already mentioned, soldiers were supposed to pay for the food delivered to the army.
84 'Deklaratia wojska wszystkiego J. Królewskiej Mości na kole generalnym przy J. Mści Panu Hetmanie będącym pod Grudziądzem, dnia 16 maja 1628', *Pamiętniki o Koniecpolskich*, p.69.
85 Od Pana Hetmana do Xiędza Kanclerza. Z obozu pod Gniewem, dnia 27 lipca 1628, *Pamiętniki o Koniecpolskich*, p.99.
86 *Zbiór pamiętników do dziejów polskich*, volume IV (Warszawa, 1859), List starosty cehowskiego, Pawła Marchockiego, do podskarbiego wielkiego koronnego Hermolausa z Bobku Ligenzy, p.131.
87 *Ibidem*, p.131.
88 Riksarkivet, Extranea IX Polen, 135, Z listu P. Wojewody Chełmińskiego debata 23 May 1629 o Woyjsku Cesarskim z Arneimem w Prusiech.

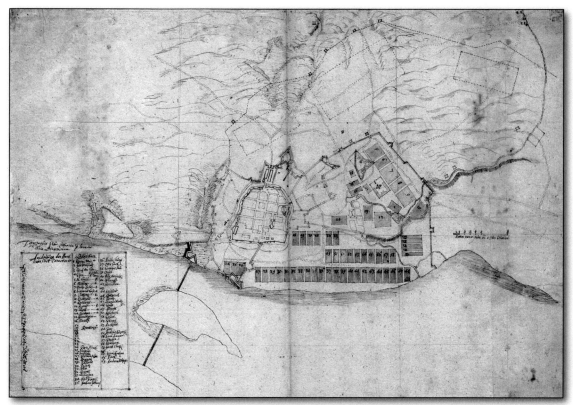

Swedish army in camp near Tczew (Dirschau) in 1628. (Krigsarkivet, Stockholm)

continued despatching his cavalry to Swedish-held territories in order to gather supplies. At the beginning of July that year, Mikołaj Moczarski led 400 cavalry through a ford on the Vistula river and the ravaged areas of Dutch settlers, taking a few hundred cattle.[89] At the end of same month, more than 30 retainers from Mikołaj Łysakowski's cossack banner, led by a local Dutch guide, sneaked behind the Swedish positions and snatched another few hundred cattle from areas around Elbląg, bringing them to the Polish camp.[90]

By that time all three armies, Swedes, Poles and Imperials, were suffering due to shortages of food. As mentioned before, many supplies for Koniecpolski's troops were transported from other areas in Poland through the Vistula. With the main Polish camp far away from the river, it led to 'great hunger in the camp, especially [lacking] bread and oats'.[91] Polish foragers had to travel three to four miles to get supplies; it was even worse for the Imperial allies, who had to travel up to eight miles to Grudziądz. Such difficult conditions led to severe losses, with hunger, sickness and desertions eroding the armies' strength and manpower. It was especially desperate for the Imperials, who were losing hundreds of soldiers. They became so desperate that small groups were leaving their positions, ambushing travellers from Gniew, Grudziądz and Kwidzyn and even supply convoys moving to the

---

89   'Kontynuacja Diariusza', pp.434.
90   *Ibidem*, p.444.
91   *Ibidem*, p.434.

Polish camp, 'taking all the clothes, horses, food and everything else' and 'pretending to be ... Swedish soldiers'.[92] It became such a big issue, that the Poles had to send two banners of cavalry to Grudziądz with the sole mission of escorting supply convoys to and from the main camp. Over a dozen Imperial marauders were captured and hanged for attacking travellers.

Conditions of the Service

Next to the shortage of food, lack of proper quarters and inability to replace lost equipment was always a problem. In a relatively short period of time after the beginning of the war it started to affect the condition of Koniecpolski's troops in Prussia. The Polish army spent a 'very harsh winter in poor shelters'[93] from 1626 to 1627. Already in January 1627 Hetman Koniecpolski wrote to Sigismund that due to bad conditions 'many banners have less than half [of their strength]' and he pointed out the desperate situation of his unpaid foreign infantry that would have no other option than 'to die [from starvation] or flee'.[94] The situation did not improve much during the following years. Royal Prince Władysław, in his letters to Lithuanian Field Hetman Krzysztof II Radziwiłł, complained about the inactivity of Polish army. In February 1627 he wrote that 'here in Prussia it is the same old [situation], little is done at all, our army is getting smaller and [the soldiers] are not eager to fight'.[95] He repeated this sentiment in another letter from September 1627, when he mentioned that in the army camp near Tczew 'there's not much I can write as there are no miracles happening here. While we had quite a lot of troops, they are stationed in the wrong place and have little effect [on the Swedes]'.[96] Many soldiers, especially in the cavalry, decided to leave Prussia – both due to lack of pay and the difficult conditions of the service. In March 1627, during a skirmish at Dzierzgoń (Kiszpork), the Swedes captured Lieutenant Paweł Struś from Mikołaj Łysakowski's cossack banner. In his testimony[97] he mentioned that some companies/banners lost 20, 30 and even 70 men who left the ranks and returned home. Many officers – especially of *rotmistrz* rank – were also not present, as they followed their soldiers in order to gather them and bring them back to Prussia. Bazyli Judycki wrote in March of the same year, that 'many Companions and retinues left the [cavalry] banners, while from amongst the Foreigners many fled or died'.[98]

When on October 1627 the army sent a few officers as envoys to the *Sejm*, many points of their instruction mentioned the extremely difficult conditions of their service, related to lack of pay, food and proper quarters. 'We are sending [envoys] for the third time, humbly begging Your Royal Highness

92 *Ibidem*, p.439.
93 *Kronika Pawła Piaseckiego biskupa przemyślskiego*, p.328.
94 Adam Szelągowski, *O ujście Wisły*, p.83.
95 *Listy Władysława IV do Krzysztofa Radziwiłła*, p.82.
96 *Ibidem*, p.84.
97 Krigsarkivet Stockholm, Gustav Adolfsverket, Bearbetningar, B15–17, Volym 75b, *Fälttåget i Preussen 1626-1627*, *Vinterfälttåget 1626-1627*.
98 AGAD, AR, V, no 6171, Kawaler Judycki do Zygmunta Karola Radziwiłła, 2 III 1627 obóz pod Tczewem, p.3.

Battle of Tczew (Dirschau), 17–18 August 1627. At the bottom we can see the Polish camp. Drawing by Abraham Booth. (Author's archive)

for [all those previous] years, so [finally] this great privation will stop killing more of us then the enemy itself, as we do not have horses, nor equipment, nor servants...'[99] During the winter of 1627/1628 Koniecpolski's army was spread between many different quarters, 'as in the previous year's campaign [1627] all yields were destroyed while still growing, so [the soldiers] lacked grain and forage'.[100] Because of such difficult conditions, the troops were very slow in gathering during spring 1628, not eager to leave their winter billets. One of the Polish Commissioners negotiating with the Swedes in January 1628 mentioned in his letter, that probably there would not be any main actions from the Polish side until June, as the troops did not want to leave quarters 'until grass [appears] in June' and that lack of pay was a very severe issue.[101] Hetman Koniecpolski wrote in his petition to the Polish districts, that the situation of his soldiers was very bad. He mentioned that during winter 1627/1628 the army suffered hardship 'not only [due to] fighting

---

99   AGAD, Teki Naruszewicza, volume 119, no 40, p.168. Instrukcja posłów od wojska w Prusach będącego na sejm Warszawski 1627.

100   *Kronika Pawła Piaseckiego biskupa przemyślskiego*, p.333.

101   AGAD, Teki Naruszewicza, volume 120, no 1, p.3. List jednego z Komisarzów strony traktatów ze Szwedami, 5 Stycz. 1628.

against the Enemy but also due to destitution and [weather] elements'.[102] The desperation of unpaid troops can be clearly seen in their message sent to the *Sejmik* of Poznań and Kalisz Voivodships in May 1628:[103]

> ... you know to what destruction, misery and privations were the soldiers of His Royal Highness brought here ... through the whole time of our service in Prussia our full pay never reached the army, we've unhappily received just pieces of it. So we've lost horses, servants, equipment and all things that are needed for military enterprises ... Those of you that know military ways understand, [how difficult it is] for soldiers to stand worthily on their muster, if they do not have good horses and when some do not even have poor [horses], have to fight on foot, as war does not give birth neither to men and horses, as [the latter] are killed by an enemy and die of starvation. Not to mention the equipment and all soldiers' necessities, that are destroyed during such a difficult wartime [as] without them a soldier is not a soldier, as horse and equipment are what make a good soldier.

There was even talk of mutiny, with soldiers considering *związek wojskowy*, which was a traditional Polish name for an official mutiny of the army due to delayed pay. The personal intervention of Hetman Koniecpolski averted the crisis. Not only did he promise to sort out the issue of outstanding pay but also to discuss increasing it for future campaigns and to organise delivery of supplies from Poland.[104] He praised his officers, especially colonels, who also used their personal charisma (and often their own money) to calm down the soldiers and prevent any attempts of organised mutiny.

Desertion from the Crown army, especially amongst cavalry retainers and infantry, was so high that in summer 1628 the *Sejm* issued a special resolution 'About deserters from the Prussian army'. It stated that if any soldier 'without a confirming letter from a hetman or colonels, *rotmistrz*(s), lieutenants' arrived in a town or burgh, he should be arrested and sent back to the army in Prussia.[105] It is highly unlikely that such captured deserters were punished however, the idea was to rather have them returned to the ranks, to strengthen depleted units. Of course the problem was not just with low-ranking soldiers and servants. On 25 February 1629 Sigismund III issued a special order to high-ranking commanders[106] to return to their units in Prussia.[107]

The English envoy in Prussia, Sir Thomas Roe, described the miserable situation of both armies in September 1629:

102 Biblioteka Kórnicka, BK 341, *Diariusze z lat 1625–1630 oraz korespondencja dyplomatyczna*, pp.309–310v, *Manifestatio Ie Mci Pana Hetmana Polnego Koronnego cu solennni Protestatione podana do Xiąg Grodzkich Warszawkich y inszych w Koronie*.
103 'Legacja dana posłom od skonfederowanego pod Grudziądzem wojska na Sejmik przedsejmowy województw poznańskiego i kaliskiego w Środzie 5 czerwca 1628, z 16 maja 1628 r., Włodzimierz Dworzaczek (ed.), *Akta Sejmikowe województw poznańskiego i kaliskiego*, pp.260–261.
104 *Kronika Pawła Piaseckiego*, p.333.
105 *Volumina Legum*, volume III, p.278.
106 Especially of *rotmistrz* rank.
107 *Akta grodzkie i ziemskie z czasów Rzeczypospolitej Polskiej* (Lwów: Towarzystwo Naukowe, 1884), volume X, p.221.

We treate from one army to another, now lodged in one, now in the other, in the field of Golgotha; the plague so hott in both that I never saw such a mortalitye in Turky, India, not I thinke can be in Cayro, the seat of the plague, for the number. All the countrye is dispeopled; in 80 English mile not a house to sleepe safe in; no inhabitants except a few poore women and children *vertendo stercorarium* to find a corne of wheate. I have begun to have my part, one of my kitchin being stroken dead; the French Ambassador hath lost 3; the King of Swede 60 servants of his bodye and all his cookes, many of his officers. Our new regiment of English [in Swedish service] halfe dead and not able to muster 200. Of all his Ma[jesty Gustav Adolf's] subjects, consisting of at least 13 regiments new and old, they cannot march 1,500; more dye, or as many, of famine as of plague, inseparable companions, bread and water is the best dyet; and I heare nothing but lamentations, nor see varietye but of dead bodyes.[108]

Drummer of the Polish infantry from the beginning of the seventeenth century. 'Stockholm Roll'. (Author's archive)

In one of the next letters he added: 'I am glad to-morrow to go to Danzig, for this town – Elbing – is a furnace of contagion, and I have walked these last days between death rather between armies, lying in the field in such want, danger and nastiness that it will offend any cleanly ear to hear.'[109] Of course illness could also affect units in many different ways. At the end of July 1629, Łukasz Żółkiewski, *rotmistrz* of a hussar banner and de facto commander of Hetman Koniecpolski's cavalry regiment, decided to leave the army camp for a while. According to eyewitness, Żółkiewski was ill himself (although he later recovered) but a few of his servants, two companions and a few retainers from his banner died due to plague. An anonymous report from Prussia, written in August 1629, mentioned that the majority of allied Imperial troops died due to starvation and diseases, also that Polish troops were affected by 'bad air'[110] and suffered a lot because of it. Many officers commanding infantry and dragoons seemed to be affected: newly arrived Colonel Rosen and his lieutenant, Lieutenant Colonel Fittinghoff from Denhoff's regiment, and Master of the Ordnance Bazyli Judycki, were mentioned amongst those ill in September 1629, with the latter dying due to plague.[111] Plague was here called 'camp fever', which was one of the

Piper (*dudziarz*) of the Polish infantry from the beginning of the seventeenth century. 'Stockholm Roll'. (Author's archive)

108 Samuel Rawson Gardiner (ed.), *Letters relating to the mission of Sir Thomas Roe to Gustavus Adolphus 1629–30* (Westminster: Camden Society, 1875), pp.37–38.

109 *Ibidem*, p.39.

110 A common name for any plague during the period.

111 Riksarkivet Stokholm, Extranea IX Polen, 140, 36, Z obozu pod Prabutami, 18 Septembris 1629.

common names for typhus fever.[112] An epidemic of this disease occurred in many war-affected territories, especially during the Thirty Years' War.

Military Discipline

The Polish army had a long history of official disciplinary regulations, normally issued by the king or hetman at the beginning of the campaign. There were many normative acts, usually called 'Articles of War', from both the sixteenth and seventeenth centuries. Often they were tailored to the needs of the campaign, depending on the organisation of the army. Some rules were specific to 'national' troops, especially cavalry, as highlighting the special status of nobles serving there. 'Articles of War' regulated many aspects of military life, from the way that soldiers should behave during the march and in camp, through correct approaches to the local population and other soldiers, to regulations on the presence of woman, merchants and servants in the army. There were also fairly strict rules regarding sentencing officers and nobles to the death penalty, but as we will see in a moment, during the 1626–1629 war Hetman Koniecpolski could easily override them. One of the most serious penalties was so-called *wytrąbienie* (trumpeting out), which was disciplinary discharge from the service.

An important tool of military discipline was the semi-official institution of so-called 'gatherings'.[113] Two main types were 'military gatherings' (*koła wojskowe*) and 'general gatherings' (*koła generalne*). The first could be done on many levels, for example just within one banner or within the whole *pułk* (regiment) of national cavalry. Companions would discuss many different problems, including dealing with minor disciplinary matters, such as resolving quarrels between companions. A 'general gathering' was a major event, where deputies sent by 'military gatherings' from the whole army would discuss with the hetman and his commanders. It was a sort of big rally, when such important topics as overdue pay, problems with lack of equipment and supplies would be talked over. During this meeting major disciplinary events could take place as well: discussions about the death penalty and *wytrąbienie* (trumpeting out) from the army ranks. In late autumn 1626 a 'general gathering' decided to expel from the service more than 30 companions from *lisowczycy* banners, including *rotmistrz* Kalinowski and Ślężyński.[114] Another *wytrąbienie* took place in 1627, when several companions were expelled due to 'different excesses'.[115] A 'gathering' could also deal with the death penalty. When in August 1627 dragoon Captain Andrzej Ratke (Radke) killed another foreign officer, Captain Owen, in a duel, it was a 'gathering' that initially sentenced him to death. Three days later army representatives

---

112 AGAD, Teki Naruszewicza, volume 121, no 92, p.310.
113 The Polish word for them is *koła*, which means circles, as in 'gathering with a circle of equals'. We decided to use the term 'gathering', to represent the essence of the word, as a direct translation would be confusing.
114 'Diariusz albo Summa spraw...', p.16.
115 *Ibidem*, p.37.

managed to convince Hetman Koniecpolski to stop the execution. After the battle of Tczew (Dirschau) the officer was released 'to show his bravery' and he did successfully serve until the end of the war.[116] Another important task of a 'general gathering' was to elect army envoys, who represented soldiers' interests during both the *Sejmiki* and *Sejm*. They were normally presenting captured standards, sometimes also more important prisoners, and delivered before the King and Senate petitions from the army, asking for delivery of delayed pay, royal favours for veteran soldiers, and support. Sometimes a 'gathering' also chose those soldiers who were to discuss important matters with the hetman himself. In May 1628, when the army was on the verge of the mutiny due to lack of pay, each cavalry unit sent their lieutenant and one of the companions to confer with Koniecpolski and to look for any possible solution to this problem.

Discipline in the field often depended on the person of the commanding officer. When in summer 1626 Tomasz Zamoyski led a regiment composed of his own private soldiers and banners raised by few other nobles, he was trying to impose very strict discipline on the troops. His diarist mentioned that during the siege of Gniew, one of Zamoyski's companions was heavily drinking with a woman well after night curfew was announced in the camp. The noble was punished 'with some heavy words', while in an act of extreme uneven treatment, the woman had her nose cut off and was banished from the camp.[117] At the end of 1626, when Hetman Koniecpolski left the army and was visiting Gdańsk, Zamoyski – who was still staying in Prussia – ensured he kept the soldiers on their toes. He tended to take a few servants and every night do a round of the sentries: 'where he found order and alertness, he praised them, where he found wickedness and negligence, he reproved.'[118] Koniecpolski returned after a few days and Zamoyski, due to ill health, received from King Sigismund the right to leave Prussia.

Hetman Koniecpolski on the one hand was known as a supporter of strong discipline, on the other hand he had to be wary to not antagonise his unpaid and often unruly army. He seemed to be well liked by the soldiers though, as during the campaigns he often shared their hardship and if needed he led from the front, as on the first day of the battle of Tczew. The Hetman also always took his soldiers' side during the *Sejm* and in exchanges of correspondence with Sigismund III. There were some situations, though, when the guilty could not avoid his wrath. When on 5 September 1628 French Captain La Montaigne surrendered to the Swedes the strategically vital town of Brodnica (Strasburg), the Hetman decided to make an example of him. In the official relation from the campaign[119] he called him a 'traitor who decided to make accord [with the Swedes] and chose to keep his word [given] to the enemy than to keep [one given] to His Royal Highness'. As the capture of Brodnica was the only Swedish success during the disastrous campaign of 1628, Koniecpolski saw La Montaigne's decision as the worst

---

116 *Ibidem*, pp.31–32.
117 *Żywot Tomasza Zamoyskiego*, p.108.
118 *Ibidem*, p.116.
119 'Relacja IMP. Wojewody Sendomirskiego…', p.426.

kind of treachery, as it happened despite his specific order and when the main Polish field army was in the vicinity of the town. The fate of the French officer was then sealed, 'he did not avoid the executioner's hand'.[120] There was even a rumour, mentioned by Albrycht Stanisław Radziwiłł, that the Swedes bribed the Frenchman. The diarist also confirmed, that 'by the order of the Hetman [La Montaigne] was sentenced to be beheaded and [that way] punished for his treachery'.[121] The captain was the highest-ranking officer of the Polish army sentenced to death during the war however, others were usually soldiers or servants executed due to pillaging. There were also cases of captured spies, who could rarely count on mercy. On 21 October 1626 in the Polish camp 'they sentenced to death one traitor, who was giving away passwords and other secrets to an enemy and a few times sneaked to our camp. He was from Gdańsk and [was] quartered and hanged.'[122]

The Royal Fleet had its own disciplinary regulation, regulated by the Royal Naval Commission. Punishments of course varied and depended on the severity of the crime. Sometimes it could be just a verbal or written warning but we also read about demotion from officer rank, expulsion from the fleet and even the death sentence (although it was rarely used). For example, captain of the Royal Fleet Jan Rost, for an act of naval piracy, was 'attached by the rope to the boat and three times dragged through the water between Grand Krantor[123] and Green Bridge, and then as a dishonoured man to be expelled, without pay and documents, from the Royal Fleet'. His quartermaster Henrich Kuhl, for the same crime, was to be three times thrown from the ship's mast yard but he was to be retained in service.[124] Captain James Murray, after thorough investigation, was discharged for avoiding combat during the battle of Oliwa. Interestingly enough, he retained his rank as a captain of infantry and continued to serve in Koniecpolski's army until the end of the war. A final example comes in April 1628, when a court of commissioners and ships' captains sentenced a few sailors for attempts of mutiny and common brawls. Bosun Lorenz Kröger was to be keelhauled twice and for thee months demoted to cabin boy. Quartermaster Jacob Neuman was to be keelhauled twice and for three months demoted to bosun. Quartermaster Franz Wessel was to be keelhauled once and demoted to bosun. Constable Joachim Lizaw to be thrown from the ship's mast yard once.[125] Naval regulation did not cover any disciplinary breaches committed by the infantry attached to the ship. Such cases had to be handled by the officer in charge of the unit on board.

---

120 *Ibidem*, p.426.
121 Albrycht Stanisław Radziwiłł, *Rys panowania Zygmunta III*, p.123.
122 *Diariusz Wojny Pruskiej*, p.379.
123 (Pol.) *Wielki Żuraw*, a gate in Gdańsk known from a large port crane (known also under German name Krantor).
124 Wiktor Fenrych (ed.), *Akta i Diariusz*, pp.50–51.
125 *Ibidem*, pp.184–189.

Uniforms

Foreign troops in Polish service (infantry, dragoons and reiters) would be wearing clothes similar to Swedish or (especially) Imperial armies of that period, so the reader is referred to other books in Helion's Century of the Soldier series, where those armies are mentioned in more detail.[126] We would like to devote some space to Polish clothing of that time, though,[127] to describe the most typical articles of 'uniform'. When discussing Polish military uniform in the first three decades of the seventeenth century, we need to first of all remember about the (already mentioned) manner of recruiting and organising troops. Cavalry companions had to equip the whole retinue – themselves and their retainers – from their own pocket, so it is not surprising that hussar or cossack banners would not dress in uniform style. Wealthy nobles could of course equip their own soldiers in a similar colour, especially during important events like the election of the *Sejm* but it was not something that would occur in the regular army at that time. The situation was different with the infantry though, both Polish and foreign, as a part of the initial pay for the recruiting officer would be for a *barwa* (colour) which was the word used to describe uniforms. Additionally during the campaign troops could receive new cloth, from which replacement clothes were to be sewn by local tailors or even the soldiers themselves. The army *komput* agreed during the extraordinary *Sejm* of autumn 1626 mentioned that newly planned banners of Polish infantry should receive a delivery of kersey (*karazja*) and English cloth (*falendysz*),[128] also those units already in service since 1626 should receive replacement cloth.[129] In November 1628 the bill for cloth for Polish infantry in Prussia cost 44,289 zl, while at the same time English cloth (in this case probably of the better quality) for officers cost 623 zl and 28 gr.[130] Colours could vary: as early as April 1602, as part of preparation for sending troops to Livonia, blue, red and white kersey was being purchased in Prussia. Again we need to turn to the Lithuanian army, to find some more detailed information regarding how much cloth was assigned for the soldiers. In 1615 a *rotmistrz* in the Polish-Hungarian infantry was to receive eight ells[131] (approximately 4.8 metres) of English cloth. Interestingly enough, the lieutenant in the infantry was due to have 12 ells (approximately 7.2 m) although the English cloth was to be of lower quality. Finally each haiduk should receive eight ells of kersey.[132] In 1612 foreign

---

126 Specifically, Laurence Spring's *In the Emperor's Service*, and Michael Fredholm von Essen's *The Lion from the North*, vol. 1.

127 The description will focus on the most characteristic pieces of clothing used up to the early 1630s, as after that period certain items (like *żupan*) started to change their appearance.

128 The Polish name *falendysz* was the distorted German or Dutch phrase *vijn londisch*, which was used by merchants to describe good quality woollen cloth from England.

129 Riksarkivet Stockholm, Extranea IX Polen, 82, *Comput Woyjska K.J.M. Koronnego*.

130 Biblioteka Kórnicka, BK 341, *Diariusze z lat 1625–1630 oraz korespondencja dyplomatyczna*, p.341v, *Percepta w Toruniu z poborow na seymie warszawskim w roku terazniejszym uchwalonych*.

131 The *łokieć* was an old Polish measurement of 0.59 m.

132 Henryk Wisner, *Rzeczpospolita Wazów*, volume II (Warszawa: Wydawnictwo Neriton Instytut Historii PAN, 2004), p.80.

Left: Mounted drummer from the beginning of the seventeenth century. 'Stockholm Roll'. (Author's archive)
Right: Trumpeters from the beginning of the seventeenth century. 'Stockholm Roll'. (Author's archive)

soldiers in Lithuanian service were to receive seven ells of fustian (*barchan*) each that was to be used for coats, with officers and NCOs to receive the same amount but of the better quality fustian.[133] In 1634 the foreign infantry of Janusz Radziwiłł's regiment were to receive kersey and cheap cloth called *pakłak* to make *casack* coats and trousers. Additionally each soldier should have stockings and a hat.[134] While there was big problem to supply them with uniforms as planned, we have information about deliveries of red and blue kersey, also yellow cloth called *kir*.[135]

Prince Zbaraski in his *Discurs* from 1629 suggested that Polish troops trained in the 'foreign way' should not receive additional financial supplements for clothes, as soldiers should have only 'clothes from simple cloth, like Germans and all [other] foreigners do'. At the same time, though, he suggested that the Hungarian infantry should receive a special additional payment for their own clothing, which was the norm for Polish infantry of that time. During the campaign soldiers would replace worn-out clothes with items that they could purchase or pillage locally, as often we find mentions of both them and their servants taking clothes during their raids. Sadly we lack proper information about the delivery of replacement clothes or even cloth for them during 1626–1629: the cavalry could at least in theory purchase them via merchants from Gdańsk or Toruń, but the infantry would have to rely on the goodwill of their commanders or on their own initiative.

---

133 Urszula Augustyniak, *W służbie hetmana*, p.82.
134 Przemysław Gawron, 'Koszty wystawienia', p.151.
135 *Ibidem*, p.154.

A brief description[136] of the most characteristic parts of Polish dress starts with the *żupan*, the main garment, worn by both cavalrymen and infantrymen. In was in fact the most common piece of clothing used by males in both Poland and Lithuania, used by all social classes, from wealthy magnates to poor peasants. The *żupan* that could be seen in the 1620s amongst soldiers in Prussia would have long sleeves and collar, normally at least to below the knees, and long rows of decorative buttons called *guzy*, which could be made from cheap metal such as brass, or thread-covered, or were much more distinct and expensive. The cavalry often used a shorter version finishing at the knee, known as a *żupanik*. The material that was used for such an important piece of clothing depended on the wealth of the owner. Royalty and wealthy magnates could afford a silk-based *żupan*, made from brocade, damask or satin. These were usually in more bright and expensive colours, for example different shades of red or blue. The majority were made from woollen cloth or silk, with linen, silk or cotton used for the lining, sometimes in combination (i.e. part silk, part wool). Wealthier townspeople, especially merchants, could afford better quality woollen cloth or even silk. Peasants would have to rely on those made from wool or the cheapest cloth. The colour of the *żupan* also varied, depending on the material and requirement (or rather the available funds) of the owner, from bright red and yellow being most expensive, to white (linen) and grey being the cheapest. Generally red was associated with nobility and often used by those serving in the cavalry, although on paintings from the period we can also find hussars or cossacks with *żupan* in different shades of green. In regard to the infantry, blue was the most common colour associated with their *żupan*, mentioned in sources. For example in the army muster in 1581 we have three banners of *wybraniecka* infantry in that colour; Sigismund III's Guard haiduks in 1596 and some banners of Polish infantry fighting in the armies of False Dmitry I and II are also wearing blue *żupan*. Other colours of that piece of 'uniform' used by the infantry would be red, green and white – depending on the *rotmistrz* and the circumstances in which troops would be recruited and clothed.

Over the *żupan* Poles and Lithuanians would normally have another outer garment, known as a *delia*. It could take the form of a longer or shorter cloak, usually with elbow-length unsewn sleeves. Some *delia* would have a fur collar, although others could be without it. It could be made from a variety of materials, from velvet to wool, often lined with fur. As with *żupan*, colour may varied, iconography and primary sources supply us with information about red, yellow (those of course more expensive) and blue (again fairly common with the infantry). There were also more 'specialised' types of cloaks, that could be worn instead of *delia*. The *kopieniak*, which was another piece of Hungarian influence, was a sleeveless cape, normally

---

136 Based on: Maria Gutkowska-Rychlewska, *Historia ubioru* (Wrocław-Warszawa-Kraków, 1968), pp.402–406; Zofia Stefańska, 'Polskie ubiory wojskowe z XVI i XVII wieku', *Muzealnictwo wojskowe*, pp.295–315; Władysław Czapliński, Józef Długosz, *Życie codzienne magnaterii polskiej w XVII wieku* (Warszawa: Państwowy Instytut Wydawniczy, 1976), pp.106–107; Michał Paradowski, *'Barwa' piechoty polskiej w XVI–XVII wieku. Wypisy źródłowe* (available on Academia.edu). The author would like to thank Rafał Szwelicki for additional comments for this part of the text.

made from cheap wool, which could be worn when travelling as it served as a 'raincoat'. *Szuba* and *szubka* were names used for different types of fur coats used during the winter.

Trousers, usually fairly tight, were made from cloth. As with other items of clothing, they could also be in different colours. Iconographical sources bring us a variety of red, violet, blue, green and black. Shoes would be normally made from leather but yet again both materials and colours depended on the wealth of the owner. Yellow or red ones, made from Saffian (Moroccan) leather were the most popular with nobles, so we often see it with officers and companions in the hussar and cossack cavalry. Their length could vary, some were just above the ankle while others could reach the knee. The majority of soldiers would have to rely on much cheaper shoes though, usually made from black or brown leather. Still popular, especially with the infantry, were short shoes without laces, often black or brown but, especially with private troops, we can sometimes find haiduks in yellow ones as well. Most shoes were made from calf and goat leather.

Headgear was a very important piece of clothing and it came in a large variety of shapes and types. Very common were different types with fur trim folded over, making it distinctly visible, and they could have fur or cloth within. The reign of Stephen Bathory brought popularity for the Hungarian *magierka* hat, which became part of the national dress and is often seen worn by Polish infantrymen. Caps and hats were very often adorned with feathers. Most common were those from herons, cranes and birds of prey such as eagles or falcons. More exotic and expensive were the feathers of ostriches and parrots.

Standards

Each cavalry and infantry banner/company had a flag/standard, which was the most important symbol of a unit's identity. Some larger independent units, such as Polish infantry banners or foreign free companies (numbering 400 men or more) could in fact have two or even more flags, for each of the sub-units.

The most common pattern was square, usually unfringed. Hussars, also possibly certain cossack banners, usually had a flag with tails or a tongue-shaped fly. Cossack cavalry could sometimes have a flag with a semicircular end but their standards were normally a smaller square one, sometimes ending with tails. Some surviving examples are also shaped as a triangle. Dragoons had smaller square cornets, often very similar to those of cossacks. Infantry ones were the biggest, the majority were shaped as a large rectangle.

Hussars would have the largest flags amongst all the cavalry, those that have survived to our time in Swedish collections have dimensions of 120 × 300 cm, 150 × 300 cm, 200 × 300 cm. Cossacks and dragoons: 100 × 110 cm, 110 × 170 cm, 125 × 115 cm, 150 × 240 cm, 112 × 137 cm, 170 × 230 cm. 35 × 112 cm, 100 × 110 cm, 120 × 160 cm, 77 × 125 cm, 55 × 55 cm (dragoons), 60 × 60 cm (dragoons), 150 × 80 cm (dragoons). Examples of infantry flags clearly show how the size of their standard varied from unit to unit: 345 × 275 cm, 690 × 400 cm, 320 × 255 cm, 155 × 150 cm, 320 × 159 cm, 205 × 180 cm.

As for the details on the flags, both 'national' and religious motifs were the most common. When in summer 1626 Sigismund III was due to leave Warsaw and lead the army to Prussia, he asked Archbishop of Gniezno, Wawrzyniec Gembicki, to bless the Royal banner 'where under the Cross it was written with golden letters *Mecum et pro te*.'[137] The Knight's Cross, usually red on a white background or white on red (or other) background was often used in the cavalry. A white Eagle was present on banners of all formations. The Madonna with the Infant Jesus could be used for cavalry banners, especially hussars. The Burgundian Cross/St. Andrew's Cross, usually red or white, was present on many infantry flags. References to mythology (for example, Fortuna), saints (St George defeating the dragon) or even to known enemies (the head of a Turk) were also sometimes present. Coats of arms of the nobles leading the units were most likely the commonest motifs in privately raised troops but could also be present with flags in the standing army. Such symbols were often accompanied by a wreath, usually green, red or black. Throughout the whole seventeenth century it was very common in the infantry to see the usage of horizontal lines in alternate colours, usually three, sometimes mixed with additional emblems (for example the Madonna or Burgundian Cross). Three standards of cossack cavalry captured by the Swedes at Dzierzgoń (Kiszpork) in 1627 were described as yellow-red (*rotmistrz* Annibal's banner), white with a black wreath (*rotmistrz* Łysakowski's banner) and black-red with the head of a Turk (*rotmistrz* Boki's banner).

The standard was an important part of the unit's identity and, especially in Polish cavalry banners, was treated as a point of identification and for the gathering of troops. Losing a flag in battle was always a severe blow, but even worse was when such a loss happened outside of the battlefield. In winter 1626, when Tomasz Zamoyski was acting as temporary commander of the army, checking camp guards during the night, he encountered a rather unusual sight. Soldiers of Samuel Łaszcz's cossack banners, feeling very secure within the camp's perimeter, 'all companions and retainers dismounted, stuck their flag in the ground and were [all] sleeping'. He quietly walked amongst the troops, took away their standard and sent it with one of the servants to his own tent. Then he ordered the camp guards to keep silent about his nightly ventures and returned to his quarter. Soon after, officers of Łaszcz's banner arrived at Zamoyski's tent, where he pretended to have just woken up and asked them about news. They reported the loss of the flag, so Zamoyski mentioned that he would announce it during the day in front of the whole army, asking if anyone had seen it. Of course the officers were mortified, 'falling to their knees, tearfully begging to save them from such shame, disgrace and infamy amongst the troops'. Believing the lesson had been learnt, Zamoyski ordered their flag returned, admonishing them and advising them to improve in their service.[138]

137 (Latin) With me and for you. Albrycht Stanisław Radziwiłł, *Rys panowania Zygmunta III*, p.118.
138 *Żywot Tomasza Zamoyskiego*, pp.116–117.

Albrycht Stanisław Radziwiłł provides a slightly different version of this story. He pointed out that Łaszcz's banner belonged to the 'quarter army' whose soldiers looked down on royal troops fighting in Prussia since summer 1626, mockingly claiming that 'they did not do anything glorious so far [and] at the same time praising their own actions, vigilance and boasting that they will certainly banish Gustav [Adolf from Prussia]'. Tomasz Zamoyski was trying to find some way to show newly arrived soldiers their place, and Łaszcz's sleeping standard-bearer gave him the perfect opportunity. The 'captured' flag was then put into … a pie and served to the *rotmistrz* during a banquet for the officers. Zamoyski was to say that 'such a thing never happened to our soldiers, so [the newly arrived] should not despise us here and stop being so proud'.[139] It was definitely a good lesson in humility, at the same time showing how the unit's flag was important for the morale of the soldiers.

It could be interesting to at least attempt to estimate both flag losses and trophies of the Polish army during the war. At the battle of Gniew Sigismund III's army lost two or rather (partially) three hussar standards. Based on a few period sources we can identify them as belonging to the banners of Mikołaj Wejher and Jan Działyński, with a partial standard belonging to Paweł Niewiaromski's unit. The fighting at Dzierzgoń (Kiszpork) in 1627 brought the Swedes a haul of three cossack cavalry flags, from the banners of Mikołaj Annibal Strocy, Jan Boki and Mikołaj Łysakowski. It is also probable that at least one of the haiduk units lost their banner there, but we lack detailed information. The skirmish at Długie Pole (Langfelde) in the same year ended with the Poles losing four banners (according to the Swedes) but the Poles admitted to losing three, all from the cossack units of Samuel Łaszcz, Jerzy Kruszyński and Gabriel Kuliczkowski. The run of bad luck in that year continued, when foreign infantry surrendering to the Swedes at Kiezmark (Käsemark) lost between two to four flags. Some small consolation is that one of them survived to our time and we can still admire it in the collection of the Armémuseum in Stockholm. Finally, during the battle of Tczew (Dirschau), the Polish army lost two further hussar flags, from the units of Royal Prince Władysław and Jan Potocki. According to Chancellor Axel Oxenstierna, the Poles also lost one cossack flag, although it is not confirmed by Polish sources.

In 1628, probably due to the focus on 'small war', losses were very low and based only on a Swedish source. According to that source, during the skirmish near Rypin that took place at night from 28 to 29 September, reiters managed to capture a 'beautiful flag'. We know that a group of cossack cavalry banners, led by *rotmistrz* Stanisław Suliszowski, did indeed clash with Swedes there. Suliszowski died leading the charge but his force managed to force the Swedish reiters to retreat. Polish sources do not confirm if any flag was lost during the fight.

Finally in 1629, during the defeat at Górzno, the Hetman's own hussar banner lost its flag. Interestingly enough, a few months later it was recovered during the battle of Trzciana – more detail below. There is one Polish source

---

139 Albrycht Stanisław Radziwiłł, *Rys panowania Zygmunta III*, p.122.

that also mentions that the flag of Royal Prince Władysław's hussars was lost during this battle, but there are some doubts regarding the veracity of this relation, so it could be that its author confused the loss of this standard during the battle of Tczew. Considering that a few hundred German and Polish infantry were captured by the Swedes at Górzno, it is highly probable that they lost some flags as well. Unfortunately none of the sources that we have access to provide any information in that matter.

After all those losses, it is time to have a look into trophies taken by the Polish army during the war. There are three confirmed occasions when Koniecpolski's troops captured such valued spoils of war. The largest came into Polish possession during the capitulation of the Swedish force at Czarne (Hammerstein) on 15 April 1627. A detailed relation of the triumph mentions 13 infantry standards and 13 reiter cornets. As the source may be of interest for many readers, a translation is provided in Appendix IX.

On 23 October 1628 near Ostróda (Osterode) the cavalry regiment of Colonel Wulf Henrik von Baudissin, newly arrived to the Swedish army, was ambushed by Polish cavalry and infantry. Despite the fact that the unit was composed of veterans of the recently disbanded Danish army, they were not ready for Polish tactics and took heavy losses, with the colonel, 50 soldiers and three cornets captured.

Trzciana (Honigfelde) on 27 June 1627 brought a high number of trophies. When writing to Sigismund the day after the battle, Koniecpolski mentioned that his troops captured 10 Swedish cornets. Von Arnim, writing after the battle, mentioned 11 cornets. The difference can be easily explained by the (already mentioned) fact, that the Poles managed to recover Hetman Koniecpolski's hussar flag, captured by the Swedes at Górzno. It was attached to the lance of the standard bearer of Colonel Hans Wrangel's company, that was captured after its colonel's death. Writing two days after the battle, Koniecpolski mentioned an additional five cornets that were recovered during a search of the battlefield. So in total the Polish and Imperial troops managed to capture 15 of them.

Exchange of Prisoners

The length of the conflict, with long periods of inactivity or limited small-scale actions, had to lead to situations when both sides were engaged in prolonged negotiations and talks. A very important part of such discussions was always the issue of exchange and ransom for prisoners. We have detailed information regarding such activities in February and March 1628, when Field Marshal Herman Wrangel was dealing with the Royal Naval Commission.[140] Letters were being delivered every few days between the Swedish headquarters in Malbork (Marienburg) and the Commission's headquarters in Gdańsk. Wrangel mentioned that previously he had already exchanged prisoners with Lieutenant Colonel Gerhard Denhoff, therefore

---

140 Wiktor Fenrych (ed.), *Akta i Diariusz*, pp.139–150.

he would prefer it if the Poles could ransom their remaining soldiers. He changed his mind, though, when the Commission agreed to send him back the body of Admiral Nils Göransson Stiernsköld, killed during the battle of Oliwa. After arranging details and giving mutual assurances of safety, on 28 February 1628, near Sobieszów, representatives of the Polish and Swedish army met to exchange prisoners of war. The Polish envoys were Lieutenant Colonel Gerhard Denhoff, Major Arthur Aston and fleet captain Adolph von Arzen. Twelve Swedish infantrymen were returned to their army, while the Poles brought home with them 12 soldiers from Aston's company. At that point they still had another 60 Swedish prisoners that they were very eager to exchange, as the cost of their keep was far too high for the already strained Polish resources. The Swedish side also wanted to get rid of captured Poles, one of the letters from Wrangel mentioned that they had been kept in prison for a year now. At the beginning of May 1628 the Commission advised the Swedes that there were still Swedish soldiers in Polish captivity, then provided a list with the names of 27 soldiers and 18 sailors. All the named men seem to be native Swedes and Finns, which could explain why, unlike their German colleagues, they did not switch sides and join the Polish army or Royal Fleet.[141] The main problem with all negotiations was the ratio in which soldiers could be exchanged. Whilst a minor problem when dealing with infantry, as they were swapped 1:1, it was much more difficult with cavalrymen. The Swedes were reluctant to exchange Polish nobles serving as companions for their own captured reiters in a 1:1 ratio, thinking it unfair. It appears that Sigismund III agreed with Hetman Koniecpolski the conditions upon which the soldiers should be released from Polish captivity, though unfortunately letters with detailed information about this arrangement have not survived to our time.

It is interesting to note that meetings leading to discussions and exchanges could also happen in rather unusual circumstances. On 22 July 1629, Polish and Swedish cavalrymen after a short skirmish decided to meet for a round of negotiations. Both sides 'asked to lay down muskets and [other] weapons, so they can speak freely'. As Polish musketeers were positioned nearby, the Swedes asked for them to be moved away, while at the same time sending back their own infantry support. Once that was done, the cavalrymen from both armies sat down and talked about a possible prisoner exchange. The Swedes also passed the message that Field Marshal Herman Wrangel wanted to meet in person with *rotmistrz* Hermolus Aleksander Przyłęcki, as it appeared that the Swedes held Przyłęcki's brother in their captivity. The end of the meeting really highlighted how bizarre the whole Polish–Swedish conflict sometimes was: 'At the end the Swedes brought a bottle of vodka from Malborg and shared it with us. After having a drink and [being] merry for a while, [both sides] again mounted their horses and shot at each other at skirmish for almost the whole day.'[142]

A prisoner swap was not only limited to live soldiers. On certain occasions dead ones (especially officers) were exchanged or even returned

---

141 Wiktor Fenrych (ed.), *Akta i Diariusz*, pp.225.
142 'Kontynuacja Diariusza', p.440.

with military honours to their own army. In mid January 1628 *rotmistrz* Andrzej Śladkowski's cossack banner clashed with a Swedish picket between Elbląg (Elbing) and Brodnica (Strasburg). The Polish unit was completely broken and scattered. One of the companions, named Słuzieński, died during the fight and his body was abandoned when the rest of the unit fled before the Swedish reiters. Soon afterwards the Poles sent a letter to Elbląg, asking 'what is happened to the body, is it captured [by Swedes], or buried or still laying there [on the battlefield]', hoping for some explanation and recovery of the body.[143] As mentioned before, on 1 March 1628 Polish captains von Arzen and Gerhard Friedrichson led a delegation that brought to the Swedes the body of Admiral Nils Göransson Stiernsköld. During the meeting both sides shared their willingness for a future exchange of deserters switching sides. The Swedish officers even presented the Poles with a list of 43 soldiers that had gone AWOL from Johan Banér's infantry regiment.[144] A year later, the day after the battle of Trzciana, Gustav II Adolf sent trumpeter to von Arnim, asking for permission to bury numerous Swedish dead and to start talks about paying ransoms for prisoners. At that point the Imperials had at least 200 captured Swedish reiters, with Polish troops capturing even more. Gustav's envoy was also probably trying to enquire about the fate of some of the officers, not knowing if they were killed in the battle or captured.[145]

---

143 Israel Hoppe, *Geschichte des ersten*, pp.254–255.
144 Wiktor Fenrych (ed.), *Akta i Diariusz*, pp.149–150.
145 'Relacja bitwy trzciańskiej posłana od P. Hetmana', p.431.

Chapter 5

Combat Experience: Battles, Skirmishes and Sieges

It is important to realise that Polish–Swedish battles in Prussia were fairly small encounters, especially when we compare them to battles from the Thirty Years' War. At Gniew (Mewe) in 1626 Polish army had initially approximately 11,000 men, in the later stages approximately 15,000 men – but only 6,000–7,000 saw fighting at any point. The Swedes in the same battle had initially approximately 8,000 men, later just above 10,000, but also here the element that took part in the fight was fairly small, with no more than 3,000 men at any given time. The Swedish force marching from Mecklenburg and captured by the Poles at Czarne (Hammerstein) in 1627 was 2,500 men strong, with the Polish forces fighting against it numbering, 3,000–4,000 men. In the same year at Tczew (Dirschau) Koniecpolski's army had probably at least 4,000–5,000 soldiers, while Gustav Adolf had 11,000–12,000 soldiers but he only used half of this force in the first day of the battle. In 1629 at Górzno the Polish army was again between 4,000 and 5,000 men strong, while the Swedes had 6,000 men. Finally during the battle at Trzciana (Honigfelde) Koniecpolski deployed 2,000–2,500 Poles, supported by 2,000 Imperials led by von Arnim. The Swedes had 5,400 cavalry and 1,400 infantry, but while the majority of their cavalry did take part in the fight, only 50 musketeers had a chance (and the bad luck) to engage allied forces as well.

Each of those battles was also a rather unique type of encounter. Gniew (Mewe) in 1626 was in fact three small-scale battles that took place on 22 September, 29 September and 1 October, with both sides taking some losses but at the same time unable to decisively defeat their opponents. Czarne (Hammerstein) in 1627 saw a Swedish force raised in Mecklenburg marching through Pomerania and Prussia, harassed by Polish cavalry and finally surrounded and forced by the main Polish army – led by Hetman Koniecpolski – to surrender on 17 April 1627.

The battle of Tczew (Dirschau) in same year was a two-day encounter, with a very distinct battle scenario each day. On 17 August after some initial skirmishing a strong group of Polish cavalry spent the whole day in front of the Swedish field fortifications, trying to lure the Swedes into pitched battle that they were not eager to start on Polish terms. Only once Koniecpolski decided to return with

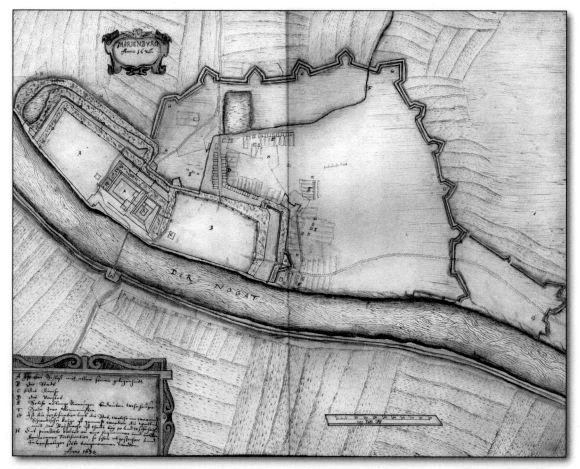

City plan of Malbork
(Marienburg) in 1626,
drawn by Heinrich Thome.
(Krigsarkivet, Stockholm)

his soldiers to his camp did the Swedes finally move into action, attacking the Polish rearguard when it was moving through dikes on the Motława (Mottlau) river on its way back to the main positions of the Polish army. In the ensuing cavalry battle, despite some initial successes, the outnumbered Poles were hard pressed, with Koniecpolski himself losing his horse and in danger of being captured. Luckily for the Polish side, at the crucial moment of the fight foreign infantry and dragoons protecting the village of Rokitki (Rokittken) provided cavalry with much needed fire support and brought some relief. Both sides, tired after the brief (approximately two hours) but fierce encounter, retreated to their camps. The second day of the battle, on 18 August, took a completely different turn. After a long and rather uneventful artillery fire exchange the Swedish troops managed to dislodge the Polish troops from Rokitki, but the fight continued on a few sconces still manned by Koniecpolski's soldiers. When the Swedish infantry was preparing for an assault against the Polish camp, Gustav II Adolf was suddenly heavily wounded by shots made from haiduks or foreign infantrymen in the Polish army (the source varies, so it is not certain who was in fact the author of the lucky shot). What is certain though, is that it was Polish captain Samuel Nadolski who identified the King as a target and pointed him out to his soldiers. Soon after that, the Swedes decided to cease further operations and returned to their camp.

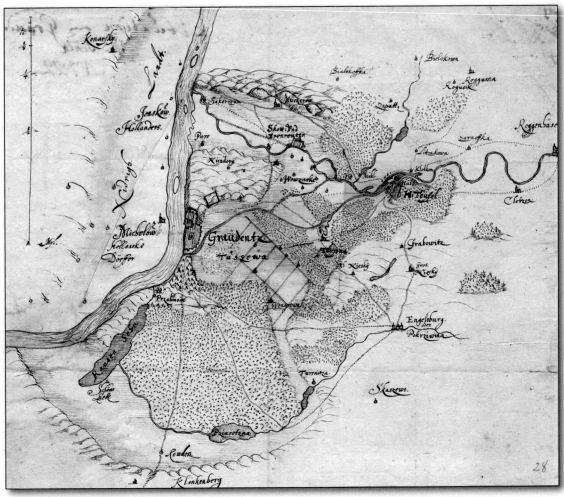

Area of Polish and Swedish operation around Grudziądz (Graudenz) in August–September 1628 (Krigsarkivet, Stockholm)

The campaign of 1628 did not see any larger battles (at least on the scale of the Prussian War), the actions instead focused on 'small war' and sieges. The 1629 campaign brought two bigger encounters, though. On 12 February 1629 the Polish field army, that since previous autumn had blockaded Swedish-held Brodnica (Strasburg in Westpreussen), was badly beaten at Górzno by a Swedish relief force. Interestingly enough, both armies lacked their nominal commanders in chief. Gustav Adolf was still in Sweden, while Hetman Koniecpolski was in Warsaw, taking part in the *Sejm*. Field Marshal Herman Wrangel did a much better job than his opponent, Colonel Stanisław Rewera Potocki, showing much better initiative and causing heavy losses to the Polish troops. The Swedes relieved Brodnica and even attempted an assault on Toruń (Thorn) but were forced to retreat, harassed by Polish cavalry.

Finally on 27 June 1629 an allied Polish–Imperial army defeated Gustav Adolf's army at Trzciana (Honigfelde). It was again mostly a cavalry encounter, where Koniecpolski practically had to force von Arnim to accompany the Polish hussars and cossacks with his cuirassiers and harquebusiers. As the Swedes were too late to beat the Imperials before they

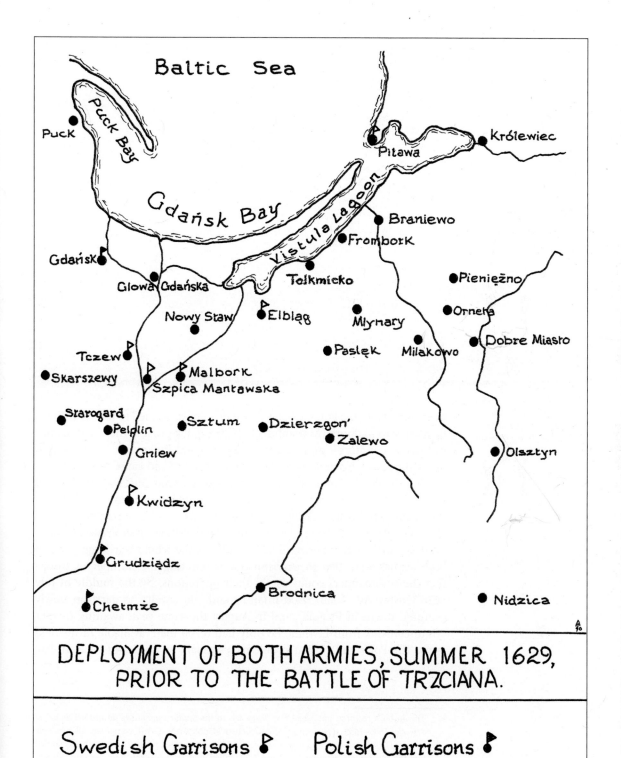

DEPLOYMENT OF BOTH ARMIES, SUMMER 1629, PRIOR TO THE BATTLE OF TRZCIANA.

Swedish Garrisons ⚑   Polish Garrisons ⚑

Source: Janusz Staszewski, *Bitwa pod Trzcianą*.

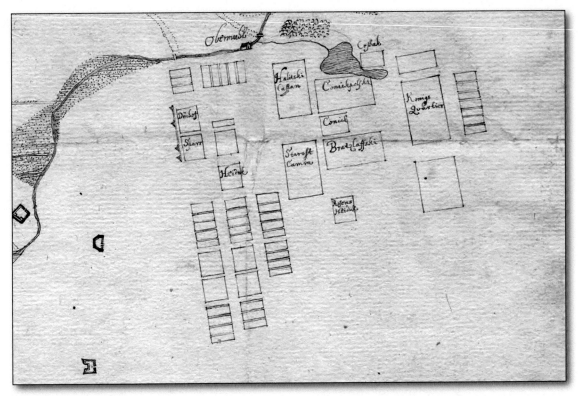

The Polish army camp facing the Swedes near Malbork (Marienburg) in July–August 1629. (Krigsarkivet, Stockholm)

managed to join the Poles, Gustav Adolf prudently decided to retreat with his field army to Malbork (Marienburg). After a quick pursuit, the allied cavalry in three encounters – at Trzciana, Straszewo and Pułkowice – managed to break the rearguard actions of the Swedish cavalry and cause it some heavy losses.[1] There were times during the battle when even Gustav Adolf himself was lucky to avoid being taking prisoner. Despite losses he managed to save the majority of his field army – especially the whole of his infantry – so this allied victory did not have a lasting effect on the situation in Prussia.

It is worth remembering that throughout the whole war large parts of both armies were tied to garrison duties, limiting the number of troops that the commanders could use in their operations. By the middle of July 1626 Gustav Adolf left 5,000 infantry and 300 cavalry to garrison newly captured towns in Prussia,[2] and in August the same year, awaiting further reinforcements from Livonia, he only had 6,700 men[3] available in his field army. The Poles had similar problems, especially in 1627 and 1628. In late

---

1   The author's research published few years ago in his *Studia i materiały do historii wojen ze Szwecją 1600–1635* (Oświęcim: Wydawnictwo Napoleon V, 2013) compared all available sources (Polish, Swedish and Imperial) regarding this topic. Beforehand many authors claimed that the Swedes lost between 1,000 and 1,500 killed soldiers, while this new research brought lower but more accurate and source-based figures, with an estimate of 500–700 killed and at least 200–300 prisoners of war.

2   *Polska kriget*, pp.263–279.

3   *Ibidem*, p.279.

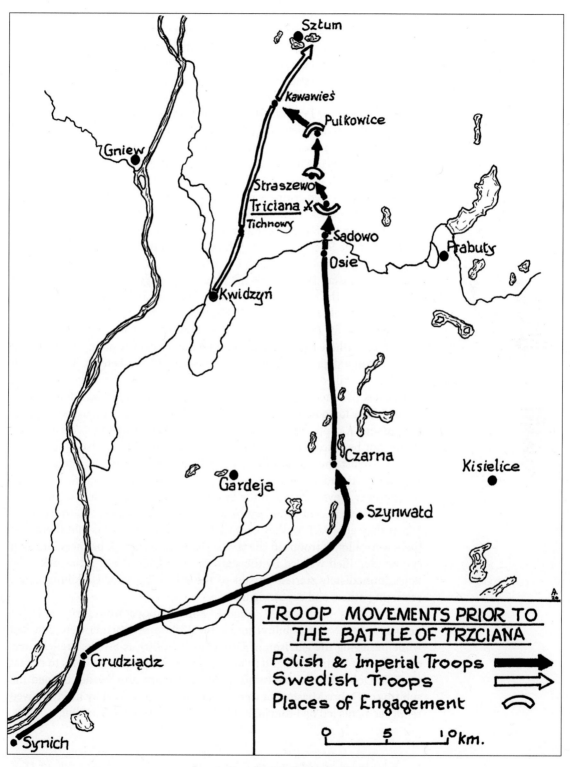

Source: Janusz Staszewski, *Bitwa pod Trzcianą*.

1627 more than 4,000 infantry and almost 1,500 cavalry[4] were deployed as garrisons, which significantly reduced the number of infantry available for Koniecpolski to use in any pitched engagement against the Swedes.

It is not surprising though, that 'small war', with all its skirmishing, foraging actions and cavalry raids, became practically the major part of the conflict. Some interesting examples of the 'small war' from the first year of the conflict, prior to and after the battle of Gniew (Mewe), can be found in the Polish *Diary of Prussian War against Gustav…*[5] The anonymous author was well informed, which indicates that he could possibly be one of the royal courtiers. We can look at some actions and skirmishes, as seen from the Polish perspective, as it gives an interesting view of how that type of warfare was conducted in Prussia.

On 9 August two banners of cossack cavalry of the starost of Malbork (Marienburg) under command of Dębiński set up an ambush in the forest two miles from the Swedish camp near Tczew (Dirschau). Then they captured a servant of the Swedish captain, who told them that soon his master would be travelling to Sobowidz (Sobit, Sobbowitz), as he received this village from King Gustav II Adolf for his bravery during the capture of Malbork (Marienburg). The prisoner also revealed that Gustav II Adolf himself, with a bodyguard of only 100 reiters, would be travelling this road soon. The cossack cavalry waited for four days but no one showed up. After that they marched to Sobowidz where they had encountered the previously mentioned Swedish captain with a detachment of eight reiters and 30 musketeers. The Swedish infantry was killed, an officer and horsemen captured. The Swedes sent six companies of reiters from their camp to chase the Poles, but the cossacks divided their force in two and after a few miles of running managed to evade the pursuit. A captured Swedish captain told them, that the Swedish reiters would not be able to catch them, as they did not ride as fast as the Poles. On 23 August the cossacks arrived with prisoners into the camp, where Sigismund III had 'polite conversation with the Swedish captain'.

The next move belongs to the Swedes, as on 24 August a few cornets of their reiters were sent to pillage Nowe Miasto (Neumark in Westpreussen). When they approach it, they captured a Polish soldier who told them that there were a lot of troops in the town. There were cossack banners, one that can be identified was led by the starosta of Bratian, Paweł Działyński. The Poles immediately started pursuit of the retreating Swedes, 'killing many, scattering others and capturing three'.

Three days later, on 27 August, Polish troops from Prussia (most probably the levy of nobility) under the Bishop of Warmia were attacked while besieging the garrison of Orneta (Wormditt). A Swedish relief force, composed of both reiters and infantry, managed to force the Poles to retreat towards Dobre Miasto (Guttstadt). Hot in pursuit, the Swedes burned the suburbs of Dobre Miasto, but were in turn forced to retreat by newly arrived reinforcements led by Lithuanian reiter *rotmistrz* Henryk Szmeling.

---

4   Biblioteka Uniwersytecka Wrocław, *Polonica varia*, volume 2, p.226, *Presidia wojskiem J.K.M. opatrzone w Pucku.* See Appendix IV.

5   *Diariusz…*, pp.354–379.

City plan of Elbląg (Elbing) 1626–1629. (Krigsarkivet, Stockholm)

Fights around Nowe Miasto broke out again on 28 August. A few Swedish cornets and a few companies of foot moved next to the town. The majority of this force lay in ambush, while two or three cornets tried to lure the Poles into it. The Polish garrison of Nowe Miasto is described as a few banners of cavalry[6] led by the starosta of Bratian, Paweł Działyński and German infantry under Gerhard Denhoff and Balthasar Rosenstein, so probably a few hundred cavalry and approximately 300 musketeers. A few Polish banners engaged the Swedish cavalry, then the reiters feigned retreat and lured the Poles into an ambush. The cossacks were able to fight with the Swedes for more than an hour, until reinforcements from the town arrived. The Swedes then quit the field, leaving some dead reiters and one prisoner. It seems that their retreat was well organised, as they managed to take their wounded with them. Polish losses are mentioned only from Działyński's banner – one companion and four retainers killed – but it is more than probable that other

---

6   Probably cossacks.

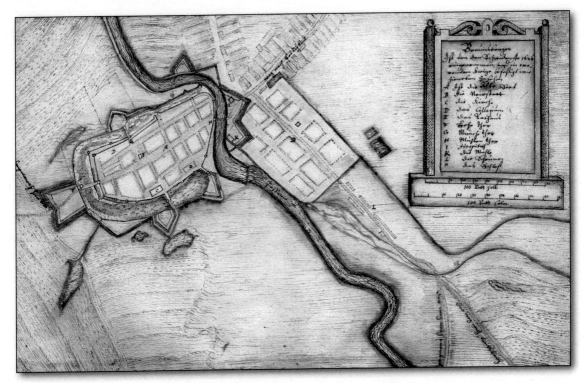

City plan of Braniewo (Braunsberg) in 1626, drawn by Heinrich Thome. (Krigsarkivet, Stockholm)

units also had some dead and wounded. Additionally many horses were shot (killed and wounded).

On 9 September *rotmistrz* Mikołaj Moczarski returned with two banners of his *lisowczycy* from the raid near Swedish camp. He reported a heavy skirmish with the Swedes 'a few days earlier'. According to Moczarski his troops destroyed almost completely two cornets of Swedish cavalry. The Swedish prisoners killed in this skirmish were taken to camp 'on a few wagons'. He brought few prisoners.

Further actions took place in October, after the battle of Gniew. On 8 October *rotmistrz* Falencki, who with his cossack banner was stationed near Puck (Putzig), sent to the Polish camp 11 prisoners captured in the area. One of them was a Polish deserter, who had earlier fled to Swedes. He was put on trial and beheaded as a traitor. The next day another *rotmistrz* of *lisowczycy*, Idzi Kalinowski, brought four Swedish prisoners. On 10 October a few Swedish cornets and a few hundred infantry were sent from Tczew to capture food and forage. They were surprised and defeated by the Poles, losing all the supplies and more than 30 men. Three days later some cossack cavalry captured three Swedes near Gniew. On 20 October Idzi Kalinowski and his cavalry attacked a group of Swedish infantry gathering cabbage in a garden next to a Swedish camp. The Poles killed all their enemies except three, who were taken prisoner. They reported that the Swedish soldiers were starving.

The Swedes were learning quickly though, so no surprise, then, that soon the Poles were to receive a harsh and painful lesson in the conduct of 'small war'. A good example of it is the fight at Dzierzgoń (also known as Kiszpork, Polish version of German name Christburg), that took place on 26 March

1626. Soon after the arrival of the 'quarter army' in Prussia in November 1626, Hetman Stanisław Koniecpolski sent a strong force to the Prince-Bishopric of Warmia to ensure that the 'enemy was not able to rest'.[7] This 'division' was composed of three cavalry regiments: Marcin Kazanowski's,[8] Mikołaj Kossakowski's and Stanisław Potocki's, supported by some infantry. In total there were eight hussar banners, 10 cossack banners, one reiter company, one dragoon company and at least four banners of Polish-Hungarian and *wybraniecka* infantry. The Poles recaptured Orneta (Wormditt) and Pieniężno (Meelsack), then took winter quarters in Warmia, staying there until spring 1627 and protecting it from Swedish raids. In March 1627, facing Swedish reinforcements approaching from Mecklenburg and with a large part of his force tied up besieging Puck, Hetman Koniecpolski requested Kazanowski to send back part of his force from Warmia. However, Colonel Kossakowski with a few banners of cavalry and infantry had many problems in his march, due to difficult weather (thaw and flood from Vistula river), his troops, accompanied by tabor wagon, being stuck on a poor road. On 24 or 25 March he finally arrived in Dzierzgoń, where he decided to give the soldiers some rest. On the morning of 26 March the Poles were surprised by a Swedish raiding force sent from Malbork, led by Colonel Franz Bernhard von Thurn. Israel Hoppe[9] estimated the Polish contingent as two banners of hussars (Kossakowski and Szkliński), four banners of cossacks (Łysakowski, Annibal, Boki and Struś) and some haiduks. After a short encounter the Poles were to lose half of their soldiers killed and captured. According to the same source, the Swedes captured a large tabor wagon, many horses, one cavalry and one haiduk flag. Thurn's force allegedly lost 50 reiters, 15 dragoons and 14 musketeers, which would indicate that it was not just cavalry but rather more combined troops that he led against the Poles.

More detailed information about the composition of the cavalry of the Polish force can be found in the testimony of Lieutenant Paweł Struś, who became the personal prisoner of von Thurn in Elbląg.[10] It allows correction of Hoppe's version, as Kossakowski was in fact in charge of his own and Szkliński's hussar banners, four banners of cossacks: Rogulski, Annibal, Boki and Łysakowski (Struś was his lieutenant). It is probable that Miękiński's Polish-Hungarian banner was present as well. As this unit did not figure in the Polish army in the 1628 muster, it is possible that it took such heavy losses at Dzierzgoń that it had to be disbanded.

The official report about the situation in Prussia, sent to Sigismund III at the beginning of April 1627, provides the Polish point of view on the event.[11] Colonel Mikołaj Kossakowski led a group of cavalry near Malbork and then set up camp in nearby Dzierzgoń. The Poles felt very secure and did not set

---

7   *Diariusz albo summa*, p.14.
8   He was in overall command.
9   Israel Hoppe, *Geschichte des ersten*, pp.164–165.
10 Krigsarkivet Stockholm, Gustav Adolfsverket, Bearbetningar, B15–17, Volym 75b, *Fälttåget i Preussen 1626–1627, Vinterfälttåget 1626–1627*; AGAD, Teki Naruszewicza 118, document 147, pp.679–680, Nowy z Gdańska.
11 AGAD, Teki Naruszewicza, volume 118, no 140, pp.642–643, Doniesienie Królowi Jmci o Szwedach.

up many guards, the cavalry unsaddled their horses, the soldiers laid down their weapons and equipment. One day (there is no exact date in the text) between noon and 1:00 p.m., two cornets of the Swedish cavalry charged into town and encountered 90 haiduks camping near the gate. The haiduks fired at the Swedes, killing the captain, ensign and a few reiters – this detailed list of losses sounds rather odd, considering that the Polish side was defeated and scattered soon after. The relation at that point gives an exaggerated number of attackers, 'from one gate came 3,000, from other 9,000 Swedes', although it mentions that those figures are based on information received from the mayor of Kiszpork. The Poles chose to fight a smaller group of Swedish soldiers to break through, and allegedly killed up to 300 Swedes while doing so. Polish losses are depicted as 117 killed and only 20 captured, with 100 tabor wagons and 'many horses' lost as well. Clearly, as it was reported to the King, the Polish defeat was played down, with their own losses being lowered and Swedish strength and losses exaggerated.

Another Polish relation,[12] written more than a week after the battle, is more candid and mentions that a group of eight banners from Kazanowski's and Kossakowski's regiments camped in Kiszpork. The Polish soldiers were reckless, and despite the proximity to the Swedish garrisons in Malbork and Elbląg they settled in town without many precautions. The Poles were then surprised by 20 cornets of Swedish cavalry that 'slaughtered them as a cattle', banners were scattered with heavy losses and still, despite it happening more than week before, the exact number of survivors is not known. The anonymous author of the relation makes a very interesting observation, pointing out that Polish soldiers were not prepared for the new Swedish style of warfare:

> God forgive for such dishonour, more even than loss of life; our Polish Soldiers, or rather [I should call them] Polish geese,[13] think that they [still] fight against Tatars, where you can sleep safely next to any place, [while now] it is against good soldiers and I think that they will teach us how to fight properly, as the Lithuanians already did.

Stories of such encounters are of course much more interesting if we can read about it in sources from both sides, and so see and compare their perspective. In July 1627 Koniecpolski, after capturing Gniew, sent a large group of his cavalry – it looks like it was a reinforced regiment under command of Mikołaj Potocki – to check rumours of Swedish forces grouping near Kiezmark (Käsemark). The Polish cavalry set up camp near the village of Grabiny and during the night-time despatched *rotmistrz* Paweł Czarniecki with eight banners of cossack cavalry in search of the Swedes. In the morning of 14 to 15 July the Poles were to encounter 12 Swedish cornets 'also sent to capture prisoners or to forage'. A Polish source[14] claimed that Czarniecki's cossacks broke the Swedes and forced them to retreat towards their own camp. During

---

12 AGAD, Teki Naruszewicza, volume 118, no 137, pp.628–629, *Miłościwy Panie Pisarzu…*
13 Here the goose is used as a symbol of a silly animal.
14 *Diariusz*, p.29.

the pursuit the Poles were ambushed by a few hundred Swedish infantry. After a prolonged fight, Czarniecki decided to withdraw. Three of his banners lost their flags (from the units of *rotmistrz* Samuel Łaszcz, Jerzy Kruszyński and Gabriel Kuliczkowski), also four companions were killed and six captured. Interestingly enough, no losses amongst retainers were mentioned and they were often much higher than companion losses. It is very likely that the Poles lost many more killed, wounded and captured there.

The second source that we can use is Israel Hoppe's chronicle,[15] as he would have plenty of information from the Swedes. Hoppe described the Polish force as two banners of hussars and 13 of cossacks. The Swedish side was, according to him, much weaker, though. It was led by 'Achiatus Tott' (Finnish lieutenant colonel Åke Tott), who had with him *3 seinen Compagnien zu Ross* (three companies of reiters) and *2 Comp. von Lessels Regimente zu Fuss* (two companies from the Swedish national infantry regiment from Kronoberg, under command of Colonel Alexander Leslie). A chronicler from Elbląg mentioned that the Swedes forced the Poles to retreat, capturing four standards.

Finally a very important source is a letter from Chancellor Axel Oxenstierna to his brother Gabriel Gustafson, written one day after the encounter.[16] He mentioned the name of the place where the skirmish took place, the village of Długie Pole (Langfelde). Tott had with him 150 Finnish reiters, Leslie 180 musketeers from his regiment. This supports the number of companies mentioned by Hoppe, as due to attrition, sickness, etc. they would be well below their 'paper strength'. Tott and Leslie were securing the flank of the main Swedish force that was to attack Polish and Gdańsk's position at Kiezmark. There's a big difference in the size of the Polish force here, as Oxenstierna mentioned 14 companies: three hussars, nine cossacks and two dragoons. But according to him only five companies of cossacks took part in the fight, so it appears that 14 companies was just the size of the main cavalry group, not Czarniecki's vanguard. In his relation, the desperate Finns managed to stop the Polish cavalry long enough for Leslie's musketeers to shoot from their ambush site on the flank of Poles. That sudden fire, which could cause significant losses in both men and horses, broke the Polish resolve and they retreated. The Swedes lost three killed (one reiter and two musketeers) and eight to 10 wounded. They managed to take nine prisoners (including one ensign bearer) and four flags, with 150 Poles (killed and wounded) left on the battlefield.

Another interesting action was a night attack by a combined force led by *rotmistrz* Paweł Czarniecki, in November 1628.[17] As the loss of Brodnica (Strasburg) to the Swedes was a big blow to Koniecpolski, it is not surprising that he tried to recapture the city. On the evening of 3 November Paweł

15 Hoppe, *Geschichte des ersten*, pp.185–186.
16 Axel Oxenstierna to G.G. Oxenstierna, 16 July 1627, *RAOSB*, volume I, part 3 (Stockholm, 1900), p.586.
17 The description of the events is based on Adam Kersten, *Stefan Czarniecki 1599-1665* (Lublin: Wydawnictwo Uniwersytetu Marii Curie-Skłodowskiej, 2006), pp.78–80, *Pamiętniki o Koniecpolskich, passim*.

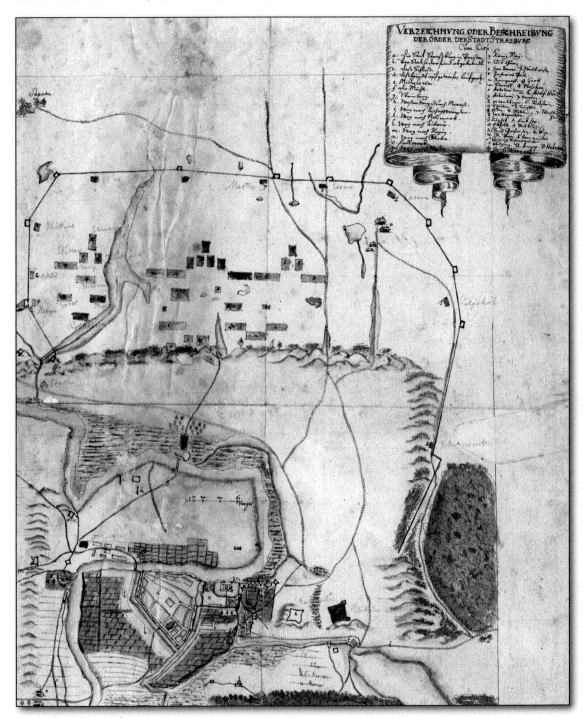

The Swedish siege of Brodnica (Strasburg) in September 1628. (Krigsarkivet, Stockholm)

Czarniecki, one of the best commanders of cossack cavalry in the army, led a combined group of troops into Brodnica. He had already made a few reconnaissance missions into the area, and it seems that after checking the defences he asked the Hetman for permission to attack. The size of his force is not entirely clear, and depends on sources that vary between 600 and 1,000 soldiers. The bulk of the group was composed of foreign infantry, 'drafted from different companies' (probably even from different regiments as well) and Polish-Hungarian infantry. There were also two or three cossack banners, it is almost certain that one of them was Czarniecki's own. The troops quickly marched towards the town, crossed the river Drwęca and after a short but fierce fight forced the Swedish guards from the sconces outside Brodnica. With a few soldiers Czarniecki then broke into one of the houses, and was able to capture and open the gate to allow the rest of his troops into the suburbs. The Poles captured three standards, while the remaining Swedish soldiers,[18] not knowing the size of the attacking force, locked themselves in the castle. At approximately 10:00 p.m. Czarniecki realised that he did not have enough troops to attempt to capture the castle, but it appears that for some strange reason he waited the whole night to send a messenger to the Hetman asking for reinforcements. Unfortunately the *rotmistrz* had problems keeping his soldiers in order. Polish sources tend to put the majority of the blame on the German infantry that, instead of holding positions, started to loot houses. In a way it is understandable though, as the entire army was in poor shape by then, lacking pay for such a long time. When in the morning the Swedes saw the disorder in the Polish ranks they counter-attacked, we even have a description of the Swedish pikemen leaving the castle gate and spearheading the attack.[19] After two hours of intense shooting, where clearly the Swedish musketeers had the upper hand over the Polish force, some of Czarniecki's troops panicked and ran. One of the town's bridges, used as way of escape, collapsed under the retreating soldiers, adding confusion to whole situation. At that time reinforcements from the main army arrived – the Hetman's own regiment, led by Łukasz Żółkiewski – but all they could to was cover the retreat of Czarniecki's defeated force.

Musketeer from Friedrich Jungermann's *Paraten Schlachtordung,* dated between 1617–1625. (Biblioteka Cyfrowa Uniwersytetu Wrocławskiego)

The Poles took heavy losses, with up to 70 killed and more than 100 infantrymen taken prisoner. Amongst the dead were *rotmistrz* Rybiński[20] and two 'German captains',[21] with many veteran soldiers counted amongst the lost. Jakub Maksymilian Fredro, describing the events of the attack, put emphasis on the actions of the German troops, going so far as to claim that they were trying to warn the Swedes about the incoming attack. Supposedly they were, against orders, lighting up their match cords, 'pouring some powder on them, so they light up better, and they also coughed [loudly] and gave all the signs of their unwillingness [to fight]'.[22] Both Koniecpolski and Fredro praised the bravery of the other troops, the latter was even very positively surprised by the 'Hungarian infantry' (which clearly means the Polish infantry here). Paweł Czarniecki was

---

18 The garrison was composed of one squadron from the elite *Hovregementet.*

19 Od P. Jak. Mak. Fredra do Xiędza Kanclerza, dnia 5. Listopada 1628, *Pamiętniki o Koniecpolskich,* p.147.

20 From either Polish-Hungarian or *wybraniecka* infantry.

21 The sources do not mention their names.

22 Od P. Jak. Mak. Fredra do Xiędza Kanclerza, dnia 5. Listopada 1628, *Pamiętniki o Koniecpolskich,* p.147.

blamed by many for this defeat, though obviously he put all the blame on unruly infantry. Yet he was at least partially responsible for the defeat: he was a very good cavalrymen but lacked skills in using infantry, especially in such difficult and demanding conditions as a city fight at night. The descriptions of the action do not name any experienced infantry officers, such as Nadolski, Butler or Denhoff, as being present, so it seems that Czarniecki did not have proper support in command of those troops. It is possible that if the Polish troops had been better led, and if more troops had arrived in time to support Czarniecki, Brodnica could have been recaptured.

During the war both sides were engaged in many siege operations, fighting for vital towns and castles. Here the Swedes were in a much better situation, as throughout July 1626 they managed to capture many such locations, practically without any opposition from the Polish and Prussian (Brandenburg) side. One of the towns captured during those operations was Puck (Putzig), the Baltic port that surrendered to the Swedes on 29 July. The Poles were very eager to recapture Puck, seen as a perfect location for the Royal Fleet (which was not warmly welcomed by the burghers of Gdańsk). On 7 November 1626 Hetman Koniecpolski sent to the area around Puck three banners of cossack cavalry, under Colonel Jan Bąk-Lanckoroński,[23] with orders to harass the Swedish garrison and prevent its foragers in their missions in neighbouring locations. They joined one Polish unit already stationed in the vicinity of Puck. It was a company of foreign infantry under command of Wilhelm Appelman, numbering approximately 300 soldiers. It seems that even before the arrival of the cavalry Appelman attempted first an assault on the city, supported by ships of the Royal Fleet arriving from Gdańsk. It was a rather ill-advised attack that was beaten back by the Swedes, with the Polish infantry taking heavy losses.

Another assault, this time attempted by Bąk-Lanckoroński's cavalry, took place soon after their arrival into the area. The cossacks tried to take the defenders by surprise but the Swedes and the burghers supporting them managed just in time to close the gates and the attack failed.[24] The Poles then started proper siege operations, building field fortifications manned by more units of infantry that started to arrive near Puck. We can identify the companies of Thomas du Plessis (approximately 100 soldiers)[25] and Arthur Aston (350 soldiers). Additionally Gdańsk sent troops, artillery and supplies, in order to support Koniecpolski's troops. Siege operations were led by Appelman, an experienced engineer who in 1621 was responsible for the Polish fortifications at Chocim (Khotyn) against the Turks, while the overall command of all troops was in Bąk-Lanckoroński's hands.

The Polish commanders were attempting to capture Puck before winter forced them to limit their operations to a blockade. The Swedes seemed to

---

23　He was also *rotmistrz* of one of them, numbering 100 horses, Rest of the ad hoc created regiment was composed of banners of Jan Bogusz (125 horses) and Krzysztof Faliński (150 horses).

24　Wacław Odyniec, 'Lądowo-morska obrona', p.454.

25　Reinhold Curicke, *Der Stadt Dantzig Historische Beschreibung: Worinnen Von dero Uhrsprung, Situation, Regierungs-Art, geführten Kriegen, Religions- und Kirchen-Wesen außführlich gehandelt wird* (Amsterdam, Dantzigk, 1687), p.222.

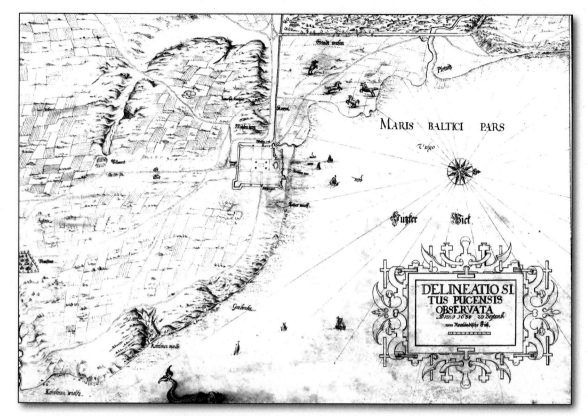

Area of Puck (Putzig) on the drawing of Fryderyk Getkant from 1634. (Krigsarkivet, Stockholm)

think that Koniecpolski's troops would not be a serious danger to the defence, and decided to evacuate part of the garrison. The remaining force, under command of governor Klas Kristersson Horn af Aminne, was composed of:

- James Seaton's infantry squadron, four companies
- Half of Fritz Rosladin's infantry squadron, two and a half companies
- Three reiter companies: Horn's, Rosladin's and Wilhelm Grey's[26]

In total it was approximately 900 men, with at least 30 cannons, mostly 2- and 3-pounders. The garrison was well supplied with food and ammunition, and was also hoping for support from the Swedish fleet. The Polish side attempted two assaults on 14 and 15 December, moving their troops against Mill Gate (*Brama Młyńska*) towards the main Swedish position – the castle and church. Attacking such a strong position would seem to be rather risky, but there was good reasoning behind it: the Poles approaching next to the Baltic coast were able to dig their trenches fairly close to the walls, also this part of the town was not protected by a moat. The attack was supported by heavy artillery fire, which led to many fires in the city. Both Polish assaults were unsuccessful however, and the Swedes also followed up with counter-attack that managed to capture one cannon and 25 Polish soldiers. Appelman,

---

26 Axel Oxenstierna to King Gustav Adolf, Marienburg, 5 April 1627, *RAOSB*, volume I, part 3 (Stockholm, 1900), p.515.

who led the assaults, had two horses shot from under him, *rotmistrz* Faliński leading one of the cossack banners was mortally wounded, and up to 100 Polish soldiers were killed during those two days. This bloody failure led to a change of Polish tactics. Until the end of 1626 Bąk-Lanckoroński's troops harassed the defenders, 'in day and night preventing the Swedes from having rest and sleep'.[27] Hoping that almost a full month of such activities would badly affect the Swedish garrison, the Poles on 8 January 1627 started preparation for a new assault. For two days the town came under heavy fire from cannons and muskets, followed by an attack from the Polish infantry and dismounted cavalry. An attempt to destroy one of Puck's gates with a mine was prevented by the defenders, and the Poles yet again were repulsed, losing approximately 100 killed.

The siege continued through the winter, while the besiegers again received reinforcements from Gdańsk, including a few heavy cannons.[28] The city walls next to Mill Gate were badly damaged, making perfect entry points for further assaults. On 8, 13 and 23 February the Polish infantry even managed to access the city, but each time the Swedes pushed them back. Both sides took heavy losses, with the garrison slowly running out of food and ammunition. Hetman Koniecpolski sent even more infantry to support the siege, urging the Polish officers to attack Puck simultaneously from two sides and to prepare new mines. He wanted to capture Puck before spring, to make sure that it would not be reinforced in time by a Swedish contingent marching from Mecklenburg or by a relief force from the field army camped near Elbląg.

In early March the Swedish garrison finally managed a successful sortie, engaging the Polish and Gdańsk troops in their camps and then capturing a newly arrived supply convoy that was left without any guard. It was the swansong of Horn, Seaton and their troops, however. The Poles were very determined to finally capture Puck, and Koniecpolski himself decided to intervene. On 23 March, before Koniecpolski's arrival, Appelman and Bąk-Lanckoroński attempted one more assault on the city walls, and were again repulsed with the loss of 100 men.[29] The Hetman was already on his way, though, bringing with him all available Polish and foreign infantry from his army and further troops from Gdańsk.[30] Additionally he organised support from the Royal Fleet, with six ships arriving from their base in Wisłoujście to help during final assaults.

Attacks started on 29 March and were continued the following day. As Koniecpolski had under his command around 4,000 infantry and a few hundred dismounted cavalrymen, he decided to stretch the defenders by attacking all four city gates and the castle gate. Supported by heavy cannons and fire from galleons, the besiegers were hardly pressing the garrison. Even

---

27 'Diariusz albo summa', p.20.

28 Reinhold Curicke, *Der Stadt Dantzig*, p.222.

29 One starts to wonder how accurate were the losses described by Hoppe, as he seems to claim almost the same number of killed besiegers in each of the assaults.

30 200 mercenary musketeers, a few heavy cannons and engineer Paweł Rudel.

though the Poles took some heavy losses, including engineer Rudel being killed and engineer Herneck wounded, the Swedes asked to start negotiations.

> Seeing that it would be hard to continue [with the defence], knowing that Hetman [Koniecpolski] was here and [that] he approached with all his soldiers; seeing ships with their mighty artillery [and] on land [around Puck] trenches and fortifications being dug everywhere, full of soldiers and cannons, losing their hearts [the Swedes] sent a trumpeter to His Grace Hetman, asking for a truce, which was, with some conditions … allowed to them, as they gave up the town and all traitors [from their ranks] to His Grace Hetman.[31]

The official surrender was signed on 2 April 1627. The garrison was allowed to march to Piława (Pillau), escorted by two banners of cossacks and one company of dragoons. As Hetman Koniecpolski wrote to King Sigismund III, '[they marched] with folded flags, silent drums and muskets carried under arms'.[32] Wounded and sick Swedes were sent on barges to Pillau as well. The siege had taken its toll on the garrison: according to Koniecpolski 'there were 900 survivors including the sick, and through whole siege they lost 600 men'.[33] As we already mentioned in Chapter 3, some Swedish soldiers decided to switch sides and join the Polish army. Koniecpolski's troops captured 31 cannons, five barrels of gunpowder and some remaining food supplies (mostly cheese and dried fish). Bąk-Lanckoroński was nominated by Koniecpolski as governor of Puck. He had under his command three banners of cossack cavalry and between four and six companies of foreign infantry, in total up to 450 horse and 1,000 infantry.[34]

Capturing Puck was a big Polish success, providing them with another base for the Royal Fleet. It was a costly affair though, it is estimated that Polish losses were up to 800 killed and wounded. The whole operation shows very clearly the typical problems affecting Koniecpolski's army during the war: lack of heavy siege artillery, a very small number of engineers and often the reckless disregard of Polish commanders towards their own infantry and its losses.

A very interesting and rather unusual action of Koniecpolski's army took place during the night of 25 to 26 July 1629. Polish units were attempting to capture two sconces built by Swedes at the forefront of their camp near Malbork (Marienburg). We have very detailed information about this event from Polish sources, supported by some from the Swedish side as well.[35] While the Poles were preparing to attack the Swedish positions, allied Imperial forces were due to attack secondary defence points at Cypel Mątowski (Montawshe Spitz) although for various reasons von Arnim decided to stop his attack.

---

31 'Diariusz albo Summa', p.20.
32 Stanisław Koniecpolski do Zygmunta III, Puck, 3 kwietnia 1627 roku, *Pamiętniki o Koniecpolskich*, p.45.
33 *Ibidem*, p.45.
34 Biblioteka Uniwersytecka Wrocław, *Polonica varia*, part 2, *Presidia wojskiem JKM opatrzone w Pucku*, p.226.
35 'Kontynuacja Diariusza', pp.441–442, *Polska kriget*, pp.547–548.

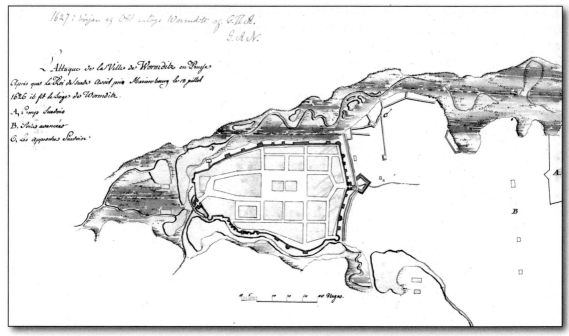

Swedish attack at Orneta (Wormditt) in October 1627. (Krigsarkivet, Stockholm)

Infantry was to play a main part in the Polish action. The idea was to attack two sconces manned by Swedish troops, and if successful to push towards the main camp of Gustav Adolf's troops. The 'great sconce', built near the mill, was garrisoned by four companies from Matts Kagg's Swedish regiment. The 'small sconce' is more problematic, as the sources mention there three 'English' companies. There were no English troops in the Swedish field army at that point, unless someone simply made a serious error and identified Scots as English. The Polish relation mentioned Ruthven but he of course was a Scot, additionally he was in charge of Swedish native infantry, not a unit from the British Isles. It is possible, then, that the three companies in the 'small sconce' were his Swedish musketeers. They were also supported by a squadron of four reiter companies, stationed near Nowa Wieś Malborska (Tessendorf).

After one day of heavy artillery fire exchange, Koniecpolski decided to commence an attack 'after dusk' on 25 July. It was to be led by units from all three foreign infantry regiments: Gerhard Denhoff's, Friedrich Denhoff's (formerly Gustav Sparre's regiment) and James Butler's. A few banners of Polish infantry were present as well. The troops crossed three bridges over the small Młynówka river and marched against the Swedes. The first unit was Major Putkamer's company (from Gerhard Denhoff's regiment) led by the lieutenant, then the colonel's company from Friedrich Denhoff's regiment also led by its lieutenant. The infantry came under heavy Swedish fire, but the Poles did not open their own fire until they were near the Swedish 'small sconce'. They managed to push back the defenders from that position, and the Swedes retreated to the 'great sconce'. The Poles pursued and were engaged in a heavy fight here but some troops stayed behind to destroy the 'small sconce'. The fight was very fierce, as we can imagine with such a bloody infantry encounter fought during the night-time. Colonel James Butler was wounded in the throat; one of his captains – Gall – was wounded by musket fire. Another captain, called 'Fityng' (most likely Lieutenant Colonel Ernest Fittinghof from Gerhard Denhoff's regiment) was injured in the arm 'by hit of the pickaxe'.

On the Polish right flank the Swedish cavalry attempted a counter-attack. Three or four companies of reiters were trying to outflank the Polish infantry then attack it in the rear. The Swedes did not know, though, that Polish cavalry lay in ambush there. After the infantry moved through Młynówka, two regiments of cavalry crossed it to protect the main attack. They were a regiment of national cavalry under Mikołaj Potocki and Mikołaj Abramowicz's regiment of reiters (five companies). Initially the Swedes were able to push back one banner of cossack cavalry, but their advance was halted when the cossacks were supported by Abramowicz's reiters. Then the main force of Potocki's cavalry, most likely including a few banners of hussars, joined the fray and the Polish cavalry forced the Swedes to retreat.

At the same time the Polish infantry was still engaged against the defenders of the 'great sconce', managing to push the majority of them outside their positions. Koniecpolski's troops did not progress towards the main Swedish camp, though. It seems that no one expected that the initial attack would have some success, and the commanders did not know if they should continue moving towards the Swedes. 'Maybe due to the darkness of the night, maybe due to [the expected] ambush by the enemies, maybe due [to the] lack of [a local] guide', the momentum of the attack stalled and the troops did not attack the Swedish camp. It was also very difficult to fight in unknown and muddy terrain. The retreat of the Swedish infantry was stopped by Field Marshal Wrangel himself, who came from another camp near Elbląg (Elbing), leading a force of cavalry. The Swedish horsemen stopped their fleeing comrades 'with sticks', Wrangel lost his horse and was wounded in the leg. The Poles were able to capture the 'small sconce' but it seems the Swedes managed to hold the 'great sconce'. Too many Polish units advanced towards the Swedish camp and none of the officers coordinated a final attack on the defenders of the 'great sconce'. The main force of the Polish infantry exchanged fire with the Swedes near their camp throughout the rest of the night, then at dawn returned to their own camp. Due to their surprise there were no Polish troops in the 'great sconce', instead the Swedes held firmly this position. It is no surprise that eyewitnesses described this fight as a 'wild and messy brawl'.

In the early morning of 26 July the Swedes tried to rebuild the destroyed 'small sconce' and came under heavy fire from the Polish infantry. Then after two hours Colonel Friedrich Denhoff led a counter-attack on the Swedes busy with rebuilding, and once again pushed them back towards the 'great sconce'. For the whole day until sunset the infantry exchanged fire, also there were some small skirmish actions between cavalry.

Polish losses 'for the last three days and one night' (24–26 July) were '43 killed and 100 and a few wounded' from the ranks of the foreign infantry alone, but the Polish infantry units 'also lost many men', including the wounded *rotmistrz* Horzelski. Losses amongst the cavalry were not mentioned but were most likely minimal. The Swedish witness mentioned his army's losses as 50 killed, but even the authors of *Polska kriget* commented that it was too low an estimate. Colonel Matts Kagg was killed while leading the defence. Of course the Polish estimate of Swedish losses was much higher: according to deserters fleeing Gustav Adolf's army, during the three days of fighting the Swedish infantry lost up to 400 killed and many wounded.

While it met with limited success, the night attack from 25 July is a very interesting example of infantry action, fought in difficult conditions, more similar to Spanish–Dutch fights in Flanders than to other actions during the Polish–Swedish wars. It was also the last main encounter in the 1626–1629 war, as both sides reached the limit of their offensive capabilities, with their armies ravaged by plague, hunger and desertion.

Conclusion

The 1626–1629 war was a completely new chapter in the history of the conflicts between the Polish–Lithuanian Commonwealth and Sweden. Previous wars and campaigns took place on the rather distant battlefields of Livonia and Courland, far away from Polish mainland. Despite the fact that Swedish preparations for the invasion of Prussia were not a huge surprise for Warsaw, still the Poles entered the war woefully unprepared and at a serious disadvantage. The main armed force, the 'quarter army', led by the best Polish commander, Hetman Stanisław Koniecpolski, was stationed on the far border of Poland and did not arrive at the theatre of war until November 1626. As such, the first line of the defence was held by a ramshackle mix of Brandenburg/Prussian allies, private troops (raised by Sigismund III and some of the wealthy magnates and nobles), the Royal Guard, reinforcements sent from the Lithuanian army, district troops and a local levy of nobility. The Swedes held the initiative for the first few months of the war and it had a huge impact on the initial moves of the conflict. Gustav Adolf's army, facing very weak resistance, managed to capture many vital towns and locations, bringing under their control territory that they managed to hold practically until the end of the war.

Circumstances forced the Polish side to adjust the organisation and size of their army. The Swedes, who were up to this moment seen in Poland as a 'peasant army' supported by Western European mercenaries, showed huge resilience and, based on their experience from Livonia in 1621–1625, made many changes that improved the quality of their troops. With a shift in both strategy and tactics, the Poles no longer could count on achieving such victories in open battles as happened in Livonia during the 1600–1611 war. Luckily for the Commonwealth, Hetman Koniecpolski was the right man in the right place. Charismatic, well liked by his soldiers, he guided the army during a period of necessary adjustment required in Prussia. While the cavalry, especially hussars and cossacks, still played a vital role during the campaigns, it was infantry and dragoons that came to the fore now. Large numbers of foreign troops had to be recruited in order to balance the Swedish infantry, to garrison vital places, and serve as 'marines' on the ships of the Royal Fleet. Dragoons were deployed in large numbers, ideally suited to support the Polish cavalry during field operations. There were just not enough experienced officers and NCOs to raise a larger number of native Polish infantry; additionally, due to the early stages of the Thirty Years' War, recruitment of the so-valued Hungarian *haiduks* was practically impossible. Only during the final stage of the war did the idea of Western-style units recruited in Poland come to life, although on a rather limited scale. It clearly shows, though, that the Poles learned from the experience of the war and were willing to adjust the composition and recruitment of their army. The episode of the Royal Fleet, although short-lived, proved how important naval warfare was and how it could influence any conflict in the area surrounding Baltic Sea. Sadly, in Poland it was seen as part of a wide range of royal attempts to spread Crown influence over the vital Baltic coast and of Sigismund's long-term plans to regain the Swedish throne. As such it did not have many supporters outside the Royal Court and it was facing strong opposition amongst the nobility.

The Prussian war laid the foundations of a new type of Polish–Lithuanian army, which started its transformation under the leadership of Hetman Stanisław Koniecpolski and under the royal patronage of King Władysław IV between 1632 and 1635, during a series of new conflicts against Muscovy, the Ottoman Empire and Sweden. Polish recruits started to fill the ranks of 'foreign' infantry and dragoons, drilled by officers and NCOs that learned their trade in Western Europe and during the 1626–1629 war. After 1635 the Commonwealth armies developed a new system of two contingents (known as *autoramenty*), based on the method of recruitment and types of troops. The Polish section, called 'national' (*autorament narodowy*) included hussars, cossack cavalry, light cavalry (Wallachian and Tatar) and Polish-Hungarian infantry. The western section, known as 'foreign' (*autorament cudzoziemski*) was composed of foreign/German infantry, dragoons and reiters. Severe problems with the quality and quantity of Polish artillery during the conflict in Prussia led to massive changes initiated by Władysław IV. The post of the Master of the Ordnance (*starszy nad armatą*).[1] later known as General of the Ordnance (one for Poland and one for Lithuania) was reintroduced unofficially in 1632 in Poland and in 1634 in Lithuania, with the official announcement in 1637. The *Sejm* agreed on a new regular tax, designed to finance artillery corps and royal armouries. Production of new cannons and unification of the artillery park was also the purview of the specialist holding this new post. The period 1626–1629 was also a great 'military school' for many officers, who would play an important role in Polish armies during future conflicts. Colonel Mikołaj Potocki in 1637 became Crown Field Hetman, then in 1646 was promoted to Crown Grand Hetman. Another of Koniecpolski's colonels, Marcin Kazanowski, was between 1633 and 1636 Crown Field Hetman. Finally the famous hero of the 1655–1660 'Deluge' war against the Swedes, Stefan Czarniecki, learnt his craft during 1626–1629 war serving in his brother Paweł Czarniecki's cossack banner.

At the same time the conflict against Sweden revealed the main weakness of the Polish army: a massive problem with financing long-term military effort. An inefficient fiscal system, combined with the unwillingness of

---

1   Until now an officer was nominated to the position, just for the purpose of the campaign.

the Polish nobles and clergy to pay increased taxes, led to huge debt that negatively affected military operations. Unfortunately not much changed in this regard, as throughout the rest of the seventeenth century the Polish army would be still to some extent affected by financial problems, even during times of peace.

Appendix I

Names of the main towns and villages in Ducal Prussia (Prusy Książęce/Herzogtum Preussen) and Royal Prussia (Prusy Królewskie/Königlich-Preußen)

Polish name	Seventeenth-century German name
Barczew	Wartembork/Wartenburg
Biała Góra	Weissenberg
Biskupiec	Bischofsburg
Braniewo	Braunsberg
Brodnica	Strasburg
Chełmno	Culm/Kulm
Chojnice	Konitz
Ciepłe	Warmhof
Cypel Mątowski (Mątowska Szpica)	Montawshe Spitz
Czarne	Hammerstein
Człuchów	Schlochau
Długie Pole	Langfelde
Dobre Miasto	Guttstadt
Dobrzynek	Frydland
Działdowo	Soldau
Dzierzgoń (Kiszpork)	Christburg
Elbląg	Elbing
Frombork	Frauenburg
Gardeja	Garnsee
Gdańsk	Danzig
Głowa Gdańska	Danziger Höftt, Danziger-Haupt
Gniew	Mewe
Gronowo	Gronau
Grudziądz	Graudenz

Polish name	Seventeenth-century German name
Iława	Deutsch Eylau
Jastarnia	Heisternest
Kiezmark[1]	Käsemark
Kisielice	Freystadt
Kiszpork – see Dzierzgoń	
Królewiec	Königsberg
Kurzętnik	Kauernik
Kwidzyn	Marienwerder
Lębork	Lauenburg
Lidzbark	Lautenburg
Lubawa	Löbau
Malbork	Marienburg
Nowa Wieś Malborska	Tessendorf
Nowe Miasto Lubawskie	Neumark
Nowe nad Wisłą	Neuenburg
Nidzica	Neidenburg
Olsztynek	Hohenstein
Orneta	Worditt
Osie	Osche
Ostróda	Osterode
Pasłęk (Holąd Pruski)	Preußisch Holland
Pelplin	Pelplin
Pieniężno	Mehlsack
Piława	Pillau
Prabuty	Riesenburg
Primorsk	Fischhausen
Puck	Putzig
Pułkowice	Pulkowitz
Starogard Gdański	Stargard
Starogard	Stargordt
Stary Targ	Altmark
Straszewo	Dietrichsdorf
Sztum	Stuhm
Sulicice	Sulitz
Susz	Rosenberg
Szymbark	Schönberg
Tczew	Dirschau
Tolkmicko	Tolkemit
Toruń	Thorn
Trzcianą	Honigfelde
Warcimierz	Wartzimir
Walichnowy	Falkenau
Wrzoski	Grünhof
Zastawa	Lochstedt

---

1   Often incorrectly called Kieżmark, which is in fact a town in Slovakia.

Appendix II

Muster of nine thousands soldiers in front of His Royal Highness between Arciberz and Pszczew. 4 Nov[ember 1626][1]

After the battle of Gniew (Mewe) the composition of Polish army in Prussia drastically changed. All district troops and the majority of private ones left the theatre of war, as their time of service was at an end. At the same time the royal army was reinforced by those private units that were late for the battle of Gniew, and additionally a few units of cavalry and foreign infantry paid from the Royal Treasury also finally joined the main army. While waiting for Hetman Koniecpolski and his 'quarter army', King Sigismund III reviewed the remaining troops at the army camp at Warcimierz (Wartzimir), near Tczew (Dirschau). On 4 November 1626 the Poles organised a muster of all units left under the King's command.

A surviving document shows the unusual composition of the army at that time. It was an odd mix of Royal Guard, private troops, soldiers paid from the Royal Treasury, and Lithuanian reinforcements and units raised for the 'quarter army' but never sent to Podolia. Additionally the clerk composing the army list had a tendency to write some words, especially Polish ones, in a rather distinct way (*Arcibierz* instead of Warcimierz, *Pszczew* instead of Tczew), which make direct translation into English almost impossible. Instead the decision was made here to present the full army list in edited form, where possible identifying and adding full details of officers and the provenance of their units. Unit strength appears to be 'paper' one, not the actual one. For example two banners of reiters – Szmeling's and Dönhoff's – took part in the battle of Gniew and took losses during the fight, yet here they are shown with full 200 horses each. On the other side, though, Abramowicz's reiters were 400 horses before the battle but on the muster are reported as

---

1   Biblioteka Narodowa w Warszawie, BOZ 1173, p.150, *Popis Woiska dziewiąci tysięcy przed Królem Je. M. pod Arciberzem a Pszczewem 4 Nov.*

358 horses. The muster is titled as depicting 'nine thousand' soldiers, while total strength of reviewed units was in fact 8,625 horses and portions.

A. Reiters
Wyszbierz, 200 horses
Ernest Denhoff, 200 horses
Otto Denhoff,[2] 200 horses. Royal Guard unit
Henrik Szmeling, 200 horses. From the Lithuanian army
Rosnopst Meden, 20 horses[3]
Mikołaj Abramowicz, 358 horses. Livonian unit from the Lithuanian army

B. Dragoons
Bazyli Judycki, 355 portions. Private unit
Andrew Keith, 82 portions. Part of the units raised by the King
Gabriel Ceridon, 193 portions. Part of the units raised by the King

C. German infantry
(all units raised by the King)
Adrian Fuldrops, 172 portions
Friedrich Denhoff, 238 portions (it was in fact Gerhard Denhoff's unit under the command of Friedrich)
Otton Fittinghof, 264 portions
Ernest Fittinghof, 264 portions
Walter Butler (Older), 194 portions. Unit raised by Jan Weyher, voivode of Malbork
Walter Butler (Younger), 229 portions
Jan Forde, 180 portions
Baltazar Rotenstein, 178 portions
Tomas Duplessis, 103 portions
Wilhelm Keith, 137 portions

D. His Majesty's Infantry
(these are foreign troops paid by the King from his treasury to serve as 'marines' on ships. In the muster they are described as 'fighting on the sea'):
Arthur Aston, 500 portions
Wilhelm Appelman, 300 portions

E. Husaria
Jan Baranowski, 150 horses
Paweł Niewiarowski, 160 horses. Lithuanians
Michał Woyna, 115 horses. Lithuanians
Andrzej Stanisław Sapieha, 156 horses. Lithuanians
Mikołaj Kendzirzewski, 96 horses
Royal Prince Władysław Waza, 200 horses
Andrzej Mniszech, 100 horses

---

2   He died during the battle of Gniew but the unit was still mustered 'under' his name.
3   If it is not clerk's typo, it would indicate that Meden brought only a strong retinue and not a full banner.

F. Arkabuzerzy
Mikołaj Gniewosz, 200 horses

G. Cossack cavalry
Jan Baranowski, 150 horses
Andrzej Mniszech, 192 horses
Mikołaj Moczarski, 228 horses. Lisowski's cossacks (*lisowczycy*)
Idzi Kalinowski, 297 horses. Lisowski's cossacks (*lisowczycy*)
Żaliński, 187 horses
Mostowski, 150 horses
Kuczborski, 108 horses
Wojciech Baranowski, 100 horses
Jan Worytko, 200 horses
Piotr Bujalski, 200 horses
Władysław Śledziński, 206 horses. Lisowski's cossacks (*lisowczycy*)

H. Polish infantry
Jan Porembski, 227 portions (or 275). Lithuanians
Józef Rabi, 200 portions. Lithuanians
Wojciech Kuropatwa, 137 portions. Paid from the Royal Treasury
Maciej Jeliński, 195 portions. Paid from the Royal Treasury
Piotr Śmieszyński,78 portions. Paid from the Royal Treasury
Jan Szacko (Szacki), 144 portions. Paid from the Royal Treasury

Appendix III

Muster from 29 August 1627

In Chapter 2 was mentioned Abraham Booth's description of the muster of the Polish army, that took place on 29 August 1627.[1] Presented here is a comparison of the Dutchman's figures with known units present at that time in Prussia, with the aim of judging how accurate his description could be.

> [The Polish army] being with new-arrived German foot-troops, not stronger than 16 companies of hussars, 24 companies of cossacks, 6 companies of German riders, 4 companies of dragoons, 29 companies of haiduks and 32 companies of German infantry, making together one hundred and eleven companies, who have a great number of whores and boys and a lot of baggage with them. Close to midday the entire army was in order, very far spread out.

It should be remembered that private units could also take part in this muster, and as they were not part of the official army records it could lead to some discrepancy within the numbers.

Hussars: in the summer of 1627, the army had (depending on sources) 16 to 19 banners, so evidently the overwhelming majority of the units are gathered here. One cavalry regiment – which could include 2–3 banners – operated in this period in Warmia, which could explain the difference.

Cossacks: Booth mentioned 24 of (at least) 29 banners serving under the command of Koniecpolski. Three banners were part of the garrison in Puck, others were operating in Warmia at that time. It was also the time where at least four short-lived units joined the army, so they could be included in this muster.

Reiters (called here 'German raiders'): Abramowicz's regiment probably already had five companies, thanks to ex-Swedish soldiers switching sides at Czarne (Hammerstein) a few months before. After the battle of Tczew the banners of Denhoff, Opoczyński and Prince Pruński joined the field army

---

1   Abraham Booth, *Journael van de Legatie in Jaren 1627 en 1628* (Amsterdam, 1632), pp.40. The author would like to thank E.J. Blaauw for his enormous help in translation from Dutch.

as well, so in fact the number of six companies seems too low; maybe some units (whole or part of Abramowicz's regiment?) did not take part in the muster.

Dragoons: as in the case of reiters, the number seems a little too low, considering the units commanded by James Butler and Bazyli Judycki. On the other hand, some of the dragoons could be delegated to other tasks and were not present with the main army.

Haiduks: The Polish-Hungarian infantry consisted of at least nine or 10 banners, plus a few *wybraniecka* infantry banners. However, after the battle of Tczew at least one strong unit of 400 soldiers under *rotmistrz* Tryzna reached the camp. At first glance, the number of 29 banners seems to be too high but we need to give it some additional consideration. We should remember that banners of 200 or more haiduks were typically divided into 'hundreds' with their own banners, the Dutchman could actually see the majority of Polish infantry units, treating each banner as a separate 'company'.

German (Foreign) Infantry: The muster had already taken place after the arrival of both Denhoff's regiments, so despite the lower than expected strength those two units could count for between 12 and 20 flags. The Imperial regiment of Duke Adolf provides us with another 10 flags. The majority of free companies that at that time provided the bulk of foreign infantry were spread out as garrison forces so could not be present. Either way, in the case of the German infantry, the number of companies that Booth saw and mentioned is certainly not too high.

Appendix IV

Places Garrisoned by His Majesty's Troops[1]

There is another interesting document describing the Polish military effort during the war in Prussia. This time it is a list of units stationed as garrisons in towns held by Koniecpolski's troops. The document is not dated but we can at least attempt some estimates to put it in place. It mentions Gniew (Mewe) as captured by the Poles, which indicates that the list had to be written after July 1627, when Koniecpolski managed to capture this strategic town. Even more important are the names of the officers of foreign infantry, as they provide a more detailed timeline. Dittloff Tysenhaus took over the infantry company of Johan Storch, who died in a naval battle at Oliwa on 28 November 1627. Hugo O'Reilly's company did not enter the service until February 1628. The absence of the garrison of Brodnica, which was captured by the Swedish army in September 1628, would indicate that the list is in fact from late autumn 1628. To support this idea, Grudziądz is garrisoned by what seems to be part of James Butler's regiment, which was sent there by Hetman Koniecpolski in September 1628.

It is worth checking the composition of this garrison force. We will not find here any units of hussars or reiters, 'reserved' to be part of the field army. The cavalry is composed entirely from cossacks: 11 banners of the 30 present in Prussia at that time. The foreign infantry and dragoons made up the bulk of the garrisons, with 13 companies (of 36 in army), while the Polish infantry had four banners (of nine in army).

---

1   Biblioteka Uniwersytecka Wrocław, *Polonica varia*, volume 2, p.226, *Presidia wojskiem J.K.M. opatrzone w Pucku.*

Puck (Putzig)

Cavalry
Rotmistrz Jan Bąk-Lanckoroński,[2] 150 horses. Cossack cavalry
Rotmistrz Paweł Karpiński, 150 horses. Cossack cavalry
Rotmistrz Piotr Bujalski, 150 horses. Cossack cavalry

Infantry[3]
Captain Gerhard Friedrichson, 150 portions. Foreign infantry
Captain Thomas Duplessis, 150 portions. Foreign infantry
Captain James Murray, 211 portions. Foreign infantry
Captain Dittloff Tysenhaus, 154 portions. Foreign infantry

On the coast up from Oliwa (Oliva), up to (Gdańsk's) lantern:
Captain Wilhelm Appelman,[4] 370 portions. Foreign infantry
Captain Balthasar Rotenstein,[5] 260 portions. Foreign infantry

In Skarszewo to cover Gdańsk's Road and to prevent the enemy's raids:
Rotmistrz Mikołaj Moczarski, 200 horses. Cossack cavalry
Rotmistrz Jan Maliński, 100 horses. Cossack cavalry
Rotmistrz Hermolus Aleksander Przyłęcki, 100 horses. Cossack cavalry
Captain Andrzej Radke,[6] 100 portions. Dragoons

In Starogard (Stargard):
Rotmistrz Samuel Nadolski, 400 portions. Polish infantry
Rotmistrz Gaspar Śliwnicki, 200 portions. Polish infantry

In Gniew (Mewe) there should be at least [left]:[7]
100 cavalry
500 infantry

In the sconce near the bridge next to Gniew:
100 infantry

In Nowe [nad Wisłą] (Neuenburg):
Rotmistrz Albert Pepłowski, 100 portions. Polish infantry

In Grudziądz (Graudenz):
Rotmistrz Mikołaj Annibal Strocy, 100 horses. Cossack cavalry
Captain [James?] Butler,[8] 300 portions. Foreign infantry or dragoons

---

2 He was often titled as colonel, as he was serving as commander of all Polish troops in Puck.
3 All four companies from Gustav Sparre's regiment.
4 Independent company.
5 From Gustav Sparre's regiment.
6 Independent company.
7 Just number of troops, no names of officers in charge.
8 Probably James Butler's dragoons.

Captain Lesse under Keith,[9] 50 portions. Foreign infantry or dragoons

In Olsztyn (Allenstein):
Rotmistrz Władysław Lipnicki, 100 horses. Cossack cavalry
Rotmistrz Jan Boki, koni 100 horses. Cossack cavalry
Captain [deceased] Butler,[10] 300 portions. Foreign infantry
Captain Walter Butler the Younger,[11] 100 portions. Foreign infantry
Rotmistrz Stanisław Biedrzycki, 100 portions. Polish infantry

In Elzberk and Wartemberk alongside troops of Bishop of Warmia:
Rotmistrz Andrzej Śladkowski, 100 horses. Cossack cavalry
Rotmistrz Albert Rogulski, 100 horses. Cossack cavalry
Capitan Jakub Lesgewang,[12] 300 portions. Foreign infantry
Captain Hugo O'Reilly,[13] 120 portions. Foreign infantry

Summa Summarum
Cavalry, 1,450 [horses]
Infantry, 4,065 portions [it is a mistake of the clerk compiling the list, in fact
   the infantry mentioned above had 3,965 portions]

---

9   Appears to be the part of Wilhelm Lesse's company of dragoons from James Butler's regiment.
10 The deceased officer would be Walter Butler the Older, as this company – being part of Gustav
    Sparre's regiment – is also named as as 'under deceased Butler' on a muster that took place in
    May 1628.
11 From James Butler's regiment.
12 From Gustav Sparre's regiment.
13 From Gustav Sparre's regiment.

Appendix V

Deployment of His Royal Highness' Troops [Late Autumn 1628]

In this appendix is presented a very interesting document, which is to the best of the author's knowledge, not used previously by Polish researchers. It dates from late 1628, and describes the deployment of Koniecpolski's army at the end of the campaign of this year, so it can be dated as late October/ early November 1628. It shows the way that Polish troops were placed in a wide net of towns and villages blocking Brodnica (Strasburg) and keeping in check any Swedish approach to Polish-held territories. We can find here all six regiments of national cavalry, both main units of reiters, three regiments of foreign infantry (called 'German' in the text), three free companies of foreign troops and eight banners of Polish-Hungarian infantry. The Prince-Bishopric of Warmia is very well garrisoned, with two national cavalry regiments and one mixed regiment of infantry and dragoons there. Denhoff's and Sparre's infantry regiments are spread fairly wide, with their companies garrisoning places from Puck to Gniew. It is worth noting how Koniecpolski deployed his cavalry, in order to cover any possible Swedish attack. His own regiment was placed in three locations, protecting a line of approximately 23 km. Stanisław Potocki's regiment took five locations, covering approximately 25 km. At the same time Mikołaj Potocki's regiment, with troops in four locations, had to protect almost 50 km, while Stefan Koniecpolski's regiment, in three locations, had to cover just above 50 km.

Deployment of His Royal Highness' Troops[1]

Cavalry

Hetman's regiment – Działdowo (Soldau), Olsztynek (Hohenstein) and Nidzica (Neidenburg)

Stanisław Potocki's regiment – Nowe Miasto Lubawskie (Neumark), Lubawa (Löbau), Kurzętnik (Kauernik), Biskupiec (Bischofsburg) and Lidzbark (Lautenburg)

Marcin Kazanowski's regiment – Prince-Bishopric of Warmia

Mikołaj Potocki's regiment – Grudziądz (Graudenz), Gardeja (Garnsee), Prabuty (Riesenburg), Susz (Rosenberg)

Stefan Koniecpolski's regiment – Starogard (Stargordt), Nowe (Neuenburg), Skarszewo

Mikołaj Kossakowski's regiment – Prince-Bishopric of Warmia

Mikołaj Abramowicz's reiter regiment – Dąbrowa

Lieutenant Colonel Ernest Denhoff's reiter squadron/regiment – Kisielice (Freystadt)

German Infantry

Gerhard Denhoff's regiment – Kwidzyn (Marienwerder), Gniew (Mewe), Nowe, Prabuty

Gustav Sparre's regiment – Puck (Putzig), Sulicice[2] (Sulitz), Szymbark[3] (Schönberg), Iława (Deutsch Eylau), Lubawa, Dąbrowa, Olsztynek

James Butler's regiment – Prince-Bishopric of Warmia *where needed*

Remaining Infantry (both German and Polish)

Bazyli Judycki's foreign infantry

Roki [which could be either Andrzej Ratke's dragoons or David Rotkier's foreign infantry]

The text indicates that both units were deployed in Chełmno (Culm)

Aleksander Czopowski's Polish infantry – no information about deployment place

Wilhelm Appelman's foreign infantry – *with the ships*

Samuel Nadolski's Polish infantry – Starogard

Piotr Kurecki's and Albert Pepłowski's Polish infantry – Grudziądz

Mikołaj Bobiatyński's and Jakub Bukowiecki's Polish infantry – Nidzica and Działdowo

Kacper Śliwnicki's and Stanisław Biedrzycki's Polish infantry – Nowe Miasto Lubawskie

---

1   Biblioteka Kórnicka, BK 341, *Diariusze z lat 1625–1630 oraz korespondencja dyplomatyczna*, pp.337–337v, *Rozłożenie stanowiska Woyska J.K.M.*

2   Village near Puck.

3   Village near Puck.

Appendix VI

The Crown Army in Prussia, According to a Bill Presented to the *Sejm* in January–February 1629

A document presented by Hetman Koniecpolski at *Sejm* in January–February 1629. The most interesting aspect of it is the organisation of each of six regiments of national cavalry, supporting the theory that Koniecpolski kept a very similar structure during the whole war. Existing units were mentioned only by the name of their *rotmistrz*/colonel, only 'paper strength' was provided with the Polish infantry.[1] Additionally new enlistments planned during the *Sejm* are mentioned, but most of them joined the army in late summer 1629 and did not take part in the fighting against Swedes.

Old Enlistments [pre–1629]

Hetman Stanisław Koniecpolski's Regiment (*pułk*):
Four banners of hussars (Stanisław Koniecpolski, Royal Prince Władysław Waza, Łukasz Żółkiewski, Adam Kalinowski)
Four banners of cossack cavalry (Stanisław Suliszowski,[2] Mikołaj Herburt, Andrzej Jeżewski, Aleksander Cetner)

Marcin Kazanowski's Regiment (*pułk*):
Three banners of hussars (Marcin Kazanowski, Władysław Myszkowski, Władysław Lipnicki)
Seven banners of cossack cavalry (Władysław Lipnicki, Jerzy Budziszewski, Walerian Włodek, Albert Roguski, Andrzej Radkowski, Jerzy Łowczycki, Andrzej Syrakowski)

---

1   We decided to ignore it though, as it is mentioned in Chapter 3.
2   Banner still noted under his name, even though he died in September 1628. Unit was taken over by Borzysławski.

Stanisław Potocki's Regiment (*pułk*):
Three banners of hussars (Stanisław Potocki, Zbigniew Oleśnicki, Stefan Potocki)
Six banners of cossack cavalry (Mikołaj Annibal Storcy, Mikołaj Łysakowski, Paweł Karpiński, Jan Boki under Lieutenant Minor, Piotr Łabęcki under Lieutenant Struś, Piotr Bujalski under Lieutenant Górski)

Mikołaj Potocki's Regiment (*pułk*):
Three banners of hussars (Mikołaj Potocki, Tomasz Zamoyski, Jan Działyński)
Six banners of cossack cavalry (Jan Bąk-Lanckoroński, Jan Odrzywolski, Samuel Łaszcz, Stefan Wieruski, Samuel Temruk, Stefan Nadarzycki)

Stefan Koniecpolski's Regiment (*pułk*). After his death, under Samuel Żaliński:
Four banners of hussars (Stefan Koniecpolski, Samuel Żaliński, Andrzej Sapieha, Mikołaj Krzyczowski)
Six banners of cossack cavalry (Paweł Czarniecki, Baltazar (Balcer) Męciński, Mikołaj Moczarski, Jerzy Krasiński, Hermolus Aleksander Przyłęcki, Daniel Maliński)

Mikołaj Kossakowski's Regiment (*pułk*):
Three banners of hussars (Mikołaj Kossakowski, Andrzej Kossakowski, Mikołaj Gniewosz)

Reiters (*Equitibus Germanis Sclopetaris*)
Regiment of Mikołaj Abramowicz
Banner/regiment of Ernest and Jan Denhoff
Banner of Aleksander Octavian, Prince Pruński
Banner of Gotthard Bodembroch

German Infantry (*Peditibus germanis*)
Gustav Sparre's regiment. After his death, under Friedrich Denhoff and Gabriel Posse[3]
James Butler's regiment (infantry and dragoons)
Gerhard Denhoff's regiment
Bazyli Judycki's free company/banner
Wilhelm Appelman's free company/banner
David Rotkier's free company/banner
Andrzej Ratki's dragoon free company/banner

Polish Infantry (*Peditibus Polonis*)
Banners of Samuel Nadolski, Aleksander Czopowski, Mikołaj Bobiatyński, Florian Uleniecki, Albert Pepłowski, Piotr Kurecki, Gaspar Śliwnicki, Jakub Bukowiecki, Stanisław Biedrzycki

---

3   Dual command is mentioned, as Posse would be in charge of units attached to Royal Fleet ships.

New Enlistments Planned for 1629

Hussar banner of Jerzy Prince Zasławski, 200 horses
Arkabuzeria (*arcabuseros*) banner of Prince Jerzy Zasławski, 150 horses
Hussar banner of Aleksander Prusinowski, 200 horses
Hussar banner of Ferdynand Gonzaga Myszkowski, 150 horses
Hussar banner of Jan Bąk Lanckoroński, 100 horses
Dragoon banner of Captain Jan Stanisław Janikowski, 200 portions
Dragoon banner of Jan Żółtowski, 200 portions
Infantry regiment (recruited in Poland but trained in 'German fashion') of
     Reinhold von Rosen, 1,000 portions
Polish infantry banner of Mikołaj Sadowski, 200 portions
Polish infantry banner of Jan Dąbrowski, 200 portions
Polish infantry banner of Jakub Chorzelski, 200 portions
Polish infantry banner of Dobek, 200 portions
Polish infantry banner of Prince Jerzy Zasławski, 200 portions
Polish infantry banner of Feliks Psarski, 100 portions
Polish infantry banner of Andrzej Wybicki, 100 portions
Polish infantry banner of Jan Gratiani, 100 portions
Polish infantry banner of Szymon Czwelin, 100 portions

Appendix VII

Muster of Polish and Imperial Troops in Front of King Sigismund III, 17 July 1629

On 17 July 1629 the joint Polish and Imperial armies took part in a muster in the presence of the recently arrived King Sigismund III and Royal Princes Władysław and Jan Kazimierz. An anonymous eyewitness, most likely one of Władysław's courtiers, left a very interesting description of this event.[1] The royals were accompanied by the Court hussar banner and half a mile before the main Polish camp were greeted by Royal Prince Władysław's hussar banner from the regular army. The allied army presented the muster near the Polish camp, as due to the closeness of the Swedish positions Hetman Koniecpolski did not want to risk moving the troops too far away. Units are presented as per the relation, with some additional comments identifying officers and providing some additional information.

The order of the troops was as follows:

- Seven companies of Imperial cuirassiers
- The Imperial infantry (no details in regard to the number of companies)
- Imperial reiters (probably the author meant harquebusiers, again no information about their numbers)
- A few companies of Polish reiters under Abramowicz and Denhoff (possibly seven if both units were presented in full)
- Three banners of hussars – the Hetman's own (still without the lances lost at battle of Trzcianą), Łukasz Żółkiewski's and Adam Kalinowski's
- Two companies of dragoons from Colonel James Butler's regiment
- German infantry regiment of Colonel Gustav Sparre
- 'Twenty and a few more' cossack cavalry banners (no names of their officers given)
- Polish infantry (probably haiduks, least likely that it would be *wybraniecka*). Again no information about officers and number of units

---

1   'Kontynuacja Diariusza', pp.437–438.

- Part of the German infantry regiment of Colonel Gerhard Dönhoff
- 'Infantry and dragoons of chavalier Judycki' (Bazyli Judycki had at that point free company of dragoons under his command, it is possible that due to lack of horses part of his unit was fighting as infantry)
- More Polish infantry (once again no details)
- Another part of Colonel James Butler's regiment (possible infantry companies)
- Captain Patrick Gordon's dragoons (company)
- A few more hussar banners (no details but it appears that one of the may be Mikołaj Potocki's – see below)
- A few more cossack banners (no details)

To prevent any possible Swedish attack, the Poles posted very strong pickets composed of 'hussars, reiters, cossacks and dragoons', unfortunately the author of the relation did not provided any further details regarding those troops. The mustered armies greeted the King and his sons with three musket salvoes, while the Imperials 'lowered their cornets and their pistols in front of Royalty, tipping their hats'. The Swedes limited their attempts to interrupt the muster to frequent artillery fire aimed towards the Polish sconces and the gathering of the allied armies. For the most part this cannonade was more nuisance than any danger. Only once the troops were returning to camp after the muster finished, did a heavy cannonball[2] hit in front of Mikołaj Potocki's hussar banner. It narrowly missed the unit's flag, then bounced and broke many of the hussars' lances, killed two soldiers, then flew between the tents of the Imperial soldiers, killing one infantryman.

---

2   Once recovered in the Polish camp it was found to weigh 45 pounds.

Appendix VIII

Small Polish–English Dictionary of Seventeenth-century Warfare

The original version, including Polish letters with diacritics (ą,ć,ż,ó, etc.). If any of those letters are used then the version without them is given as well, in brackets (as often used in non-Polish text), followed by the English version and, if required, an explanation of the term. An attempt has been made to include terms used not only during the Polish–Swedish wars but also the conflicts against the Muscovites, Ottoman Turks, Tatars and Cossacks.

Comments:

(S) – singular form
(P) – plural form
(F) – form used as description of type of formation, example:
dragon – dragoon (S)
dragoni – dragoons (P)
dragonia – dragoons (F)
[-] – English version unknown

amunicja – ammunition
arkabuzer/arkebuzer – harquebusier (S)
arkabuzeria/arkebuzeria – harquebusiers (F)
arkabuzerzy/arkebuzerzy – harquebusiers (P)
arkebuz – harquebus/arkebus
autorament – section/contingent of Polish/Lithuanian army to show difference between:
　　– *autorament narodowy* – 'national autorament' (Polish/Lithuanian cavalry and infantry)
　　– *autorament cudzoziemski* – 'foreign autorament' (Western style troops – infantry, dragoons, reiters)
bandolet – harquebus, light musket (used by cavalry)

berdysz – berdish-axe

bej – bey

bitwa – battle

bojar – boyar (S)

bojarzy – boyars (P)

buława (bulawa) – mace, symbol of the Hetman's rank

buzdygan – mace. Symbol of high officer's rank

brygada – brigade

chan – khan

Chanat Krymski – Crimean Khanate

chorągiew (choragiew) (see also rota) – banner:
  – unit's standard/flag
  – basic unit of organisation of the Commonwealth cavalry and infantry (except 'foreign' troops), usually between 50 and 200 horses (cavalry) and 100–300 portions (infantry)

chorąży (chorazy) – standard bearer

czeladź (czeladz) – servants and camp followers

dezercja – desertion

dezerter – deserter (S)

dezerterzy – deserters (P)

dragon – dragoon (S)

dragoni – dragoons (P)

dragonia – dragoons (F)

dywizja – division

działa (dziala)/armaty – cannons (P)

działo (dzialo)/armata – cannon (S)

forteca – fortress

garnizon – garrison

gwardia – guard (as in Royal Guard)

haiduk – haiduk (S) – Hungarian infantry

hajducy – haiduks (P)

halabarda – halberd

hełm (helm) – helmet

hetman – [-] Highest commander of troops in Poland and Lithuania, there were two ranks, with a separate pair for Poland and for Lithuania
  – Hetman Wielki – Grand Hetman
  – Hetman Polny – Field Hetman

husaria – hussars (F)

husarz – hussar (S)

husarze – hussars (P)

janczar – janissary (S)

janczarzy/janczarowie – janissaries (P, F)

jazda kozacka – cossack cavalry (F)

jazda tatarska – Tatar cavalry

jazda wołoska (woloska) – Wallachian cavalry

jazda/kawaleria – cavalry

kałkan (kalkan) – [-] Eastern-type of round shield

kampania – campaign

kapitan – captain

kapitulacja – surrender

karakol – caracole

kirasjer – cuirassier (S)

kirasjerzy – cuirassiers (P)

kirys – cuirass

kiryśnicy (kirysnicy) – [-] Name sometimes used to describe both cuirassiers (for example Swedish in the first half of the century) and better-equipped husaria units (P, F)

kiryśnik (kirysnik) – [-] See above, (S)

kolczuga – chainmail

kompania – company

koncerz-estoc/panzerstecher – additional weapon (long sword) used mainly by hussars

kornet – company (foreign troops – cavalry and dragoons)

komunik – [-] Style of all-mounted army (for example Tatars, Poles or Lithuanians) marching fast without tabors and infantry

komputowa armia – [-] the Crown army since 1652. *Komput* was the size and organisation of the standing army set by the *Sejm* (see) for each year

kontrmarsz – countermarch

koń (kon) – horse (S)

konie – horses (P)

kopia – lance (used as a name for the hussars' weapon)

korpus – corps

Kozacy (Zaporoscy, Dońcy) – Cossack (Zaporozhian, Don)

kusza – crossbow

kwarciane wojsko/armia – 'quarter troops/army', the standing army in Poland, in service between the 1560s and 1652. It was maintained by a quarter ('kwarta') of revenues from the King's estates. Replaced by 'komputowa armia' (see)

Litwa – Lithuania

łuk (luk) – bow

muszkiet – musket

muszkieter – musketeer (S)

muszkieterzy/muszkieterowie – musketeers (P)

niemiecka/cudzoziemska piechota – German/foreign infantry

oberszter – colonel, commander of a foreign regiment (infantry, dragoons, reiters)

obersztlejtnant – lieutenant colonel – second in command of a foreign regiment (infantry, dragoons, reiters)

oblężenie (oblezenie) – siege

ordyńcy (ordyncy) – [-]

pancerni – [-] medium Polish cavalry, the name started to be used for cossack-style cavalry after 1648, to distinguish between them and Zaporozhian Cossack rebels

pałasz (palasz) – pallasch. Additional hand weapon, popular amongst cavalry (especially hussars)

petyhorcy – [-] Lithuanian medium cavalry, equipped with a rohatyna (see) or half-lance (see półkopia), often seen as the equivalent of pancerni cavalry

piechota – infantry

pika – pike (S)

piki – pikes (P)

pikinier – pikeman (S)

pikinierzy – pikemen (P)

pistolet – pistol (S)

pistolety – pistols (P)

poczet – retinue – basic sub-unit of a cavalry banner, composed of one companion and between one and five retainers

pocztowi – retainers (P)

pocztowy – retainer (S)

Polska (Korona) – Poland (Crown)

polska piechota – Polish infantry

polsko-węgierska piechota – Polish-Hungarian infantry

porucznik – lieutenant – second officer in a cavalry banner, often a real commander when *rotmistrz* was only nominal

pospolite ruszenie – levy, in Poland and Lithuanian used almost exclusively as a noble levy

potyczka – skirmish (small size fight)

porcje – portions (P), it was used to describe the 'paper strength' of Commonwealth's infantry unit.

porcja – portion (S)

półkopia – half-lance, used by petyhorcy (see)

pułk (pulk) – literally 'regiment' but term was used to describe the formation (often created ad hoc), composed from between 3 and 20+ 'banners' of national cavalry (hussars, cossacks, pancerni). It did not have a large headquarters and regular organisation like cavalry regiments in Western countries

pułkownik (pulkownik) – colonel. Commander of a cavalry 'pulk'

rajtar – reiter (S)

rajtaria – reiters (F)

rajtarzy – reiters (P)

regiment – regiment. Only to describe foreign troops (reiters, dragoons, infantry)

regimentarz – deputy hetman, commander of the army when hetman was not present

rekrut – conscript

rohatyna – [-] Approx 2.5 metre spear used by different types of Polish cavalry

rota – in the sixteenth and first half of the seventeenth century, the basic unit of organisation of the Commonwealth cavalry and infantry (except 'foreign' troops), usually between 50 and 200 horses (cavalry) and 100–300 portions (infantry), used interchangeably with chorągiew (see)

rotmistrz – commander of cavalry and Hungarian/Polish/Lithuanian infantry banner, equivalent of captain.

rusznica – caliver

Rzeczypospolita Obojga Narodow – Polish–Lithuanian Commonwealth

Sejm – parliament

Sejmik – district parliament

siodło (siodlo) – saddle (S)

siodła (siodla) – saddles (P)

skrzydła (skrzydla) – wings (P)

skrzydło (skrzydlo) – wing (S)

skwadron – squadron, unit of two to four companies of reiters or dragoons

straty – losses

spisa – [-] a 3–3.5 metre spear used by Cossacks (both foot and mounted); the word was also often used to describe pike

spiśnik (spisnik) – [-] the name sometimes used to describe either pikeman or soldiers with spears (S)

spiśnicy (spisnicy) – [-] as above, (P)

sułtan (sultan) – sultan

szabla – sabre

szarża (szarza) – charge (of cavalry)

szwadron – squadron

Szwecja – Sweden

tabor – tabor

tarcza – shield

towarzysz – companion (S), noble serving in cavalry (usually at least 1/3 of banner's strength – see 'poczet')

towarzysze – companions (P)

węgierska (wegierska) piechota – Hungarian infantry, also hajducy (see)

weteran – veteran

wezyr – vizier

włócznia (wlocznia) – spear

wóz (woz) taborowy – tabor wagon

wojna – war

województwo (wojewodztwo) – district/palatinate/voivodship, large territorial district of Poland and Lithuania

wojewoda – voivode – governor of 'wojewodztwo'

wybraniecka piechota – the word means 'chosen' (but considering its quality it should rather be 'drafted') peasant infantry, usually used as pioneers, as they lack proper training and good command

wypiszczycy – [-] Zaporozhian Cossacks removed from regular register (P)

wypiszczyk – [-] See above (S)

zasadzka – ambush

zamek – castle

zbroja/pancerz – armour

żołd (zold) – soldier's pay

Appendix IX

Swedish flags captured by the Polish army at Czarne (Hammerstein) on 15 April 1627

As mentioned in Chapter 4, Poles captured in total 26 Swedish standards at Czarne. Thirteen of them belonged to the infantry, the remaining 13 were cavalry cornets. The Polish relation[1] provides a very detailed description of those trophies, so even though they did not survive to our time, it is interesting to include them in this appendix.

Infantry

Eight of the infantry flags belonged to one regiment, all of them from 'blue and orange *kitajka*,[2] with one of the [probably 'colonel's'] with a yellow cross on it'. The remaining five were from 'white and yellow *kitajka*, made into a chequerboard'. As they were very similar, it could indicate that all five companies were grouped into one squadron.

Reiters

Colonel Johan Streiff von Lawenstein[3] – white damask flag, on each side a salamander in fire, embroidered with golden and silver thread, Latin sentence *Me nutrit, alios extinguit* (It is feeding me [while] extinguishing the other)

---

1   'Rosprawa Jaśnie Wielmożnego Pana J.Mści P. Stanisława z Koniecpola Koniecpolskiego, Wojewody Sendomirskiego, Hetmana Koronnego, etc. Etc. Z Woyskiem Xiążęcia Sudermaoskiego Gustawa pod Amerstynem w R.P. 1627, d.17kwietnia', *Pamiętniki o Koniecpolskich*, pp.241–249.
2   Polish term used to describe thin silk fabric of Eastern origin. Word derives from *Kitaj*, used in Polish and Russian as alternative name of China.
3   Thanks to Daniel Staberg with his help in identification of the Swedish officers.

Lieutenant Colonel Fridrich von Kötteritz – yellow damask flag, with silken heart embroidered with golden and red thread, with green crancelin running out from the heart. On one side the date of raising the unit – 1627 – and German sentence *Herz ohn Giet* (heart without poison). On other side an armoured arm with sword, embroidered with silver thread and the German sentence *Trew biss in den Todt* (Faithful until death).

Lieutenant Colonel (or Major) Moritz Pensen von Caldenbach – azure damask flag, on both sides mounted the Roman hero Marcus Curtius, embroidered with golden and silver thread. In his hand he carries a mace, the horse jumping from a green field into a fire. Latin sentence *Pro Commod Publico* (For the common good).

Major Johan Groot – azure damask flag, on both sides Saint George (golden thread) on horse (silver thread) killing with his golden spear a dragon (both golden and silver thread). Latin sentence *Dum Spiro Spero* (While I breathe, I hope).

Major Johan von Breckfeldt – azure damask flag, on both sides a knight with sword (silver thread), mounted, with (golden thread) a horse on a green field. On both sides the date of raising the unit – 1626 – and the Latin sentence *Florebo prospiciente Deo, virtuti et Marte* (I will flourish due to God's Providence, Virtue and Knight's bravery)

Captain Johan Ludwig Ringe – azure damask flag, with a crane keeping a stone in his leg.[4] Latin sentence *Vigilemus* (We watch).

Captain Hans Deckert – azure satin flag, on both sides with a sword appearing from the sky, surrounded by silver rays. German sentence *Gott waldts ich wags* (God forsakes me). In upper corner (left?) letters G.A.K.J.S, in other upper corner (right? Text is not clear, so they may be opposite) letters V.S.L. At the bottom of the flag letters H.D.E.F.D.M.G.D.V.H.A.

Captain Johan Burchard von Schienberg – orange damask flag, on both sides a silver threaded lion, armed with a silver sword. Sentence *Trawe Gott undt hab ein Lewen Mudt, den Gluck wird noch werden gutt* (Trust God and have a lion's mind, then your luck with be good)

Captain Christoph a Klutzinck (did not take part in the expedition, stayed in Germany to recruit more soldiers) – white flag, on both sides Saint George (golden and black thread), on a golden horse, with a golden spear killing a dragon. Latin sentence *Dum spiro* (While I breathe)

---

4   Since the crane slept with one leg crouched, it has been believed that it had a stone in that leg, which – if the crane asleep – fell on the other leg and woke the crane. Hence the image of the crane with the stone was used as a symbol of vigilance. Thanks to Rafał Szwelicki for providing with explanation of this symbol.

Captain N. Picht – azure damask flag, on both sides a golden lion armed with a sword, surrounded by a golden wreath. Latin sentence *Omnia cum Deo* (Everything with God)

Captain Hans Christoph von Borcksdorff – azure damask flag, on both sides an embroidered cross. On one side the Latin sentence *In hoc signo vinces* (Under this sign you will be victorious), the captain's initials H.C.V.B. and the unit's recruitment date – 1626. On the other side the Latin sentence *Jesus salvator mundi sis protektor noster* (Jesues, World's Saviour, be our defender).

Captain Jakob von Borcksdorff – azure damask flag, with the German sentence *Durch Gottes Hilff undt Segen wollen wir unsere Feind erlegen* (With God's help and blessing we want to defeat our enemies)

Captain von Ahnen – red damask flag. On one side a crowned golden lion, striking with his sword a Polish soldier, who is defending himself with a sabre. Additionally the Pole has a mace in his other hand. Sentence *Gottes der Schweden und Pommeren Freundt, undt aller Polen Freundt* (God's, Swedish and Pomeranian friend, and enemy to all Poles). On the other side a mounted Captain van Ahnen and a girl handing him a wreath. On top the sentence *Der von Ahnen bin ich genandt, nach Ehr undt Tugend streidt meine Handt* (My name is von Ahnen, my hand is fighting for fame and virtue). In the middle of the flag, the sentence *Meinem Cornet wirdt Gott helffen, daneben nach dieser Jungfrawen mit reputation zu streben* (God help my flag, so [that] I could with good fame ask for this girl's hand]

Colour Commentaries

1. Winged Hussars – Companion

The core of the winged hussars banner was made of companions (*towarzysze*), nobles leading their own retinues. Each companion had to purchase his own clothing, weapons and equipment, only his lance (*kopia*) was supplied by the National Treasury. As we can clearly see, this noble did not spare any expense: from rich ornaments on his horse, to the single wing attached to the saddle, the leopard pelt and good quality boots made from yellow Saffian leather. The blue shabrack called a *dywdyk* was often embroidered with gold. There was no regulation regarding clothing, so it was up to the individual what he would wear, this companion chose a red *żupan* and trousers in the same colour. The armour is typical for the 1620s, a mix of plate and chainmail with a *szyszak* helmet. Many foreign visitors mentioned the multitude of weapons carried by hussars, and we can clearly see an example of it here: a lance with red pennant, a brace of pistols, an estoc under the saddle and a sabre (on the left side of the rider, so not visible on the illustration). The leather device that can be seen under the right boot is called a *wytok* and was used to support lance during a charge. This reconstruction is based on Abraham Booth's drawing from 1627.

2. Cossack Cavalry – Companion

An example of a well-equipped noble companion from a cossack cavalry banner. He is protected by chainmail worn over a red *żupan*, with a *misiurka* helmet and *karwasz* arm-guard worn on the left hand. As with the hussar companion from Plate A, he has boots made from yellow Saffian leather. Usually regulations required a cossack to have 'three firearms' but this man decided to use a brace of pistols and a bow. The latter was often used by noble companions as a symbol of their warrior status. A quiver with arrows can be seen on his right side, with the bow and a sabre on the left, not visible on the illustration. A pelt is used as shabrack in this case.

3.1 Foreign Infantry Musketeer

Foreign infantry in Polish service was often called 'German' but is also contained English, Scottish, Irish and even some Swedish soldiers. This man's coat and breeches look well made, so probably he is just recently recruited and has not yet suffered the miseries of life during campaign. There is no evidence of such infantry in Polish service using any type of armour, even a helmet. He is equipped with a heavy Dutch matchlock musket and forked rest, a leather bandolier with pre-measured powder charges, powder horn and ammunition pouch. Match cord is for convenience worn over the left arm. His hand weapon, worn on another leather belt slung over the right shoulder, is a rapier, often imported (alongside muskets) from German-speaking countries by merchants in Gdańsk and Toruń.

3.2 Reiter in Polish Service

Reiters serving in Polish service could really vary in appearance and equipment, as there was not much regulation which could specifically define them as cuirassiers or harquebusiers, as in Western Europe. The soldier that we can see here is well equipped, probably a veteran of previous fighting in Livonia such as the men brought to Prussia in 1626 by Colonel Mikołaj Abramowicz. This man has managed to obtain a long-sleeved buff coat, over which he is wearing breastplate and backplate. His head is protected by a simple *szyszak* helmet. His attire is completed with leather gloves (worn by reiters but not by native Polish cavalry), and long leather riding boots. His brace of pistols are left in holsters with his horse; here he can be seen with a rapier and a harquebus, the latter, when he was on horseback, normally attached to the leather belt seen slung over his left shoulder. In Poland such a belt was often called a *bandolier*, while any type of firearm worn on it was usually known as a *bandolet*.

4.1 Polish-Hungarian Infantryman (haiduk)

While Polish-Hungarian infantry – known also from the Hungarian name as haiduks – was not as numerous as foreign infantry during the Prussian war, it still played a vital role during both pitched battles and sieges. Here we can see a typical example of a rank-and-file haiduk, based on the so-called *Tablica gołuchowska* from 1620. His *żupan* is sky blue, with red lining, and red thread covering for buttons. The tight-fitting trousers are also red, and short shoes black. On his *magierka* hat you can see rather unusual small attachments. Often mistaken by researchers to be pipes, they were in fact paper cartridges. His main armaments are a heavy *rusznica* caliver and sabre, but he also has a short axe that was used both as an engineering tool and a useful hand-to-hand weapon. An ammunition pouch and powder horn are attached to his belt. The unusual brown shape over his left shoulder is a cover, often made from leather, used in Poland and Hungary to protect the lock of the firearm during bad weather.

4.2 *Wybraniecka* Infantryman

While often soldiers serving in *wybraniecka* infantry had to use their own clothes, there were some attempts to provide them with proper uniforms. This reconstruction is based on a regulation for the Volhynia voivodship from 1630. A blue *żupan* with red lining, red thread covering for buttons with the blue trousers. The head is covered with a *magierka* hat. The man is also equipped with sabre and *rusznica* caliver, with a powder horn and ammunition pouch on the belt.

5.1 High-Ranking Commander in Hussar's Attire

A colonel or *rotmistrz* of Polish cavalry, leading both a banner of winged hussars and a whole regiment (*pułk*) of cavalry. We can see similarities to the winged hussars companion from Plate A. Obvious differences of his status show in the more ornamented armour, different pelt, and short leather shoes. While during the battle he may have used a helmet, here he is still wearing a *magierka* adorned with a feather. Next to the sabre he is equipped with a *buzdygan* mace, as a signature of his rank. Many examples of such officers can be seen on the 'Stockholm Roll' painting. His cuirass and unusual scale-like protection of arms is based on the tomb of Adrian Szumski (d. 1631) from St. Jacob and St. Anne's Church in Przasnysz.

5.2 Foreign Infantry Officer

Another example of a foreigner in Polish service, this time an officer – possibly a German, English or Scottish captain – in charge of the company of infantry. As with their soldiers, officers of such units were not obliged by any regulations regarding uniform. The main difference was the fact that the officer had access to soldiers' pay and any additional money issued for the unit, so it's not likely that he would be unable to afford proper clothing. The example here opts for a fashionable red and hat with white feathers. Except for a gorget he is not wearing any armour. Besides his rapier he is equipped with a partisan, used both as a symbol of his rank and a useful melee weapon. Similarly dressed and equipped officers in Polish service can be seen on the painting depicting Polish-Lithuanian army at Smoleńsk in 1634, from the collection of the Kórnik Library.

6.1 Winged Hussar – Retainer

The quality and quantity of the equipment of the retinue always depended on the companion and his wealth. On this reconstruction we can see a retainer (possibly a lesser noble) whose master did not skimp on expenses. Good quality clothes and armour, an exotic (and expensive) pelt, even an additional weapon in the form of a horseman's pick, very useful during melee. He is using an older type of helmet, however, a so-called *kapalin* or *kłobuk*, that was gradually replaced by the *szyszak* by 1630s. Pistols and an estoc would be carried on the horse, a retainer would also be equipped with a lance, just like the companion.

6.2 Cossack cavalry – Retainer

In contrast with the hussars, here we have an example from the cossack cavalry, where the equipment of a retainer is very much different to that of a companion. No armour, just a sabre and short arquebus/*bandolet*. The outer coat is blue, a colour more often associated with commoners (and infantry) than noble-related red. There is no helmet or *magierka*, instead a fur-brimmed hat adorned with feathers. A bag with cartridges, slung over the left arm, is based on a relief from the tomb of Hetman Stanisław Żółkiewski (d. 1620) in Żółkiew.

7. Engineer in Polish Service

Military engineers were highly valued and often held a double role as officers in the artillery or as captains of infantry companies. This reconstruction, based on Wilhelm Hondius' works from the period of the Smoleńsk War 1632–1634, shows a specialist who can afford proper clothing, despite the hardship of the campaign. There is some evidence that blue became the colour associated with the artillery and engineers during the reign of King Władysław IV, but even prior to that it was linked to the Vasa Royal family. This man is equipped with the tools of his trade – a compass in his left hand and ruler in his right hand. He would try to avoid direct combat, but of course he still had his rapier for self-defence.

8.1 Imperial Cuirassier

A well-equipped Imperial cuirassier, part of the allied corps that arrived in Prussia in 1629. While the majority of Polish sources called Imperial cavalry 'reiters', there are a few specific references to cuirassiers, confirming that they were also part of von Arnim's troops. With three-quarter armour and *zischägge* (*szyszak*) helmet, this man is well protected on the battlefield, as he also has a buff coat under his armour. Long riding boots and leather gloves would be useful against both Swedish weapons and bad autumn weather in Prussia. His weapons consist of a sword and a pair of pistols (with one of them left in the holster on his horse). It is possible that some of the Polish reiters could be equipped in the same way as well.

8.2 Imperial/Prussian/Brandenburg Pikeman

While there is no evidence that foreign infantry in Polish service included any pikemen, they were present in the allied armies of the Empire and Prussia/Brandenburg. Even in the late 1620s such soldiers would still be wearing armour, as per the example here, with helmet, breast- and backplate present. The Imperial infantry saw some limited actions in 1629, while Prussian/Brandenburg troops were mostly known from an infamous episode of July 1627, when their large contingent surrendered to the Swedes and switched sides. The colours of clothing and armour are based on the painting depicting the Polish-Lithuanian army at Smoleńsk in 1634, from the collection of the Kórnik Library.

Bibliography

Archival Sources

Archiwum Główne Akt Dawnych w Warszawie (AGAD) w Warszawie
Archiwum Radziwiłłów (AR), V, no 6171, 17961
Archiwum Zamoyskich (AZ), 3116
Metryka Koronna, MK 166, 174
Teki Naruszewicza, 118,119, 120, 121

Archiwum Narodowe w Krakowie
Archiwum Sanguszków, Volumin 563

Archiwum Państwowe w Gdańsku
300/29, no 105
300/53, no 48, *Diariusz Wojny Pruskiej z roku 1626*

Archiwum Państwowe w Łodzi
Archiwum rodziny Bartoszewiczów; Dokumenty, uniwersały, przywileje
Biblioteka Jagiellońska w Krakowie
Manuscript 7
Biblioteka ks. Czartoryskich w Krakowie
357
1772, *Regestrum rationis thesauri Regni in Conventu anni MDCXXIX expeditae.*
2246, *Summariusz, co brało wojsko pruskie ad rationem z skarbu Rzptej po sejmie blisko przeszłym i co mu Rzpta winna od 1 decembris 1626 a 1 septembris 1628.*

Biblioteka Kórnicka
BK 341, *Diariusze z lat 1625–1630 oraz korespondencja dyplomatyczna*
BK 1400, *Akta i korespondencja z lata 1597–1602*

Biblioteka Narodowa w Warszawie
Biblioteka Ordynacji Zamoyskich (BOZ) 1173, *Popis Woiska dziewiąci tysięcy przed Królem Je. M. pod Arciberzem a Pszczewem 4 Nov.*

Biblioteka Uniwersytecka Wrocław
Polonica varia, volume 2

Centralnyj derżawnyj istorycznyj archiw Ukrajiny, Lviv (CDIAUL)
Folio 9, 1

Krigsarkivet, Stockholm
Erik Dalhbergh, Ordres de Bataille 1600–1679
Gustav Adolfsverket, Bearbetningar, B15–17, Volym 75b, *Fälttåget i Preussen 1626–1627, Vinterfälttåget 1626–1627*

National Archives, Kew
SP/88/5/163, *Roe's account of his negotiations*

National Library of Russia in St. Petersburg
Sobranije P. P. Dubrowskiego, 166
F. 321, op. 2, manuscript 67
F. 971, op. 2, manuscript 96

Riksarkivet Stockholm
Extranea IX Polen, 80, 82, 135, 140
Skoklostersamlingen, E 8600
Skoklostersamlingen, E 8636

Printed Primary Sources

Acta historia res gestas Kozacorum Ukrainiensum illustrantia, volume I (Lwów: Nauk. Tovarystvo im. Shevchenko, 1908)

Akta grodzkie i ziemskie z czasów Rzeczypospolitej Polskiej, volume X (Lwów: Towarzystwo Naukowe, 1884)

Akta grodzkie i ziemskie z czasów Rzeczypospolitej Polskiej, volume XX (Lwów: Towarzystwo Naukowe, 1909)

Arbusow, Leonid, 'Aus dem Handbuch des Wojewoden Nicolaus von Korff auf Kreuzburg', *Jahrbuch für Genealogie, Heraldik und Sphragistik, 1911–1913* (Mitau: Kurländische Gesellschaft für Literatur und Kunst, 1914)

Booth, Abraham, *Journael van de Legatie in Jaren 1627 en 1628* (Amsterdam, 1632)

Bostel, Ferdynand (ed.), *Rachunek skarbu koronnego z r. 1629* (Kraków: Akad. Umiejętn., 1891)

Curicke, Reinhold, *Der Stadt Dantzig Historische Beschreibung: Worinnen Von dero Uhrsprung, Situation, Regierungs-Art, geführten Kriegen, Religions- und Kirchen-Wesen außführlich gehandelt wird* (Amsterdam, Dantzigk, 1687)

'Diariusz albo Summa spraw i dzieł wojska kwarcianego w Prusiech na usłudze Jego Królewskiej Miłości przeciwko Gustawowi Książęciu Sudermańskiemu będącego', Stanisław Przyłęcki (ed.), *Pamiętniki o Koniecpolskich* (Lwów, Nakł. Leona Rzewuwskiego, 1842)

Documenta Bohemica Bellum Tricennale Illustrantia, volume IV (Prague Academia, 1974)

Dworzaczek, Wodzimierz (ed.), *Akta Sejmikowe województw poznańskiego i kaliskiego*, volume I part 2 (Poznań: Państwowe Wydawn. Naukowe, 1962)

Fenrych, Wiktor (ed.), *Akta i Diariusz Królewskiej Komisji Okrętowej Zygmunta III z lat 1627–1628* (Gdańsk-Gdynia: Gdańskie Towarzystwo Naukowe, 2001)

Gardiner, Samuel Rawson (ed.), *Letters relating to the mission of Sir Thomas Roe to Gustavus Adolphus 1629–30* (Westminster: Camden Society, 1875)

Hoppe, Israel, *Geschichte des ersten schwedisch-polnischen Krieges in Preussen: nebst Anhang* (Leipzig: Duncker & Humblot, 1887)

Karola Ogiera dziennik podróży do Polski 1635–1636, part I (Gdańsk: Biblioteka Miejska: Towarzystwo Przyjaciół Nauki i Sztuki, 1950)

'Komput wojska z 1626 r.', Zdzisław Spieralski, Jan Wimmer (ed.), *Wypisy źródłowe do historii polskiej sztuki wojennej*, volume V (Warszawa: Wyd. MON, 1961)

'Kontynuacja Diariusza o dalszych postępach wojennych ze Szwedami a die 1 Julii (1629)', Otto Laskowski (ed.), *Przyczynki do działań hetmana polnego koronnego Stanisława Koniecpolskiego w Prusach Wschodnich i na Pomorzu przeciw Gustawowi Adolfowi, Przegląd Historyczno-Wojskowy*, volume IX, part 3 (Warszawa: Wojskowe Biuro Historyczne, 1936)

Kronika Pawła Piaseckiego biskupa przemyślskiego (Kraków: Drukarnia Uniw. Jagiellońskiego, 1870)

Listy księcia Jerzego Zbaraskiego, kasztelana krakowskiego, z lat 1621–1631 (Kraków: nakł. Akademii Umiejętności, 1878)

Listy Władysława IV do Krzysztofa Radziwiłła, hetmana polnego W.X. Litewskiego pisane 1612–1632 (Kraków: W. Jaworski, 1867)

Lubomirski, Tadeusz, 'Regestra skarbca książąt Ostrogskich w Dubnie', *Historya Sztuki w Polsce*, volume VI, part 2 and 3 (Kraków, 1898)

Obraz dworów europejskich na początku XVII wieku przedstawiony w Dzienniku Podróży Królewicza Władysława syna Zygmunta III do Niemiec, Austryi, Belgii, Szwajcaryi i Włoch, w roku 1624–1625. Skreślony przez Stefana Paca (Wrocław: Z. Schletter, 1854)

Okolski, Szymon, *Dyaryusz transakcyi wojennej między wojskiem koronnem a zaporoskiem w r. 1637* (Kraków: Wyd. Biblioteki Polskiej, 1858)

Okolski, Szymon, *Kontynuacja dyaryusza wojennego* (Kraków: Wyd. Biblioteki Polskiej, 1858)

Przyłęcki, Stanisław (ed.), *Pamiętniki o Koniecpolskich* (Lwów, Nakł. Leona Rzewuwskiego, 1842)

Radziwiłł, Albrycht Stanisław, *Rys panowania Zygmunta III* (Opole: Wyd. Uniwersytetu Opolskiego, 2011)

'Relacja bitwy trzciańskiej posłana od P. Hetmana', Otto Laskowski (ed.) *Przyczynki do działań hetmana polnego koronnego Stanisława Koniecpolskiego w Prusach Wschodnich i na Pomorzu przeciwko Gustawowi Adolfowi*, *Przegląd Historyczno-Wojskowy*, volume IX, part 3 (Warszawa: Wojskowe Biuro Historyczne, 1936)

'Relacja IMP. Wojewody Sendomirskiego, Hetmana Polnego Koronnego, o wojnie przeszłego roku w Warszawie, dnia 4 Februari 1629 uczyniona', Otto Laskowski (ed.) *Przyczynki do działań hetmana polnego koronnego Stanisława Koniecpolskiego w Prusach Wschodnich i na Pomorzu przeciwko Gustawowi Adolfowi*, *Przegląd Historyczno-Wojskowy*, volume IX, part 3 (Warszawa: Wojskowe Biuro Historyczne, 1936)

'Relacja z inspekcji pułku piechoty z 1627 r', Zdzisław Spieralski, Jan Wimmer (ed.), *Wypisy źródłowe do historii polskiej sztuki wojennej*, volume V (Warszawa: Wyd. MON, 1961)

Rikskansleren Axel Oxenstiernas skrifter och brefvexling, volume II, part 9 (Stockholm: Norstedt, 1898)

Rikskansleren Axel Oxenstiernas skrifter och brefvexling, volume I, part 3 (Stockholm: Norstedt, 1900)

Rolny, Wilhelm, 'Dwie taksy towarów cudzoziemskich z r. 1633', *Archiwum Komisyi Prawniczej*, volume V (Kraków: Akad. Umiejętności, 1897)

Starowolski, Szymon, *Eques Polonus* (Venice, 1628)

Starowolski, Szymon, *Polska albo opisanie Królestwa Polskiego*. Translation from Latin by Antoni Piskadło (Warszawa: Wyd. Literackie, 1976)

Szymanowski, Samuel Hutor, *Mars sauromatski i inne poematy*, edited by Piotr Borek (Kraków: Collegium Columbinum, 2009)

'Uniwersał JKMści o wybraniu piechoty w dobrach królewskich' in *Sprawy wojenne króla Stefana Batorego. Dyjaryusze, relacyje, listy i akta z lat 1576–1568* (Kraków: Akad. Umiejętności, 1887)

'Uniwersał królewski o wojsku zaporoskim z 1578 r', Zdzisław Spieralski, Jan Wimmer (ed.), *Wypisy źródłowe do historii polskiej sztuki wojennej. Zeszyt piąty. Polska sztuka wojenna w latach 1563–1647* (Warszawa: Wyd. MON, 1961)

Volumina Legum, volume III (Petersburg, 1859)

Wahrhafte und ausfürliche Warhaffte und ausfuerliche Erzehlung dess ernstlichen Treffens, welches sich unlangst in Preussen zwischen dem Koenig in Polen und Schweden nit weit von Dyrschaw begeben (Gdańsk, 1627)

Wierzbowski, Teodor, *Matieraly k istorii Moskovskago gosudarstva v XVI i XVII stoletiiakh*, volume II (Warszawa, 1898)

Zbiór pamiętników do dziejów polskich, volume IV (Warszawa, 1859)

Zernecke, Jacob Heinrich, *Das bey denen schwedischen Kriegen bekriegte Thorn oder zuverläszige Erzehlung desjenigen was sich bey dieser Stadt im Jahr 1629, 1655, 1658 und 1703 in anfällen Bloqvir – Bombardir – und Belagerungen denckwürdiges zugetragen: dabey ein nöthiger Anhang zur thornischen Chronicke* (Thorn, 1712)

Żurkowski, Tomasz, *Żywot Tomasza Zamoyskiego* (Lwów: Drukarnia Zakładu Narodowego im. Ossolińskich, 1860)

Secondary Printed Sources

Adamczyk, Władysław, *Ceny w Warszawie w XVI i XVII wieku* (Lwów, Warszawa: Kasa im. Mianowskiego, 1938)

Augusiewicz, Sławomir, *Przebudowa wojska pruskiego w latach 1655–1660* (Oświęcim: Wydawnictwo Napoleon V, 2014)

Augustyniak, Urszula, *W służbie hetmana i Rzeczypospolitej. Klientela wojskowa Krzysztofa Radziwiłła (1585–1640)* (Warszawa: Semper, 2004)

Balcerek, Mariusz, *Księstwo Kurlandii i Semigalii w wojnie Rzeczypospolitej ze Szwecją w latach 1600–1629* (Poznań: Wydawnictwo Poznańskie, 2012)

Czapliński, Władysław; Długosz, Józef, *Życie codzienne magnaterii polskiej w XVII wieku* (Warszawa: Państwowy Instytut Wydawniczy, 1976)

Czołowski, Aleksander, *Marynarka w Polsce: szkic historyczny* (Lwów, Warszawa, Kraków: Wydawn. Zakładu Narodowego im. Ossolińskich, 1922)

Duda, Paweł, 'Działalność oddziałów Hansa Georga von Arnima w Rzeczypospolitej z punktu widzenia nuncjusza papieskiego Antonia Santacrocego', *Od Kijowa do Rzymu. Z dziejów stosunków Rzeczypospolitej ze Stolicą Apostolską i Ukrainą* (Białystok: In-t Badań nad Dziedzictwem Kulturowym Europy, 2012)

Duda, Paweł, *Krzyż i karabela* (Katowice: Wydawnictwo Uniwersytetu Śląskiego, 2019)

Filipczak-Kocur, Anna, *Skarbowość Rzeczpospolitej 1578–1648* (Warszawa, 2006)

Frost, Robert, *The Northern Wars: War, State and Society in Northeastern Europe, 1558–1721* (Harlow: Longman, 2000)

Gawron, Przemysław, 'Koszty wystawienia regimentu piechoty cudzoziemskiej w Wielkim Księstwie Litewskim w pierwszej połowie XVII wieku', *Rocznik Lituanistyczny*, volume 5 (Warszawa, 2019)

Generalstaben, *Sveriges Krig 1611–1632. Band 2, Polska kriget* (Stockholm, 1936)

Górski, Konstanty, *Historya artylerii polskiej* (Warszawa: Wende E. i Spółka 1902)

Gutkowska-Rychlewska, Maria, *Historia ubioru* (Wrocław-Warszawa-Kraków: Arkady, 1968)

Hoszowski, Stanisław, *Ceny we Lwowie w XVI i XVII wieku* (Lwów, 1928)

Huflejt, Marian, *Bitwa pod Oliwą 1627, fakty i mity* (Olsztyn: Wydawnictwo Mantis, 2019)

Jany, Curt, *Geschichte der königlich preussischen Armee bis zum Jahre 1807*. Volume I, von den Anfängen bis 1740 (Berlin: K. Siegismund, 1928)

Kaczorowski, Eugeniusz, *Flota polska w latach 1578–1632* (Warszawa: Wyd. MON, 1973)

Kaczorowski, Eugeniusz, *Oliwa 1627* (Warszawa: Bellona, 2002)

Kersten, Adam, *Stefan Czarniecki 1599–1665* (Lublin: Wydawnictwo Uniwersytetu Marii Curie-Skłodowskiej, 2006)

Łoziński, Władysław, *Prawem i lewem. Obyczaje na czerwonej Rusi za panowania Zygmunta III* (Lwów: nakładem W. Webera, 1903)

Maroń, Jerzy, *Wojna trzydziestoletnia na Śląsku. Aspekty militarne* (Wrocław-Racibórz: Wydawnictwo i Agencja Informacyjna WAW Grzegorz Wawoczny, 2008)

Mełeń, Aleksander, *Ordynacje w dawnej Polsce* (Lwów: Pamiętnik Historyczno-Prawny, 1929)

Nagielski, Mirosław, 'Gwardia przyboczna Władysława IV (1632–1648)', *Studia i Materiały do Historii Wojskowości*, volume XXVII (Warszawa: Wyd. MON, 1984)

Odyniec, Wacław, 'Lądowo-morska obrona wybrzeża Pucka w latach 1626–1629', *Studia i Materiały do Historii Wojskowości*, volume I (Warszawa: Wyd. MON, 1954)

Paradowski, Michał, *Studia i materiały do historii wojen ze Szwecją 1600–1635* (Oświęcim: Wydawnictwo Napoleon V, 2013)

Sygański, Jan, *Historya Nowego Sącza od wstąpienia Dynastyi Wazów do pierwszego rozbioru Polski*, volume I (Lwów, 1901)

Seredyka, Jan, 'Wezwanie posiłków cesarskich do Polski w 1629 roku', *Zeszyty Naukowe Wyższej Szkoły Pedagogicznej im. Powstańców Śląskich w Opolu, Seria A, Historia XIV* (Opole, 1977)

Seredyka, Jan, 'Wypłata żołdu armii cesarskiej w Polsce po rozejmie altmarskim (1629–1631)', *Śląski kwartalnik historyczny Sobótka*, year XXXI, no 1–4 (Wrocław-Warszawa-Kraków-Gdańsk, 1976)

Seredyka, Jan, *Sejm w Toruniu z 1626 roku* (Wrocław-Warszawa-Kraków: Zakład Narodowy im. Ossolińskich, 1966)

Seredyka, Jan, *Sejm zawiedzionych nadziei* (Opole: Wyższa Szkoła Pedagogiczna im. Powstańców Śląskich w Opolu, 1981)

Sikora, Radosław, *Kłuszyn 1610* (Warszawa: Instytut Wydawniczy Erica, 2010)

Skowron, Ryszad, *Olivares, Wazowie i Bałtyk* (Kraków: Towarzystwo Wydawnicze 'Historia Iagellonica', 2002)

Staszewski, Janusz, 'Bitwa pod Trzcianą', *Przegląd Historyczno-Wojskowy*, volume IX, part 3 (Warszawa: Wojskowe Biuro Historyczne, 1936)

Stefańska, Zofia, 'Polskie ubiory wojskowe z XVI i XVII wieku', *Muzealnictwo wojskowe*, volume II Warszawa: Muzeum Wojska Polskiego, 1964)

Szelągowski, Adam, *O ujście Wisły. Wielka wojna pruska* (Dąbrówno: Oficyna Retman, 2012)

Szelągowski, Adam, *Pieniądz i przewrót cen w XVI i XVII wieku w Polsce* (Lwów: Towarz. Wydawn, 1902)

Teodorczyk, Jerzy, 'Bitwa pod Gniewem (22 IX–29 IX–1 X 1626). Pierwsza porażka husarii', *Studia i Materiały do Historii Wojskowości*, volume XII, part 2 (Warszawa: Wyd. MON, 1966)

Teodorczyk, Jerzy, 'Broń i oporządzenie polskie w świetle cennika komisji lubelskiej, oblatowanego 22 maja 1628 r.', *Muzealnictwo Wojskowe* (Warszawa: Muzeum Wojska Polskiego, 1964)

Teodorczyk, Jerzy, 'Walki o Malbork w roku 1626, z uwzględnieniem opisu stanu fortecy, piechoty polskiej i szwedzkiej oraz politycznego tła wydarzeń', *Studia do Dziejów Dawnego Uzbrojenia i Ubioru Wojskowego*, volume 7 (Kraków, 1978)

Teodorczyk, Jerzy, 'Wyprawa szwedzka z Meklemburgii do Prus Królewskich 1627 r.', *Studia i Materiały do Historii Wojskowości*, volume VI, part 2 (Warszawa: Wyd. MON, 1960)

Tomaszewski, Edward, *Ceny w Krakowie 1601–1795* (Lwów, Warszawa: Inst. pop. polsk. twórczości nauk., 1934)

Tyszkowski, Kazimierz, 'Problemy organizacyjno-wojskowe z czasów wojny moskiewskiej Zygmunta III', *Przegląd Historyczno-Wojskowy* (Warszawa: Wojskowe Biuro Historyczne 1930)

Wimmer, Jan, 'Wojsko i skarb Rzeczypospolitej u schyłku XVI i w pierwszej połowie XVII wieku', *Studia i Materiały do Historii Wojskowości*, volume XIV (Warszawa: Wyd. MON, 1968)

Wimmer, Jan, *Historia piechoty polskiej do 1864 roku* (Warszawa: Wyd. MON, 1978)

Wisner, Henryk, *Rzeczpospolita Wazów*, volume II (Warszawa: Wydawnictwo Neriton Instytut Historii PAN, 2004)

Wisner, Henryk, 'Dwa polskie plany wojny szwedzkiej z 1629 r. (Projekty Jerzego Zbaraskiego i Krzysztofa Radziwiłła)', *Zapiski Historyczne*, volume XLII, part 2 (Warszawa: Towarzystwo Naukowe w Toruniu, 1977)

Wisner, Henryk, 'Wojsko litewskie I połowy XVII wieku', part III, *Studia i Materiały do Historii Wojskowości*, volume 21 (Warszawa: Wyd. MON, 1979)

Wrede, Alphonse, *Geschichte der K. Und K. Wehrmacht. Die Regimenter, Corps, Branchen und Anstalten von 1618 bis Ende des 19. Jahrhunderts, Band II* (Vienna: L.W. Seidel, 1898)